SO-ATA-099

FLOWCHARTING

FLOWCHARTING
A Tool for Understanding Computer Logic

NANCY B. STERN
Suffolk Community College

John Wiley & Sons, Inc.
New York • London • Sydney • Toronto

Editors: Judy Wilson and Irene Brownstone
Production Manager: Ken Burke
Editorial Supervisor: Winn Kalmon
Artist: Carl Brown

Library of Congress Cataloging in Publication Data

Stern, Nancy B.
  Flowcharting: A Tool for Understanding Computer Logic

  (Wiley self-teaching guides)
  Includes index.
  1. Flowcharts—Programmed instruction. 2. Electronic digital computers—Programming—Programmed instruction. I. Title.
QA76.6.S73   001.6'423'077,   75-11600
ISBN 0-471-82331-7

Printed in the United States of America

75 76 10 9 8 7 6 5 4 3 2 1

Preface

The primary objective of this book is to teach computer logic using the tool of the program flowchart. FLOWCHARTING is intended for a wide range of potential users who might wish to understand computer processing. There are no prerequisites for using this Self-Teaching Guide. It can be used by data processing majors, business majors, liberal arts majors, or even general readers who wish to gain conceptual knowledge of how the computer logically functions. As a supplement to an introductory data processing text, FLOWCHARTING will provide the reader with the most comprehensive and functional tools needed to understand computer processes.

After completing the book, the reader will be able to program in any programming language by simply learning the basic rules of the language. The crux of programming—the logic—is taught in this book; with an understanding of this logic, programming itself becomes a simplified task.

Unlike other flowcharting books, this book's step-by-step approach is especially designed to help the reader integrate the material through guided applications. By using the programmed instruction format, the reader progressively enhances practical understanding of the logic functions performed by a computer. The approach is basic, not encyclopedic, and is designed to provide a working knowledge of computer logic, not to overwhelm the reader with independent and unrelated topics.

I wish to express my thanks to Joan V. Hughes for her extremely useful advice on the subject matter and its organization; to Judy Vantrease Wilson, Editor at Wiley, for her invaluable assistance and advice in preparing the manuscript; and to Irene Franck Brownstone, Editor at Wiley, for her monumental efforts on behalf of this book.

And, lastly, a special word of thanks to my husband, Robert Stern, without whose profound support—both personal and professional—this book would not have been written. For this, and for so much more, I am very grateful.

Coram, New York   Nancy Stern
March, 1975

How to Use This Book

Each chapter contains: (1) a set of objective which outline the material to be covered; (2) a series of numbered frames providing a step-by-step integration of material, each including one or more questions or flowchart problems designed to test your understanding of that material; and (3) a Self-Test which will assist you in determining whether you have sufficient understanding to proceed to the next chapter, and, if not, where the problem areas exist. Each answer furnished for the Self-Test questions contains references to a series of frames to which the question applies, so that if you answer a question incorrectly, the particular area of weakness can be readily found.

The programmed instruction format of this guide is particularly suited to flowcharting since it allows you to apply your understanding throughout by both answering questions and actually drawing flowcharts. Then you can check your understanding before you go on. Following the dashed line in each frame is the correct answer or a standard flowchart solution to compare with your own. You should note that just as it is possible to provide several different logical arguments, all correct, to prove a given point, it is possible to draw several different flowcharts, all correct, to perform a given task. For this reason, your flowchart drawings may not always conform exactly to the solutions provided. Where alternatives are obvious, a note has been inserted following the flowchart, describing these alternatives. In other cases, you will need to study the given flowchart solutions to determine if your answer is basically the same. In all cases, if you can answer the questions at the end of the frames and understand the flowchart solutions provided, you will have no difficulty assessing your solutions. It is most important, therefore, that you understand each flowchart solution before proceeding to the next frame.

The time you will need to complete each chapter will vary according to the complexity of the material and your own individual working habits. In all chapters, however, because each unit is carefully structured to integrate the material presented, it is important that you work through to the end of a chapter or section rather than stop at some arbitrary point.

Contents

CHAPTER ONE
Why Computers?

The main objective of this Self-Teaching Guide is to provide an understanding of computer logic through flowcharting. The guide requires no previous exposure to data processing. It provides a step-by-step introduction to the logic used in computer processing, by utilizing the technique of the block diagram or flowchart. With an understanding of this logic the beginner will be able to program competently in any computer language by simply learning a few basic programming rules for that language.

Prior to a discussion of computer logic, however, it is important that you understand and be able to use certain fundamental terms in data processing. These terms are used throughout the book and, indeed, in all data processing centers. It is to these terms and concepts that we devote this chapter. When you complete this chapter, you will be able to:

- recognize and apply the following basic computer terms: input, output, source document, hardware, program, flowchart, data, central processing unit (CPU);

- organize data into hierarchies, from characters to files;

- show how data is organized on punched cards and on printed reports, including the length of each, the arrangement of data within fields, and use of edit symbols;

- describe how data is converted from the source document to the punched card;

- classify fields as numeric, alphabetic, or alphanumeric;

- write simple sequences of instructions for data transfer and arithmetic operations, using input areas, output areas, and storage areas;

- explain the relationship between a job description, a flowchart, and a program;

- identify various devices as input (I), output (O), or input/output (I/O);

- identify fields as variable or constant.

1.   How long would it take you to add $998,756 + 985,769$? It probably would take approximately five seconds. In the same time, a typical computer could easily perform between 50,000 and 100,000 such additions. In fact, some computers could perform over 1,000,000 additions in the same five seconds.

We have just observed one of the most compelling reasons for the great success of computers today—their speed. Computers can also perform their operations with far greater accuracy than people. But, you say, why is it that computers constantly goof? When computers are blamed, as they often are, for inaccurate results, the fault most often lies with the personnel using or programming the machinery.

The two major reasons for using computers are _____ and _____.

- - - - - - - - - - - - - - - - - - -

speed, accuracy

2.   Computers are used in two main types of processing. Business applications of computer processing are described as <u>data processing</u>. Business applications usually require relatively simple calculations to be performed on large volumes of information. For example, the calculations of paychecks for 50,000 employees is a typical business application—large volume, simple arithmetic calculations.

The more intricate type of computer processing, where relatively complex mathematical operations are performed on a relatively low volume of information, is called <u>scientific processing</u>. For example, the calculation of a moon trajectory may involve the use of only a handful of variables, but the complexity of the calculation may keep the computer busy for hours!

What are the two main areas in which computers are used? _____ _____.

- - - - - - - - - - - - - - - - - -

data processing (business applications) and scientific processing.

Our discussion of computer logic applies to both business and scientifically oriented computer processing. Let us begin with an introduction to the most fundamental forms of computer media—the punched card and the printed report.

PUNCHED CARDS AND PRINTED REPORTS

3.   This section will familiarize you with a common form of incoming computer information, the <u>punched card</u>, and with the most common form of outgoing computer information, the <u>printed report</u>. Knowing something about these computer media, you can begin to understand how data processing functions are performed.

First of all, two important terms: input and output. Incoming informa-

tion which enters a computer system is called <u>input</u>, sometimes abbreviated
I/P. Outgoing information which leaves a computer system is called <u>output</u>,
sometimes abbreviated O/P.

What is a common form of computer input? _____

What is the most common form of computer output? _____

_____

- - - - - - - - - - - - - - - -

the punched card; the printed report

4.   Information entering a computer center is called _____.

Information leaving a computer center is called _____.

- - - - - - - - - - - - - - - - -

input or I/P; output or O/P

Punched Cards

5.   The punched card is the most basic form of computer input. While many
large companies also use forms such as magnetic tape and magnetic disk (to
be discussed later), punched cards are still the most widely used form of input in small computer organizations.

Information is recorded on these punched cards by punching holes in the
form of a code. Consider the time card illustrated in Figure 1.1. The punched
holes represent information in coded form.

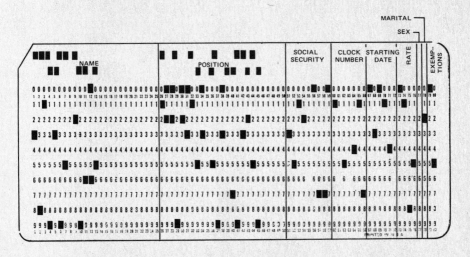

Figure 1.1. Time card.

This card represents a <u>record</u> or unit of information. The entire deck of such card records represents a <u>file</u> of information, which is the collective group of related records. Can you think of some punched card examples that you have encountered? _____

_____

- - - - - - - - - - - - - - - - - - -

Many telephone company bills, electric company bills, and gas company bills are on punched cards; so are many college course registration cards. You may have thought of other examples, too.

6.   Suppose that a telephone company sends out its bill on a punched card.

The bill you receive is called a (file, record) _____. The totality

of all bills sent out to all customers is called a (file, record) _____.

- - - - - - - - - - - - - - - - - - -

record (If you answered "file," remember that a file is a collective group
of records; generally, more than one card would be required for an entire
file.)
file (If you answered "record," remember that a record is usually a single
item.)

7.   Why do you think such cards are called <u>punched</u> cards? _____

_____

- - - - - - - - - - - - - - - - - - -

because they are coded with information in the form of punched holes

8.   Each record consists of <u>characters</u>, which make up information referred to as <u>data</u>. In computer terminology, the terms data and information are generally interchangeable. A character is a single letter, digit, or special symbol such as $, +, -, or *.

Thus, data is a combination of characters, which may consist of _____

_____, _____, or _____, or any combination

of these, that result in meaningful information or _____.

- - - - - - - - - - - - - - - - - - -

letters, digits, special symbols, data

9.   What input medium represents characters of information through the use

of punched holes? _____

- - - - - - - - - - - - - - - - - - -

_____

the punched card

10. Consider the blank card in Figure 1.2. Notice that at the very bottom of the card there are small digits numbered 1 through 80. Note also that below the first horizontal group of zeros, there are the same 80 numbers. Each of these numbers refers to a column or vertical section of the card.

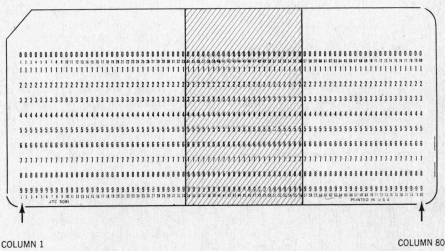

COLUMN 1   COLUMN 80

Figure 1.2. Sample punched card.

How many card columns are there ? _____

- - - - - - - - - - - - - - - - - -

· 80

11. Part of Figure 1.2 is shaded lines. That portion includes columns ____ through ____ on the card.

- - - - - - - - - - - - - - - - - -

34-56 (It is important that you understand the answer to this question, because you must be able to identify card columns. On the bottom of the illustrated card, there are 80 numbers; in the area shaded, these numbers correspond to 34 through 56. These numbers signify card columns 34 through 56.)

12. The code used for representing punched data on an 80-column card is called the Hollerith code, named for the man who developed it, Herman Hollerith.

Each column on a card is used to represent one character of information. Each column can contain one _____ , one _____ , or one special symbol. A card, then, can store or hold how many characters? ____

- - - - - - - - - - - - - - - - - -

letter, digit (in either order); 80

13. Notice in Figure 1.1 that columns _____ through _____ are referred to .
as NAME. NAME then would consist of how many characters? _____

- - - - - - - - - - - - - - - - - -

1, 25; 25

14. NAME is called a field of information. A field is a consecutive group of
characters used to represent a unit of information within a record. What are
some other fields of information on the time card in Figure 1.1? _____

_____

- - - - - - - - - - - - - - - - - -

POSITION, SOCIAL SECURITY NUMBER, CLOCK NUMBER, STARTING
DATE, RATE, SEX, MARITAL STATUS, EXEMPTIONS

15. The columns used to represent POSITION are _____ through _____.
The field POSITION consists of how many columns? _____

- - - - - - - - - - - - - - - - - -

26, 50; 25

16. The holes on the card are punched according to the _____
code representation.

- - - - - - - - - - - - - - - - - -

Hollerith

17. The time card is a (field/character/record/file) _____ of
information.

- - - - - - - - - - - - - - - - - -

record

18. How many characters are there in the field called RATE in Figure 1.1?

_____

- - - - - - - - - - - - - - - - - -

four (since there are four columns)

19. Most cards contain how many columns? _____

- - - - - - - - - - - - - - - - - -

80

For our purposes, it is not necessary to learn the actual Hollerith code representation of data on a punched card. Figure 1.3, however, gives a complete description of that code for the curious. For a more thorough discussion of the Hollerith code, see any introductory data processing book.

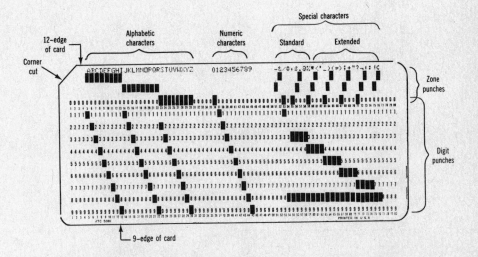

Figure 1.3. Review of punched card codes.

Note that alphabetic characters and most special characters require more than one punch in a column. Note also that the information punched in the card can also be printed on the top of the card. This printing enables data processing personnel to read the card data, and has no effect on the computer processing.

20. Now let's discuss the hierarchy of data using an illustration.

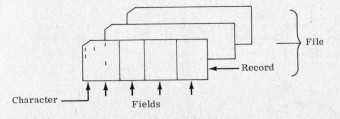

Each field consists of data items made up of _____. A group

of fields representing a unit of information is called a _____. The
entire set of information which contains all records for a particular application
is called a _____. Another name for information is _____.

- - - - - - - - - - - - - - - - - -

characters; record; file; data

Characteristics of Fields

21. Data fields can be classified in three ways.

Classification of fields	Allowable characters
numeric	digits, decimal point, + or − sign
alphabetic	letters and blanks only
alphanumeric or alphameric	any characters: letters, digits, and special symbols

What type of field is each of the following?

(a) +132. 6 _____

(b) A123 _____

(c) ABØØ (Ø means blank) _____

(d) 63 _____

- - - - - - - - - - - - - - - - - -

(a) numeric; (b) alphanumeric or alphameric; (c) alphabetic; (d) numeric
(Note that the fields in (a), (c), and (d) could be classified as alphanumeric,
since they all contain allowable characters. The field A123, however, could
only be an alphanumeric field; that is, it could not be either a numeric or an
alphabetic field.)

22. A field that will contain only digits, a decimal point, and a plus or minus
sign is called a numeric field. Such fields are generally used for arithmetic
operations. A field that will contain only letters or blanks is called an alphabetic field. A NAME field, for example, is usually considered an alphabetic
field. A field that can contain any combination of letters, digits, or special
symbols is called an alphanumeric field.
    What kind of field is an ADDRESS field, that will contain such data as

'121 MAIN ST'? _____

- - - - - - - - - - - - - - - - - -

alphanumeric, because it contains a combination of letters, digits, and
special symbols

23. What kind of field is an AMOUNT field that is to be used for an addition operation? _____

- - - - - - - - - - - - - - - - - -

numeric. Only numeric fields may be used in an arithmetic operation.

24. Would the following data be acceptable in a numeric field: 1, 235? _____

- - - - - - - - - - - - - - - - - -

no, because it contains a comma, which is not permitted in numeric fields

25. Would the following data be acceptable in a numeric field: $123. 00? ____

- - - - - - - - - - - - - - - - - -

no, because dollar signs are not permitted in numeric fields

26. If a PARTNUM field contained 12378A, how must the field be defined?

_____

- - - - - - - - - - - - - - - - - -

Because the PARTNUM field contains A, it must be defined as alphanumeric.

27. Figure 1.4 represents another sample data card. Note that the information typed on the card is for human, and not machine, readability.

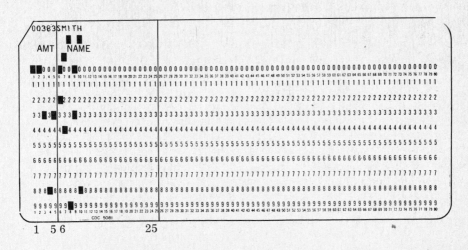

Figure 1.4. Sample data card.

Columns 1 through 5 represent a _____ called AMT. AMT is a

common data processing abbreviation for amount. The field NAME is in

columns _____ through _____ .

- - - - - - - - - - - - - - - - - - -

field; 6, 25

28. Field sizes are generally established to accommodate the longest number of characters expected. For example, a NAME field may be 20 characters long because the longest name for that application is 20 characters. However, since most names are shorter than this, part of the field will remain blank. In alphabetic and alphanumeric fields, if the data characters do not fill up the allotted number of positions in a field, the information is punched in the left-most columns of the field. In Figure 1.4, in the NAME field, in what columns

does the name SMITH appear? _____

- - - - - - - - - - - - - - - - - - -

columns 6 through 10

29. Numeric fields (consisting of numbers, decimal points, and plus or minus signs) are treated differently. If the numeric information does not fill up the field, it is right-justified. This means that the required information is placed in the rightmost positions of the field, with the remaining positions on the left being filled with zeros. In Figure 1.4, in what columns does the AMT 383

appear? _____ What is in the other two columns? _____

- - - - - - - - - - - - - - - - - - -

columns 3 through 5; zeros (in columns 1 and 2)

30. Assume that the field QTY occupies positions 11-15 of a punched card. We want to represent the number 286 in the field QTY. In what columns would

286 be punched? _____ What would appear in the other two

columns? _____

- - - - - - - - - - - - - - - - - - -

columns 13-15; zeros would appear in columns 11 and 12 (Note that only numeric data is right-justified. Non-numeric data is represented differently, as we shall see later.)

31. Represent 1143 in AMT, a numeric field in positions 31-35 of the following card.

```
 _____
|    |         |    |
|    |   AMT   |    |
|____|_____|____|
       31   35
```

- - - - - - - - - - - - - - - - - - -

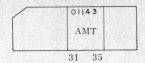

32. The rightmost positions of all fields are sometimes referred to as the low-order or units positions while the leftmost positions are referred to as the high-order positions.

If 456 is to be placed in a six-position TAX field, the low-order three

positions will contain _____ while the high-order three

positions will contain _____.

- - - - - - - - - - - - - - - - - -

the integers 456; zeros

33. Remember that field sizes are generally established to accommodate the longest number of characters expected. Alphabetic or alphanumeric data is placed in the leftmost or high-order positions, with the rightmost or low-order positions containing blanks or spaces if they are not filled. Consider the NAME field in Figure 1.4. The field has 20 positions, and the data SMITH contains 5 characters. Is this data placed in the high-order positions, or the low-order

positions? _____

- - - - - - - - - - - - - - - - - -

high-order positions

34. Represent the address 111 MAIN ST. in the following ADDRESS field.

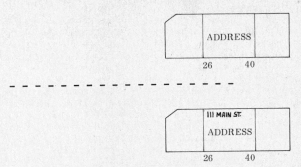

- - - - - - - - - - - - - - - - -

Source Documents and the Use of Keypunch Machines

35. Generally, data is recorded in punched cards from information supplied in a report called a source document. Invoices, purchase orders, and time sheets are examples of source documents. While there are computer machines

which can read information directly from a source document, these machines are expensive and have limitations; therefore, they are used infrequently. Thus, information from source documents must usually be converted to a medium, such as punched cards, for processing by a computer. The punched card is a relatively convenient and inexpensive method of storing data for machine processing.

A device called a <u>keypunch machine</u>, or just keypunch, is used to convert written documents to punched cards. This device, similar to a typewriter, needs an operator to press the appropriate keys representing characters, so that the machine can punch corresponding holes in the card.

Look at Figure 1.5 for an illustration of how source documents are converted to punched cards. In this case, personnel information on J. A. Brown

is converted from a humanly readable report called a _____

to a computer input medium called a _____. The

machine used to perform the conversion is called a _____

and the person who depresses the keys is called a _____.

- -

source document; punched card; keypunch machine or keypunch; keypunch operator

EMPLOYEE NUMBER	DEPT. NO.	NAME	DATE HIRED
125573	129	J. A. BROWN	8/4/75

SOURCE DOCUMENTS

PUNCHED CARDS

EMPLOYEE NUMBER	DEPT. NO.	NAME			DATE HIRED
125573	129	J	A	BROWN	080475

Figure 1.5. The keypunching of data.

36. Using a keypunch machine, the keypunch operator presses the appropriate key and a character is then punched on the card. The Hollerith code is used for punching holes. If desired, the corresponding characters are printed on the top edge of the cards. Consider the card in Figure 1.4 again. The field names AMT and NAME have been preprinted on the cards. The actual data 00383 and SMITH have been punched by the keypunch operator and also have been printed by the keypunch machine on the top edge of the card.

The punched card is generally created from information supplied on a

_____. The card has holes punched according

to the _____ code. These holes may be punched by a

_____ machine.

- - - - - - - - - - - - - - - - -

source document; Hollerith; keypunch

37. The source document is usually an established report that has been suc-
cessfully used in a business area. When a procedure is automated, the source
document is usually converted to a more efficient machine readable form, such
as punched cards or other forms of input for computer processing. Whatever
form of input is created, there is a keying device similar to a keypunch machine that can be used for the conversion.

How can data on a punched card be read by humans? _____

_____

- - - - - - - - - - - - - - - - - -

If the information punched into the card is also printed on the top edge of the
card, it can be easily read.

In the next several sections, you will learn that a punched card can be
read as input by a computer and can also be created as output by a computer.

38. We have thus far seen that there are typically 80 columns on a card. This

limits the size of most card records to how many characters? _____

- - - - - - - - - - - - - - - -

80

39. Since the information that can be included on a card is limited to 80 characters per record, one basic rule is generally followed to insure a concise
card record.

> Edit symbols such as dollar signs, commas, and usually
> decimal points are omitted, and superfluous blanks are not
> entered on input cards.

Consider the NAME field illustrated in Figure 1.5. Note that initials are
adjacent to the LAST NAME field, with no spaces or periods in between. The
LAST NAME field appears first in many card files because it is more efficient
to have major fields than minor ones for identification and sorting purposes.
All data is represented on cards with capital letters.

When this information is later printed as output, the blanks or periods
between initials will be restored for ease of reading; we'll see later how this

is done. Why are blanks, decimal points, dollar signs, and commas not included on a punched card? _____

_____

- - - - - - - - - - - - - - - - - - -

because a punched card has only 80 columns, and these edit symbols would take up columns needed for more important information

40. To insure that most card records will fit the 80-character limit, what edit symbols are usually omitted from alphabetic fields? _____

- - - - - - - - - - - - - - - - - - -

blanks and periods

41. In numeric fields, what edit symbols are usually eliminated? _____

_____

- - - - - - - - - - - - - - - - - - -

dollar signs, commas, decimal points, and blanks

42. Even though the decimal point is sometimes not included on input fields, the computer can be instructed to assume its existence through various programming techniques. In this way, decimal alignment will be maintained even without the inclusion of the decimal point. Thus an amount of $1,346.26 can be represented, as concisely as possible, as _____ on a card.

- - - - - - - - - - - - - - - - - - -

134626

43. Can you determine the meaning of 012075 in a DATE field? _____

- - - - - - - - - - - - - - - - - - -

01/20/75 (The slashes have been eliminated in an effort to save space on the card.)

Printed Reports

44. The printed report is the primary form of computer output. It is the form of output which is most commonly distributed to non-data processing personnel.
    The printed report is generally used as an end product. It is the final result of a computer run, often to be viewed by high-level management. It is printed by a computer device called the printer (see Figure 1.6).

TRIAL BALANCE

BR.	ACCOUNT NUMBER	PREVIOUS TRANS. DATE			ACCOUNT BALANCE		CURRENT DIVIDEND		UNPOSTED DIVIDENT		DIVIDENDS CREDITED THIS YEAR	
		MO	DAY	YR								
R	20001	10	01	75	4,564	14	39	93	39	93	148	08
R	20004	10	01	75	11,145	35	97	51	97	51	361	64
R	20007	10	27	75	225	98	1	96	3	92	12	10
R	20014	2	29	75	6,406	60	53	83	53	83	146	63
R	20017	1	05	76							372	29
R	20018	10	00	75	8,783	98	74	89	74	89	257	56
R	20023	3	27	74	1,944	77	17	01	125	18	63	07
R	20024	3	07	74	3,646	00	31	52	31	52	106	39
R	20027	2	09	76	6,630	49	56	15	56	15	193	05
R	20031	2	10	76	7,093	04	62	05	290	30	228	24
R	20032	2	09	72	4,000	00	26	01	26	01	36	07
R	20035	12	28	75	2,809	02	24	57	24	57	72	79
R	20036	6	15	75	113	75		98	3	47	2	60
											30	96
											119	53
											72	09
											6	44

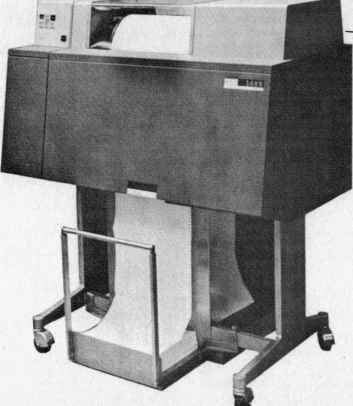

Figure 1.6. The printer. Courtesy IBM.

Other forms of output (such as magnetic tape or disk) are generally intermediate products, ultimately reentering the computer flow as input to another job. These other types of outputs are designed to be as efficient and concise as possible. Fields and records are condensed to make maximum use of the computer and its storage capabilities. The printed report, however, is written with whom in mind? _____

_____

- - - - - - - - - - - - - - - - - - - -

businessmen, non-data processing personnel, high-level management—any of these answers is correct

45. Since many computer-generated reports are read by company executives, such forms must be neat, clear, and easy to interpret. Several characteristics applicable to only printed output must be considered:

  Printing of headings
  Alignment of data
  Editing of printed data
  Spacing of forms

We will consider each of these characteristics independently.
  Printing of headings. Headings generally supply identifying information such as job name, date, page number, and field designations. These items are essential for clarity of presentation when creating printed output. Note that headings are not part of input. They are called constants or literals and are part of the set of instructions to the computer.
  Look again at Figure 1.6. The report illustrated has two headings. One identifies the _____ and the other identifies the

_____.

- - - - - - - - - - - - - - - - - - - -

title of the report, field designations

46. Alignment of data. Reports do not have fields of information adjacent to one another, as is the practice with cards. Printed output is more easily read and interpreted when data is spaced neatly and evenly across the page.
  Because output reports allow for more spaces between fields, do you think that the average printed line contains more or less positions than its corresponding data would occupy in a punched card? _____

- - - - - - - - - - - - - - - - - - - -

If you said "more," you're following the logic. Since output lines generally have more spaces, an average line allows for more characters than an average card. In fact, most computers allow for 132 characters per printed line.

47. <u>Editing of printed data.</u> A printed report must be as clear as possible. Do you think a printed report would include dollar signs, commas, decimal points, and periods even though the punched card would not? Explain your answer. _____

_____

- - - - - - - - - - - - - - - - - -

Yes. All of those edit characters would make a report easier to read and interpret.

48. The printed field $12,450.00 is easy to read. How would this data appear in a typical AMOUNT field on a card? _____

- - - - - - - - - - - - - - - - - -

12450 or perhaps 1245000 where the last two zeros are clearly decimals or fractional digits.

49. <u>Spacing of forms.</u> Printed reports, unlike other kinds of output, must be properly spaced for ease of reading. Certain lines must be single spaced, others double spaced. The printed report must contain adequate margins at both the top and bottom of the form. This requires that the computer be instructed to sense the end of a form and thus to transmit new information to a new page. Now, what information do you think would always precede data lines on a new page? _____

- - - - - - - - - - - - - - - - -

headings

50. While most cards contain (how many?) _____ characters of information, the printed report typically contains _____ characters per line.

- - - - - - - - - - - - - - - - -

80, 132

51. To align data on a printed line, we must leave numerous blanks or spaces between significant data fields. To assist in aligning the printed data, a <u>printer spacing chart</u> is often used (see Figure 1.7). It maps out those areas of a printed line that are to be filled with data.

    Printed reports that serve as computer output are sometimes referred to as <u>continuous forms</u> because they are connected together, separated only by perforations (see Figure 1.8). They are fed into the printer as one continuous form so that constant aligning of forms (as is necessary for each piece of paper in a typewriter) is not required. Each page must have its own heading so that each page can be properly identified.

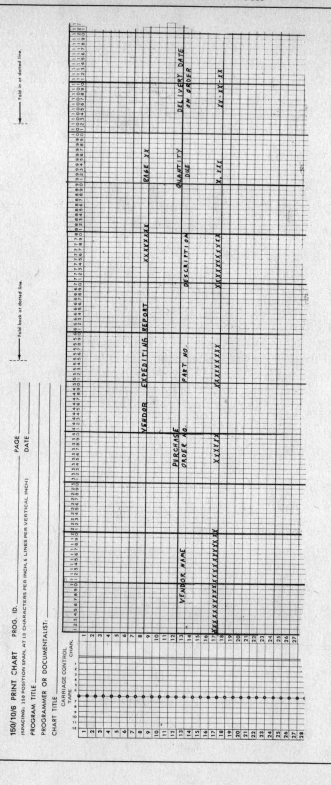

Figure 1.7. Printer spacing chart

In what print positions of Figure 1.7, on the preceding page, does the heading VENDOR EXPEDITING REPORT appear? _____

- - - - - - - - - - - - - - - - - -

41-66

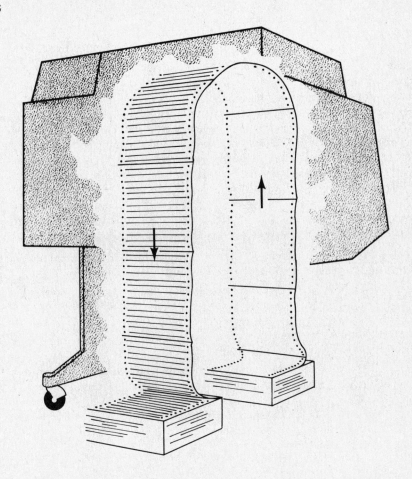

Figure 1.8. Continuous forms. Courtesy IBM.

OTHER COMPUTER MEDIA

52. In addition to the punched card and the printed report, other types of computer input and output are very often used in data processing centers. These include magnetic tape and magnetic disk, which are high speed, high volume media that are capable of storing large amounts of information in a relatively small area. For flowcharting applications, however, you don't need to know the intricacies of these media. We have discussed cards and printed output

just to give you a firm idea of how data can be entered into a computer system and how it can be produced as output. For information and details about tape and disk devices, consult any introductory data processing book.

COMPUTER SYSTEMS

53. Thus far, we have considered the fundamental characteristics of punched cards, printed reports and, to a limited extent, other computer media. It is now time to consider the way in which a computer system operates on these various forms of input and output.

A computer system is a group of machines or devices that work together to act upon data or information. Computer systems consist of a Central Processing Unit (CPU) and devices which can read and/or write information. The Central Processing Unit can rearrange information, punctuate information, perform arithmetic operations, and manipulate data in many other ways.

As we have seen, information entering the computer system is called input, and information produced as a result of the computer run is called output. Devices which can only read information into the computer system are called input devices, while devices which can only write information are termed

_____ devices. The devices which can both read and write are called input/output (I/O) devices. The CPU is the central device which operates on input data and converts it to output.

- - - - - - - - - - - - - - - - - -

output

54. A card read punch is a device that reads punched card information and punches output information. Thus, it is considered what kind of device—input, output, or input/output? _____

- - - - - - - - - - - - - - - - - -

input/output (or I/O)

55. A printer can only write information on a report. It is not capable of reading information into the computer. Thus, it is an _____ device.

- - - - - - - - - - - - - - - - - -

output

56. Tape drives are devices that are capable of both reading and writing information. Thus they are _____ devices.

- - - - - - - - - - - - - - - - - -

input/output

57. An <u>optical scanner</u> is a device that can read information from a printed document. It is a very expensive machine and thus is used only by large companies with extensive amounts of input to process. An optical scanner is an

_____ device.

- - - - - - - - - - - - - - - - - - -

input

58. CPU is an abbreviation for _____.

- - - - - - - - - - - - - - - - - - -

Central Processing Unit

59. What is the purpose of the CPU? _____

_____

- - - - - - - - - - - - - - - - - - - -

The CPU is responsible for operating on input data and converting it to output.

60. Every computer system has a Central Processing Unit. In addition, each computer system has a series of input, output, and I/O devices that are designed to provide the user with maximum use and efficiency for a specific application. The set of physical units in a computer system, including the CPU and the devices, is called the <u>hardware</u>. Each computer system has hardware designed to meet the needs of the specific user.

   (True or False.) Every computer system must have an optical scanner as an input device. _____

- - - - - - - - - - - - - - - - - - -

false—no particular input or output device is required at a given computer center

61. Must every computer system have a CPU to process data? _____

- - - - - - - - - - - - - - - - - - -

yes

62. Figure 1.9 illustrates a typical computer system. Each individual unit represents a(n) _____ or a(n) _____.

- - - - - - - - - - - - - - - - - - -

processing unit, device (input, output, or input/output)

_____

Figure 1.9. Typical computer system. Courtesy Burroughs Corp.

63. Note that in Figure 1.9 some units may be auxiliary storage units which are connected to the Central Processing Unit. Figure 1.9 is a collection of devices contained in a typical computer system. These units together are

called _____.

- - - - - - - - - - - - - - - - - - -

hardware

64. When information is read into a computer system, it is not simply held in the input device. Instead, as the following diagram illustrates, the input data is immediately transmitted from the input device (in this case, the card reader)

to the _____.

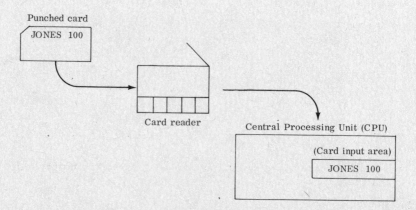

- - - - - - - - - - - - - - - - - - - -

CPU (the input area of the CPU)

65. A READ command or instruction causes the input device to physically sense or "read" the data, which is then instantly transmitted to the CPU. The CPU <u>stores</u> the data for future processing.

After the data has been operated on, or processed, by the CPU, the results are moved to the output area of the CPU. A WRITE command causes the CPU to transmit information to an output or I/O device which then physically creates the output data (punches output cards, prints reports, writes on magnetic tape, etc.).

Consider the following diagram.

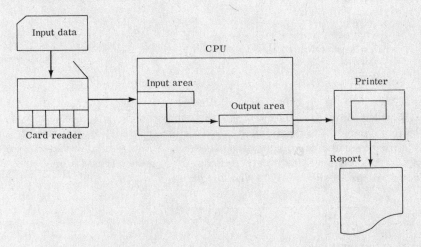

This diagram illustrates the actions required when the data in an input card is to be printed.

In your own words, what happens when a READ command is issued? ___

_____

_____

- - - - - - - - - - - - - - - - -

Data is physically read by the input device and then is immediately transmitted to the CPU (to the input area).

66. What does the CPU do with the data? _____

_____

- - - - - - - - - - - - - - - -

The CPU stores it for further processing.

_____

67. When processing is completed, the output data is transmitted from the

_____ to the _____.

- - - - - - - - - - - - - - - - - - - -

output area of the CPU, output device (in the preceding diagram, a printer)

OPERATIONS

68. The operations that the computer system can perform are classified into five major categories.

> Input
> Output
> Data transfer
> Arithmetic
> Logic

These operations are performed as called for by a programmer's instructions.
    In order to process information, the computer must be told exactly what to do in a series of instructions known as a program.   The program will be inside the computer and direct its actions at the time the information is to be processed.   Hence we say that a computer system requires a stored program. (More about programs later.) Who do you think is responsible for writing the

program? _____

- - - - - - - - - - - - - - - - - - -

the programmer

69. We have discussed input and output operations to some extent.   An input operation is one which reads data into the computer.   An output operation is one which writes data from a computer.   The computer's major task is to con- vert the input data into output data by processing it.   The processing is per- formed by data transfer, arithmetic, and logic operations.
    When input data enters the processing unit, it is stored in an input area. Similarly, output data which will be sent to an output unit is stored in an output

area.   Where are these input and output areas located? _____

_____

- - - - - - - - - - - - - - - - - - - -

in the Central Processing Unit

70. The input and output areas are located in separate areas within the pro- cessing unit.   Suppose that we wish to print information from an input card. Can you guess why the following would not be correct?

_____

READ A CARD
WRITE A LINE

- - - - - - - - - - - - - - - - - -

The data was never transferred to the output area. The READ command puts
data in the input area of the processing unit. The WRITE command causes
data that is in the output area to be printed. Since nothing was ever placed in
the output area, nothing will print. (As we will see, we must instruct the
computer to move data from input to output.)

Note that in some programming languages, the programmer must explicit-
ly indicate to the computer that a data transfer operation is required. In other
languages, however, the programmer does not use such a specific instruction;
instead, the language will automatically supply it. That is,

READ A CARD
WRITE A LINE

is acceptable in some programming languages, because the computer itself
automatically supplies the missing data transfer operation. Since our concern
here is with computer logic, and not with specific programming languages, we
will indicate the need for a data transfer operation regardless of how the computer is instructed to perform it.

71. The operation used to transfer data from input area to output area is
called a data transfer. The transfer of information, exactly as is, from one
storage area to another is performed by a MOVE command. Consider below:

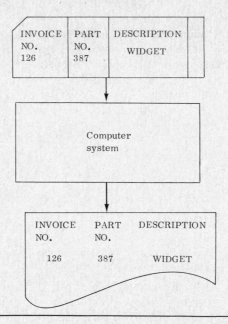

The transfer of data in the preceding illustration is performed by a MOVE operation. Now consider the following.

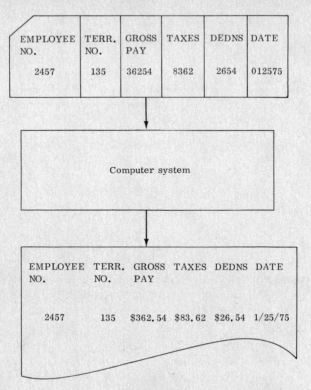

EMPLOYEE NO.	TERR. NO.	GROSS PAY	TAXES	DEDNS	DATE
2457	135	36254	8362	2654	012575

Computer system

EMPLOYEE NO.	TERR. NO.	GROSS PAY	TAXES	DEDNS	DATE
2457	135	$362.54	$83.62	$26.54	1/25/75

You will recall that input data is usually condensed with few or no edit symbols, while output reports must contain such symbols. (More about this later.) Notice, in the above example, that certain fields of information have been changed by punctuation. The data transfer operation can be used to move and punctuate information so that it is in "report form," or in a form that is more readable. This function is sometimes referred to as move and edit.

Look again at the illustration above. In what way has the input GROSS

PAY field been edited? _____ In what way

has the input DATE field been edited? _____

– – – – – – – – – – – – – – – – – –

GROSS PAY, on the report, has a dollar sign and a decimal point. DATE, on the report, has slashes between month, day, and year, and a 1 instead of 01 for month.

72. In summary, input data can be processed by transferring it to the output area, by a simple move or a move and edit function.

This is shown in the following illustration.

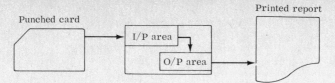

Note: I/P—abbreviation for input; O/P—abbreviation for output.

Note also that this is not really a transfer of data but a transmission of data. That is, information is not actually moved to the output area but is <u>duplicated</u> at the output area. After the move operation, the information is still available at the input area.

Suppose, then, that we wish to print a line and create a tape record from a single input card.

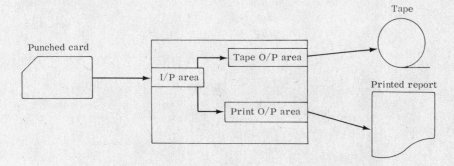

In computer terminology, a sequence is a series of instructions to be performed in a specific order. From what you know so far, is the following a correct sequence? _____

> READ A CARD
> MOVE INPUT TO TAPE OUTPUT AREA
> WRITE TAPE
> MOVE INPUT TO PRINT OUTPUT AREA
> WRITE A LINE

- - - - - - - - - - - - - - - - - -

Yes, it is, and if you understand why, you're doing great! The first three instructions create a tape record from the input card; since the transfer of data to the tape output area did not in any way alter the data at the input area, we can still move the input data to another output area. Note that the above are English instructions which, in order to run on a computer, would have to be converted to a special form. More about computer languages later.

Arithmetic Operations

73. The fourth major type of operation performed by a computer system is arithmetic operations, including adding, subtracting, multiplying, and dividing.

Consider the following diagram.

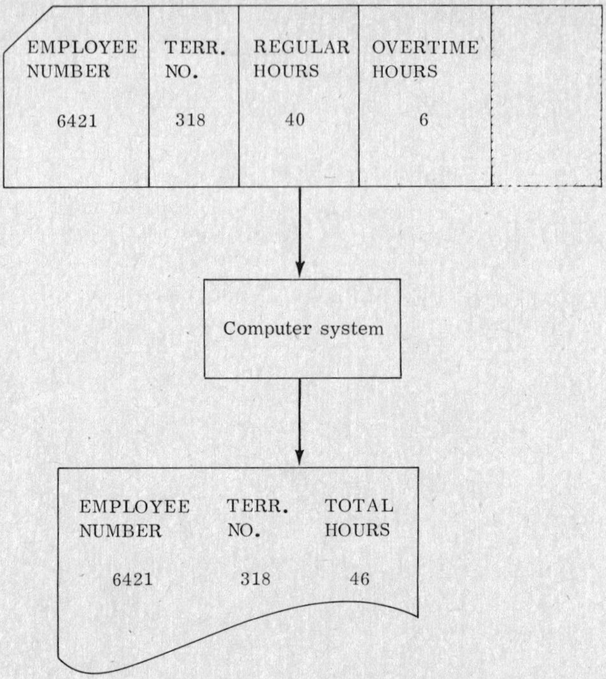

EMPLOYEE NUMBER	TERR. NO.	REGULAR HOURS	OVERTIME HOURS	
6421	318	40	6	

Computer system

EMPLOYEE NUMBER	TERR. NO.	TOTAL HOURS
6421	318	46

Here, some processing is included. Another difference between this problem and preceding ones is that in this case we are moving <u>fields</u> to the output area rather than entire input records. Any data item can be moved to the output area. Note also that the output fields don't have to be in the same sequence as input fields.

Both the input and output areas may be subdivided into corresponding fields and thus input data fields may be moved to output data fields. Try to determine the sequence of instructions that would be necessary to convert input data into output. Write your instructions in the space below.

- - - - - - - - - - - - - - - - - - -

READ A CARD
MOVE INPUT EMPLOYEE NUMBER TO OUTPUT EMPLOYEE NUMBER
MOVE INPUT TERR NO TO OUTPUT TERR NO
ADD REGULAR HOURS AND OVERTIME HOURS AND PUT ANSWER IN
  TOTAL HOURS
WRITE A RECORD

Note: Since these are not actual instructions but just the sequence of necessary instructions, the wording is not significant. That is, if you had the same
sequence but in different words, it's okay. The important point is that you
need a READ statement, two MOVE statements, and an ADD statement before
a WRITE is executed.

74. In frame 73, the individual's regular hours were added to overtime hours
to produce total hours. So there is one output line printed from how many input cards? _____

– –

one

75. Thus far, we have used single input records to produce single output records. This is not always the case. Often we wish to create a single output
record from several input records and, similarly, we can create several output records from a single input record.
    Consider the following.

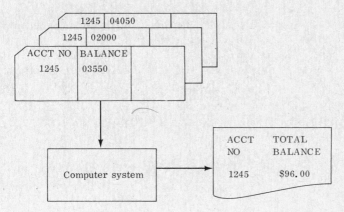

In this particular case, there is one output line printed from how many input

cards? _____

– –

three

76. For every WRITE instruction in the sequence there will be how many

READ instructions? _____

– – – – – – – – – – – – – – – – – – – –

three

77. The input BALANCE fields are in "raw" form while the output amount is in "concise" or _____ form.

- - - - - - - - - - - - - - - - - -

edited

78. The three input BALANCE fields (one from each card) are to be added together and the answer stored in an area called HOLD. This will be an area in storage, not part of input or output, that can be reserved for future processing. After the additions are performed, the area called HOLD can be moved

to the output TOTAL BALANCE area by a _____

operation.

- - - - - - - - - - - - - - - - - -

data transfer (in this case, a MOVE AND EDIT instruction)
Note: Usually programmers do not add fields in an output area since output fields require editing.

79. Now let's try to construct the sequence of instructions necessary to perform the required operations for the problem in frame 75. Notice that the ACCT NO doesn't change and needs to be moved only once. We've done the first part of the sequence for you. You should write the instructions to read the other two cards, total the balances, and produce edited output.

        READ A CARD
        MOVE ACCT NO OF INPUT TO ACCT NO OF OUTPUT
        ADD BALANCE TO HOLD

- - - - - - - - - - - - - - - - - -

READ A CARD
ADD BALANCE TO HOLD
READ A CARD
ADD BALANCE TO HOLD
MOVE AND EDIT HOLD TO TOTAL BALANCE OF OUTPUT
WRITE A RECORD

If you answered this correctly, congratulate yourself. If not, be certain that you understand the above solution before you go on. And be patient—computer expertise takes time.

80. Consider the following.

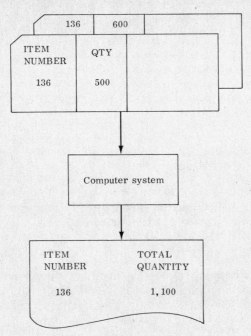

Try to construct the sequence of instructions necessary to produce the required output.

- - - - - - - - - - - - - - - - - - -

READ A CARD
MOVE ITEM NUMBER OF INPUT TO ITEM NUMBER OF OUTPUT
ADD QTY TO STORE
READ A CARD
ADD QTY TO STORE
MOVE AND EDIT STORE TO TOTAL QUANTITY
WRITE A LINE

Note that STORE could be any name. Indeed, all the instructions such as READ or MOVE have specific forms depending upon the programming language, but names of fields are typically supplied by the programmer.

81. Would a MOVE instruction be just as good as the MOVE AND EDIT in the

above example? _____

- - - - - - - - - - - - - - - - - -

_____

no, not if the output is to contain commas

82. Would the following correctly solve the problem in frame 80? _____

> READ A CARD
> ADD QTY TO STORE
> READ A CARD
> MOVE ITEM NUMBER OF INPUT TO ITEM NUMBER OF OUTPUT
> ADD QTY TO STORE
> MOVE AND EDIT STORE TO TOTAL QUANTITY
> WRITE A LINE

- - - - - - - - - - - - - - - - - -

Yes, it's fine. The item number moved is not from the first card, but from the second card. Since both cards have the same item number, there's no problem. If you had any trouble with this problem, go back and review the section.

83. Just as several input cards can be used to create a single output line, several output lines can be produced from a single input card.

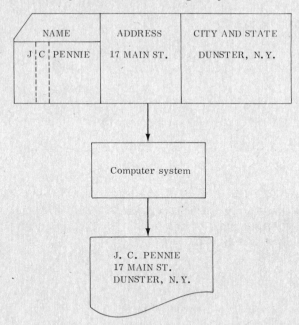

Now, for every READ command, how many output lines will be printed?

_____

- - - - - - - - - - - - - - - -

three

84. Try to construct the sequence of instructions necessary for converting input to output in the diagram in frame 83.

- - - - - - - - - - - - - - - - - -

READ A CARD
MOVE AND EDIT NAME OF INPUT TO NAME OF OUTPUT
WRITE A LINE
MOVE ADDRESS OF INPUT TO ADDRESS OF OUTPUT
WRITE A LINE
MOVE CITY AND STATE OF INPUT TO CITY AND STATE OF OUTPUT
WRITE A LINE

Note: NAME OF OUTPUT, ADDRESS OF OUTPUT, and CITY AND STATE OF OUTPUT refer to fields established in the output area.

Logic Operations

85. The fifth, and last, major type of operation is called a logic operation. A logic operation is used to test a specific condition. In this way, the computer can "make a decision or decisions" based on the outcome of a condition test. Logic operations give the computer the flexibility it needs to alter the sequence of instructions and to test for specific conditions.

The following represent the types of comparisons which the computer can make: IS A = B; IS C GREATER THAN D; IS A EQUAL 6. On the basis of the results of these operations, the computer can be instructed to either alter the sequence of instructions or to perform different operations. Computer programs gain great flexibility through using these logic operations. The next chapter will discuss them in more depth.

JOBS AND THEIR PROGRAMS

86. Each data processing problem included in this chapter may be called a job. A job is an assignment to produce specific output data from specific input data. Each job requires its own set of operations. The operations required for each job will be unique and in a different sequence than those for other jobs. The sequence of operations is critical in performing a job.

Consider the following two sequences.

Sequence 1	Sequence 2
READ	READ
MOVE	WRITE
WRITE	MOVE

Although both contain the same instructions, they represent different sequences and different jobs, because the instructions are _____

_____ .

- - - - - - - - - - - - - - - - - -

in different order

87. A job requires a specific set of instructions which tells the computer what to do. Each of the sequences in frame 86 represents a set of instructions to the computer. These are, of course, exceedingly simplified and segmented; most jobs require dozens or even hundreds of such instructions. The total set of instructions to the computer which is used to perform the job of converting input to output is called a program. Programs are written by specially trained computer specialists called programmers.

The programmer must understand the exact requirements of the job before he or she writes, or codes, the program. The programmer is usually provided with a job description which spells out the details of the job. He or she must study this job description to learn the exact specifications and requirements of the job.

To insure a complete understanding of the program to be written, the programmer must plan out the sequence of steps that are required. Programmers plan out the sequence that will be used in the program in a pictorial diagram called a flowchart or block diagram. A flowchart represents the integrated set of procedures which must be followed by the program, and flowcharting is what this Self-Teaching Guide is all about.

What is a program? _____

_____

- - - - - - - - - - - - - - - - - -

A program is a set of instructions that indicates to the computer the operations to be performed in converting input to output.

88. What is a flowchart? _____

_____

- - - - - - - - - - - - - - - - - -

A flowchart is a pictorial representation of the logic that will be required in the program.

_____

89. Is a flowchart written before the program or after it? Explain your answer. _____

_____

_____

- - - - - - - - - - - - - - - - -

Before, because it is used to help the programmer organize the data flow that will be required in the program. Once the flowchart is complete, the programmer can formalize an understanding of the job and proceed to code the program.

90. Generally, the program instructions tell the computer system how to operate on <u>fields</u> of data. That is, the content of the input and the output is <u>variable</u> and thus is not actually specified in the program, since it changes as each input record is read and each output record is created. For example, if for each input card we want to add a TAX field to an AMT field, the instruction might read ADD TAX TO AMT. Would we then need to indicate to the computer the precise content of TAX and AMT, as part of the program's instructions? Explain your answer. _____

_____

_____

- - - - - - - - - - - - - - - - - -

No. These two fields vary from input card to input card; each time the computer is instructed to add these fields, it will look for their contents in the input area.

91. Data that does not remain the same but varies from input record to input record is called _____ data.

- - - - - - - - - - - - - - - -

variable

92. Thus it can be said that programs are designed to operate on variable data. Some operations, however, also require <u>constants</u> to produce the desired output data. A constant is a predefined value that is necessary for producing output but which is not part of input.

For example, suppose we wish to compute an output field called SALES TAX by multiplying AMT, an input field, by .08, the tax rate. The instruction might appear as MULTIPLY AMT BY .08 GIVING SALES TAX.

The contents of the AMT field depends on each input record and is thus called a _____ field. Each AMT is multiplied by the preestablished value .08. The number .08, then, would be called a _____.

The output field, SALES TAX, is, like the input AMT field, a _____

field.

- - - - - - - - - - - - - - - - - - -

variable; constant; variable

93. The predefined value called a constant must be written into the program.
Programs, then, consist of instructions and constants.

Suppose that every employee at a company is given a bonus of $100 at the
end of the year. The instruction issued to the computer might read ADD 100
TO SALARY GIVING TOTAL - MONEY. What type of field, then, is SALARY?

_____ The number 100 is called a

_____.

- - - - - - - - - - - - - - - - - - -

a variable data field; constant

Notice that the amount $100 was represented in the program instruction
as 100. As a matter of convention, you will recall that numeric constants—
constants to be used in arithmetic operations—never contain edit symbols such
as dollar signs or commas, but may contain decimal points. Similarly, as a
matter of convention, non-numeric constants will be indicated in instructions
with single quote marks. Thus, if we wish to print the constant THIS PRO-
GRAM WORKED FINE on the printer, we might instruct the computer as follows.

        MOVE 'THIS PROGRAM WORKED FINE' TO OUTPUT AREA
        WRITE A LINE

There are many ways of communicating with a computer. That is, programs can be written in many different programming languages. In Chapter
7, we will learn something about the varieties of programming languages and
their major characteristics. However, flowcharting, as taught in this book,
is largely independent of any specific programming language. That is, flowcharting is a standard method of depicting computer logic and will apply to all
languages, regardless of the precise coding rules required. When a standard
is adopted, as in the above with constants, it is because that standard is appropriate to the majority of programming languages in use today. The rules
for forming field names, for example, is not a standard that can be applied to
all or most languages and thus will not be referenced in this book. You can
use any field name you desire, keeping in mind that the actual programming
language used will be somewhat more restrictive.

SELF-TEST

1. Match each of the following descriptions with the appropriate term from the column at the right.

_____ (a) information or data entering a computer system

_____ (b) information produced by a computer system

_____ (c) the originating form of information (such as purchase orders or sales slips) entering a data processing environment

_____ (d) the term used to describe the physical devices in a computer system

_____ (e) the set of instructions written by the programmer that results in reading and processing of input by the computer and creation of desired output

_____ (f) a pictorial representation of logic written by the programmer to insure understanding of the logic required in a program

_____ (g) code used for representing data on a punched card

_____ (h) a device used to convert written documents to punched cards

1. Hollerith
2. hardware
3. keypunch
4. data
5. flowchart
6. output
7. program
8. source document
9. input

2. In terms of hierarchies of data, name each of the following.

(a)

_____

(b)

NAME

_____

_____

(c)

_____

(d)

_____

3. How many columns are on a typical punched card? _____

4. A field that can contain only numbers, a decimal point, and a + or − sign is called a _____ field.

5. How would the number 62 be represented in a five-position numeric field?

_____

6. How would the name ANDREWS be represented in a ten-position alphanumeric field? _____

7. (True or False.) Edit symbols are usually omitted from input in order to make the input more concise. _____. Edit symbols are usually omitted from output in order to make the output more concise. _____

8. What is the primary form of computer output? _____
What is the name of the device that produces this output? _____

9. Match the following descriptions of storage areas and types of operations with the appropriate term from the column at the right.

_____ (a) an operation that reads data into the computer

_____ (b) an operation that produces outgoing information

_____ (c) an operation that moves data from one area of storage to another

1. output area
2. data transfer
3. flowchart
4. logic
5. input
6. input area
7. arithmetic
8. output

_____ (d) an operation that performs addition, subtraction, multiplication, or any combination of these

_____ (e) an operation that results in the computer making a decision

_____ (f) a series of storage positions within the CPU set aside by the programmer for storing input records

_____ (g) a series of storage positions within the CPU set aside by the programmer for storing output records

10. The following three cards are to produce a single output line as indicated. Write the set of instructions to perform this.

BALANCE ON HAND = BALANCE (FIRST CARD) + DEPOSITS (SECOND CARD) - WITHDRAWALS (THIRD CARD)

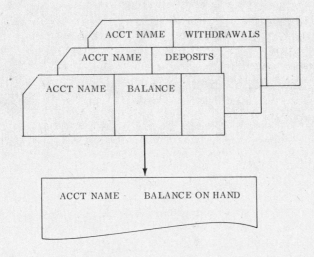

Answers to Self-Test

1. (a) 9; (b) 6; (c) 8; (d) 2; (e) 7; (f) 5; (g) 1; (h) 3
(frames 3, 4, 12, 35–37, 60, 68, 87–89)

2.   (a) character; (b) field; (c) record; (d) file
(frames 5, 6, 8, 14, 20)

3.   80 (frame 10)

4.   numeric (frames 21–25)

5.   00062 (frames 21–25, 29–32)

6.   ANDREWSₗₗₗ (ₗ is the representation for a blank) (frames 21, 22, 28, 33, 34)

7.   true; false—output, especially printed output, is often not created with conciseness in mind
(frames 39–43, 47, 48)

8. the printed report; the printer
(frame 44)

9.   (a) 5; (b) 8; (c) 2; (d) 7; (e) 4; (f) 6; (g) 1
(frames 3, 4, 37, 44, 53–57, 64, 65, 67, 68–73, 85)

10. READ A CARD
     MOVE ACCT NAME IN INPUT TO ACCT NAME IN OUTPUT
     MOVE BALANCE TO BALANCE ON HAND
     READ A CARD
     ADD DEPOSITS TO BALANCE ON HAND
     READ A CARD
     SUBTRACT WITHDRAWALS FROM BALANCE ON HAND
     WRITE A LINE
(frames 70, 72, 73–84)

Note: You might have established an intermediate work area for your calculations and then moved that work area to BALANCE ON HAND.

CHAPTER TWO
Elements of Flowcharting

The art of computer programming is based on logical integration of processing steps. This book aims to teach you how to logically integrate programming processes by using the flowcharting technique. If you can construct valid flowcharts, you should be able to program in any computer language after learning the basic rules of the language.

When you complete this chapter you will be able to:

- identify and use the basic symbols of flowcharting;

- interpret simple logical sequences represented by a flowchart;

- draw a flowchart representing simple logical sequences.

A program flowchart is a diagram, or pictorial representation, of the logical flow of data to be processed. Before you code a program, you must draw a flowchart to outline the sequence of programming steps to be coded. To master the art of flowcharting is to fully understand the nature of computer processing. So the key to successful computer processing is not in mastering the program rules but rather in understanding logic flow.

1.   A flowchart is a tool to assist the programmer in preparing the program. Its use by the programmer is analogous to the use of a blueprint by an architect. An architect draws a blueprint before a building is constructed. A programmer draws a flowchart before a _____ is written.

- - - - - - - - - - - - - - - - - -

program

2.   A blueprint illustrates the arrangement of units to be constructed in a building, and their relationship to one another. So, too, a program flowchart is a drawing that shows the arrangement of functions to be performed in a program, and their logical interrelationship.

Every different building is constructed from a different blueprint. Similarly, every different program is written from a different _____.

- - - - - - - - - - - - - - - - - -

program flowchart

3.   The programmer draws a program flowchart to insure that the steps to be coded in the program will integrate properly. A flowchart, then, consists of steps to be programmed, and the sequence in which these steps are to be performed.

What should the programmer do, before coding, to insure that his/her conceptualization of the logical integration of elements in a program is accurate? _____

- - - - - - - - - - - - - - - - - - -

draw a flowchart

4.   Flowcharts consist of <u>symbols</u>, which represent program functions, and <u>flowlines</u>, which denote the sequence in which these functions are to be performed. Instructions are written inside the symbols, but we've left those out in our example diagram below.

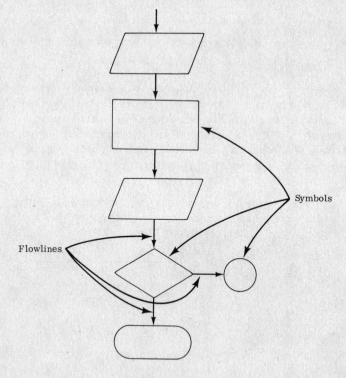

Figure 2. 1

A program flowchart is read from top to bottom, as the flowlines in Figure 2.1 indicate. The only variation to this vertical reading is if a <u>decision</u> is to be made by the computer, which causes a change in the sequence.

Flowlines are used to connect symbols of a flowchart.   These flowlines indicate that the flow of logic is usually in what direction?   _____

_____ What might change the flow of logic?   _____

- - - - - - - - - - - - - - - - - -

from top to bottom; a decision

5.   Figure 2.2 illustrates a flowcharting template, which is used for drawing all flowcharting symbols. The template is made of transparent plastic, and has cut-outs for the various symbols. The symbols noted on the template are in the standard form that is used throughout the computer industry. Since you will be constructing flowcharts using the standard form, you should buy your own template. They are available at most college bookstores and at large stationery stores.

In a flowchart, program functions are represented by _____

_____ and the sequence of functions is shown by _____.

- - - - - - - - - - - - - - - - - -

flowcharting symbols; flowlines (or arrows)

6.   We have seen that a flowchart is a series of symbols, each representing a function to be programmed. These symbols are connected by flowlines indicating the direction, or flow, of data. (Note that the phrase "flow of data" is synonymous with "logic flow.") Looking back at Figure 2.1 you will see that the first and third symbols are the same. This means that they represent the same function. While a single symbol, representing a specific function, may be used in several places in a flowchart, different operations may be required each time it is used.

For example, denotes an input/output function. Used in several places, this symbol may denote the operations of WRITE A LINE, READ A CARD, WRITE A TAPE, and so on. To indicate the specific operation for a given function, we write a note inside the appropriate symbol.

is the symbol for a processing function. Using this symbol, express the operation of ADD AMT TO TOTAL.

- - - - - - - - - - - - - - - - - -

ADD AMT
TO TOTAL

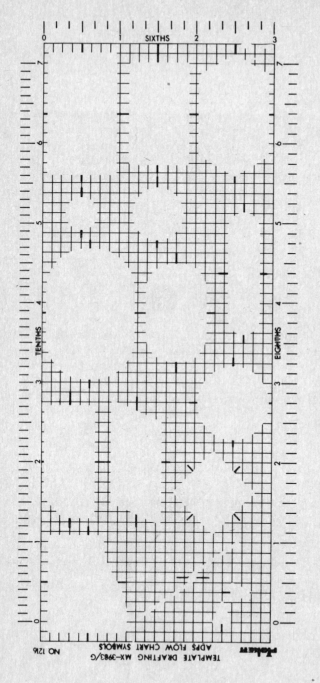

Figure 2.2. Flowcharting template.

7. From Figure 2.1 we see that a flowchart can require a function to be performed more than one time. In this figure we see that the function to be performed exactly two times is represented by which symbol ? (Draw it below.)

The actual operations noted in that symbol (must, need not) _____

be the same.

- - - - - - - - - - - - - - - -

/_____/ ; need not (This input/output function may represent differ-

ent operations. The first time it may signify a read operation; the second
time it could signify a write operation.)

MAJOR FLOWCHARTING SYMBOLS

A flowcharting template includes all symbols that are used for both systems
and programming flowcharts. The major programming symbols that we will
be using are as follows.

Symbol	Explanation
	Input/Output: used for input or output operations
	Processing: used for internal computer process-ing, usually encompassing data movement or arithmetic operations
	Decision: used for logical comparisons (always in the form of a YES or NO question)
	Connector: used for altering the normal flow of data or for specifying an entry point where the flow is to continue
	Terminal: used for start (optional), end, or interruption of a program

8.   Study the chart of major flowchart symbols. Then, match the following symbols with the appropriate names.

_____   (a) Terminal

_____   (b) Processing

_____   (c) Decision

_____   (d) Input/Output

_____   (e) Connector

1

2

3

4

5

- - - - - - - - - - - - - - - -

(a) 3; (b) 1; (c) 2; (d) 5; (e) 4

9.   Now let's put together the brief description in the chart of major flow-charting symbols with what you remember from Chapter 1 about the types of computer operations. See if you can tell which symbols would be used for each of the following operations. Name and draw the symbol.

(a) Print a line

(b) Add overtime to total pay

(c) Is M greater than 12?

(d) Stop the run

(e) Go to the End of Job routine

(f) Has the last card been read?

(g) Move name of the input to name of the output

(h) Rewind the tape

- - - - - - - - - - - - - - - - - -

(a)    Input/Output (You got this one right, I hope?)

(b)    Processing (Arithmetic operations are usually coded as processing functions.)

(c) 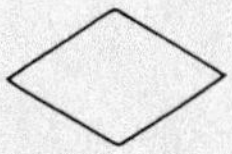   Decision (This is a common type of logical comparison. We should also note that all questions are asked in decision symbols.)

(d) 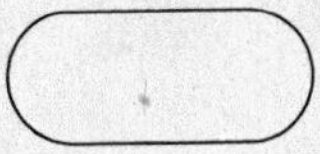   Terminal (An easy one.)

(e) 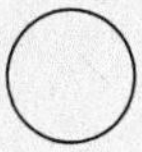   Connector (You might have said "Terminal" because you saw "End." Actually, as you'll see later, GO TO instructions alter the flow of data and are always coded in a connector symbol. In this case, GO TO directs the flow to a special set of "wrap-up" operations called the End of Job routine.)

(f) 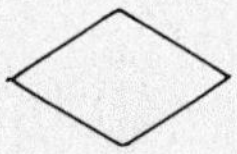   Decision (Another question. A common use of decision symbols is this last card test.)

(g)    Processing (Did you notice that move instructions are usually coded as processing functions?)

(h)    Input/Output (This one was a bit tricky. For
the record, note that any function related to an
input/output function is coded in this symbol.)

10.   Here is a sequence of instructions you wrote in Chapter 1.

READ A CARD
MOVE INPUT EMPLOYEE NUMBER TO OUTPUT EMPLOYEE
    NUMBER
MOVE INPUT TERR NO TO OUTPUT TERR NO
ADD REGULAR HOURS AND OVERTIME HOURS AND PUT ANSWER
    IN TOTAL HOURS
WRITE A RECORD

Here are the same instructions in flowchart form.

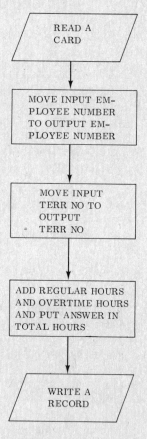

Now you try writing the following instructions in flowchart form. (To keep it
simple, we have used no decisions, connectors, or terminals.) For now, put
just one instruction in each symbol. Draw your flowchart on a separate piece
of paper.

READ A CARD
MOVE ITEM NUMBER OF INPUT TO ITEM NUMBER OF OUTPUT
ADD QTY TO STORE .
READ A CARD
ADD QTY TO STORE
MOVE AND EDIT STORE TO TOTAL QUANTITY
WRITE A LINE

- - - - - - - - - - - - - - - - -

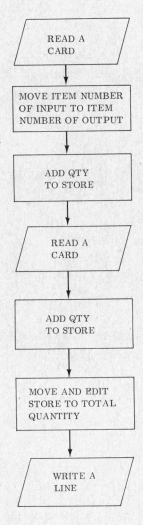

11. A matter of convention: For input/output functions, one symbol usually represents a single instruction. For processing functions, however, we can combine one or more closely related processing instructions within a single processing symbol. This method of representation enables flowcharts to be

shorter and simpler. It also makes it easier for someone reading the flow-chart to understand the function to be performed.

Thus, to calculate an AVERAGE TEST SCORE from three input scores, EXAM1, EXAM2, and EXAM3, the following, while correct, would not be considered concise enough.

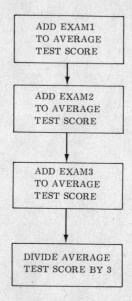

Try to construct a <u>single</u> processing symbol with a note that summarizes the operations performed above and represents them as a single function.

- - - - - - - - - - - - - - - -

Two possible solutions follow. Your solution may be worded differently.

AVERAGE TEST SCORE = (EXAM1 + EXAM2 + EXAM3) DIVIDED BY 3	or	CALCULATE AVERAGE TEST SCORE BY ADD-ING 3 EXAM SCORES AND DIVIDING BY 3

The actual wording used within each symbol is unimportant as long as the precise meaning is clear. (Of course, if your condensed instructions don't fit into one symbol, but "bulge out" instead, then use two! The aim is clarity.) As you evaluate your flowcharts throughout this book, just check to see that you have reasonably similar notes within the symbols and that you have the symbols and sequences correct. (Sequences, too, will vary in the more complex flowcharts.)

CONNECTORS

12. Here is a simple flowchart excerpt that reads a card, moves the data on that card to the print output area, and writes a line.

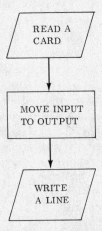

Suppose we wish to alter the above flowchart excerpt so that the sequence of steps is repeated. We could simply repeat the series as shown below.

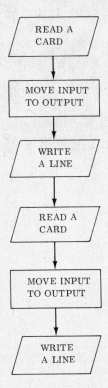

When translated into a program, the preceding sequence would work for how many cards? _____

- - - - - - - - - - - - - - - - - - -

two

13. If we had fifteen cards to process, we could repeat the sequence, or series of operations, fifteen times. You can see that this repetition of steps could become rather tedious, particularly when large volumes of data are to be processed. In reality, programmers do not repeat instructions in this way. Such repetition is not only cumbersome, but often unfeasible, since programmers generally do not know how many input records will be processed for any given run. Suppose, for example, that a program which produces payroll checks from payroll records is to be run on a weekly basis. The programmer would not know the number of payroll records to be processed in any given week, since that number changes daily as, for example, employees resign or new people are hired. Thus we must be able to indicate on flowcharts (and programs) that a sequence of steps is to be repeated for all available input records, regardless of the number.

Now suppose we wish to alter our original flowchart excerpt from frame 12 so that the series of steps is repeated for all the available input cards. How do we do that? The best technique is to issue a branch instruction after the write operation that will instruct the computer to go back to the beginning and start processing over again. A branch instruction alters the normal flow of execution and instructs the computer to continue executing at a different point. A connector symbol is used in a flowchart to depict the branch instruction:

Whenever you wish to alter the flow of a program and instruct the computer to proceed to some step other than the next sequential step, what kind of instruction do you need? _____

Draw the symbol used for that kind of instruction.

- - - - - - - - - - - - - - - - - - -

a branch instruction;

14. So far, you have been given one major use of branch instructions. (There are many other uses, as we'll see later.) In your own words, explain this major use of branching. _____

_____

_____

- - - - - - - - - - - - - - - - - -

To repeat a sequence of instructions, we can instruct the computer to begin processing again with a branch instruction. (More generally, as we'll see, a branch instruction is used when a program is to proceed to some step other than the next sequential step.)

15. As with other flowchart symbols, we specify instructions by writing notes or labels inside the connector symbol. To specify that processing should re-

turn to BEGIN, for example, we would write:

Add a connector to the following flowchart so that after a write instruction is executed, a branch to BEGIN occurs.

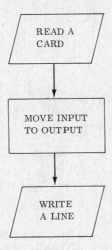

- - - - - - - - - - - - - - - -

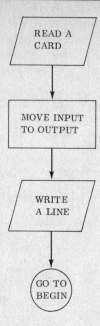

16. The GO TO BEGIN instruction in frame 15 is called a _____

instruction and it is written in a _____ symbol.

- - - - - - - - - - - - - - - - - -

branch, connector

17. The flowchart excerpt now has a branch instruction which will instruct the
the computer, when programmed, to continue executing with the instruction
called BEGIN. We must then label some instruction BEGIN, for which we also
use connector symbols. Since our aim here is to repeat the sequence of steps,
we will place a connector symbol labeled BEGIN before the first step of the
flowchart excerpt. Thus, our excerpt will be modified as shown on the following page.

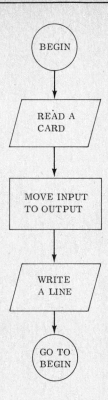

Note the direction and placement of the arrows on the connector symbols.

GO TO BEGIN ⃝ is an <u>unconditional branch connector</u>. It indicates to the computer

that the logic flow is <u>always</u> altered at this point and execution continues with the instruction labeled BEGIN. The phrase GO TO BEGIN is often abbreviated

within the symbol to BEGIN: ⃝BEGIN

⃝ is an <u>entry connector</u>, which serves as an indicator or label

corresponding to some branch connector. Thus the connector ⃝BEGIN does

<u>not</u> correspond to an instruction, but serves as a label to an instruction.

Suppose that ⃝FINISH is a symbol in a flowchart. The symbol is called

a(n) _____ connector. There must

also be a corresponding symbol called a(n) _____

connector. Draw this corresponding symbol.

— — — — — — — — — — — — — — — — — —

unconditional branch; entry; (FINISH)
↓

18. Entry and branch connectors work together as a team. A branch connector must refer to a specific entry connector. For instance, suppose that we
had an entry connector labeled PRT–RTN. (The label PRT–RTN is a common
abbreviation for PRINT ROUTINE.) Draw the symbol which would represent
the unconditional branch to that step.

— — — — — — — — — — — — — — — — — —

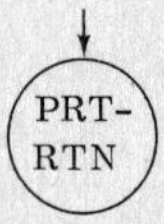

↓
(PRT–
RTN)

Note that the label name used for a branch connector must correspond precisely to a label name used as an entry connector.

19. Would the following be valid to repeat the sequence of instructions? _____

If not, why? _____

_____

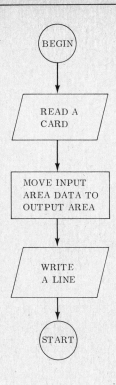

- - - - - - - - - - - - - - - - - -

No. The unconditional branch GO TO START must correspond to an entry connector with the <u>same</u> label. BEGIN is not understood by the computer to be the same as START.

20. If GO TO XXX is to be an instruction in a program, then XXX must be identified as a _____ in that program.

- - - - - - - - - - - - - - - - - -

label or entry connector

21. When a branch is to be made to the <u>beginning</u> of a sequence or routine,

is the appropriate entry connector. Sometimes, however, we don't need to repeat a complete sequence. Suppose we want to branch to some point <u>within</u> a routine or sequence. Then we would use ⟲ as the entry connector. Consider the example on the following page.

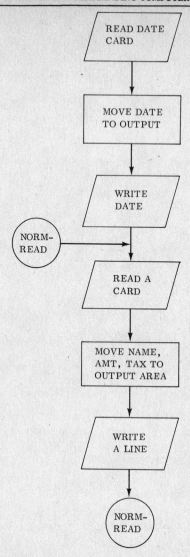

In the above flowchart how many times are the steps READ DATE CARD,

MOVE DATE TO OUTPUT, and WRITE DATE performed? _____ Is the

symbol ⟨NORM-READ⟩→ an instruction? Explain. _____

_____

After the above three instructions, a new card is read, the date moved, and

an output line is written. Processing then continues with _____

_____

- - - - - - - - - - - - - - - - - - -

once; no, it is a point of entry, a label corresponding to the unconditional

branch instruction 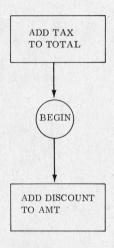 ; the reading of another <u>data</u> card (There's no

need to read a new <u>date</u> card each time.)

22. Note that an unconditional branch instructs the computer to proceed to some other point in the program. With this in mind, can you determine what is wrong with the following flowchart excerpt?

ADD TAX
TO TOTAL

BEGIN

ADD DISCOUNT
TO AMT

- - - - - - - - - - - - - - - - - -

An unconditional branch connector must be the <u>last</u> symbol in a sequence.

23. Thus far, we have used connector symbols as either unconditional branch connectors or as entry connectors. If a connector is to represent an unconditional branch, it must be the last step in a sequence, since it causes execution to resume at a different point in the program.

    If the connector in frame 22 were to represent an unconditional branch, the ADD DISCOUNT TO AMT would never be executed. Similarly, if a connector is to represent an entry point, it must <u>not</u> be coded in the middle of a

sequence but to the left of the sequence as .

    See if you can modify the flowchart excerpt from frame 22 to make it correct. (There are two possible correct answers.)

- - - - - - - - - - - - - - - - - -

Using the connector as
unconditional branch:

Using the connector
as entry point:

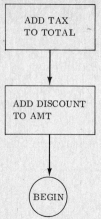

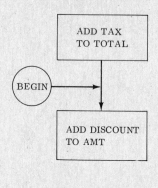

In either case, to every unconditional branch connector in a flowchart, there must correspond an entry connector.

24. Consider this flowchart excerpt.

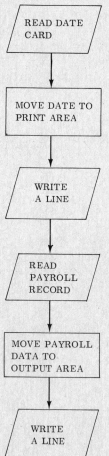

Can you determine its purpose? _____

_____

- - - - - - - - - - - - - - - - - - -

The program that will be coded from the flowchart will read a date card and then print the date; in addition, a payroll record will be read, payroll information moved to the output area, and a line written. Note that we may use the terms PRINT AREA or OUTPUT AREA synonymously when utilizing a printed output format.

25. Alter the flowchart in frame 24 so that it continues to read input payroll records. Use a separate sheet of paper for your altered flowchart.

- - - - - - - - - - - - - - - - - - -

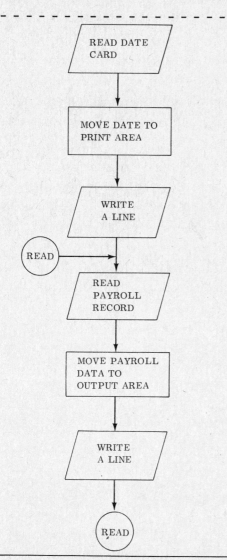

26. Suppose that you placed the entry connector, labeled READ in the preceding solution, at the beginning of the sequence. How would that have changed

the processing? _____

_____

– –

In the above solution, only one date card is read and the date is printed on just one output line. If the entry connector were placed at the beginning of the sequence, then a new date card would need to be read and printed after each payroll record were printed. This would normally not be desirable processing.

27. Draw a flowchart to read a series of cards, compute tax as 7% of SALES-AMT on each card, and print the CUSTOMER NAME and TAX for each card. Use a separate sheet of paper for your flowchart.

– – – – – – – – – – – – – – – – – – – –

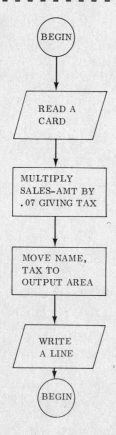

Note: The wording within each symbol need not be exactly as above. Similarly, the actual number of symbols used may vary. For example, you might

use a single processing symbol to represent both the multiply and move operations. The actual wording and number of operations performed will be defined by the rules of each specific programming language.

28. What, if anything, is wrong with the following flowchart excerpts?

(a)

(b)

(c)

(d)

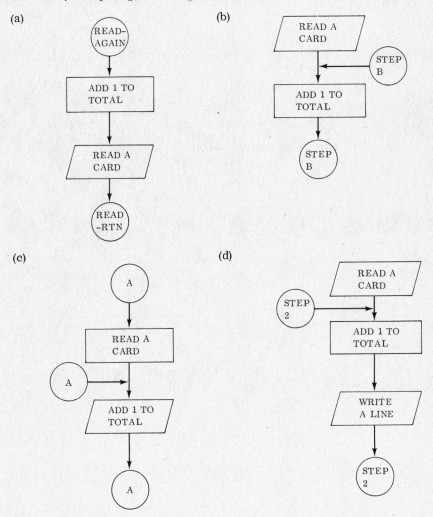

- - - - - - - - - - - - - - - - - -

(a) The label used for the entry connector must correspond exactly to the
label used for the branch connector. Since READ–AGAIN and READ–RTN
are not exactly the same, a program coded from this flowchart excerpt would
yield an error. (In more complex programs, READ–AGAIN and READ–RTN
each might correspond to other connectors, as we shall see later.)
(b) Entry connectors are drawn to the left of the sequence, not to the right.
(c) In this case, we have an unconditional branch connector labeled A and two

entry connectors labeled A. If this were coded in a program, it would confuse the computer. That is, the computer would have no way of knowing which A to branch to. A rule to follow, then, is to make certain that all entry connectors have unique labels.

(d) Although the excerpt may not appear too logical, the flowchart contains an accurate sequence of steps. (So be warned: sometimes a sequence can be coded correctly in flowcharting terms, but still not do what you want it to do!)

29. Indicate what would happen if a program were coded from the following flowchart and then executed.

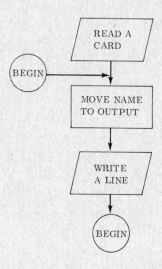

- - - - - - - - - - - - - - - - - - -

A single card would be read, the data moved to the print area, and a line printed. Then the <u>same</u> data would be moved to the print area again, a duplicate line printed, etc. In this way, the same name would be printed indefinitely!

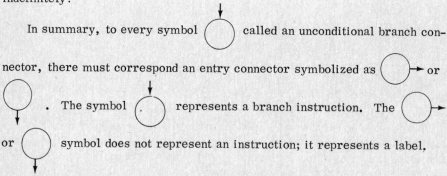

In summary, to every symbol ⬇️◯ called an unconditional branch connector, there must correspond an entry connector symbolized as ◯→ or

⬇️◯ . The symbol ⬇️◯ represents a branch instruction. The ◯→

or ◯⬇️ symbol does not represent an instruction; it represents a label.

DECISIONS

Thus far, we have considered the basic types of processing and input/output operations that a computer can perform. But with these operations alone, the computer would be little more than a sophisticated calculator. The one characteristic that sets a computer apart from most other machines is its ability to perform logic operations. That is, the computer can be programmed to make a decision based on the outcome of a specific test. It is this decision-making ability which provides the computer with its enormous potential.

The decision, or conditional, statement enables the programmer to ask the computer a question. The use of a decision or conditional branch greatly increases the capability of a program. A computer can be programmed to perform an array of input/output and processing operations until certain conditions occur, at which time the normal flow of execution can be altered. To determine if a specific condition has occurred, the programmer asks the computer a question. Here we will consider the specific types of questions which may be asked of computers in decision or conditional statements.

30. A computer can be programmed to perform a logical comparison and, depending on the results of that comparison, perform a specified operation. The types of comparisons that can be performed are:

> (1) Testing a field for specified contents;

> (2) Testing a field for high, low, equal, or unequal status compared to another field or quantity.

The following are examples of comparisons that are programmable.

(a) IS FIELD1 EQUAL TO 99?
(b) DOES FIELDA EQUAL FIELDB?
(c) IS FIELD2 GREATER THAN 150?
(d) IS FIELDX LESS THAN FIELDY?
(e) DOES TOTAL = ZEROS? or DOES TOTAL = ZERO? or DOES TOTAL = 0?
(f) DOES SEX-FIELD = 'M'?

The following statements are not stated in programmable form.

(g) IS FIELD6 A NEGATIVE NUMBER?
(h) IS FIELD7 LARGER THAN THE NUMBER OF DIGITS IN 573268?

Following the pattern of acceptable comparisons, restate (g) and (h) in

programmable form. _____

_____

- - - - - - - - - - - - - - - - - -

(g) IS FIELD6 LESS THAN 0? (Some programming languages do permit a test that compares a field to a negative number, as in IS FIELD6 NEGATIVE? However, IS FIELD6 LESS THAN 0? is acceptable in all languages.)
(h) IS FIELD7 GREATER THAN 6?

31. Which of the following represent valid decisions?

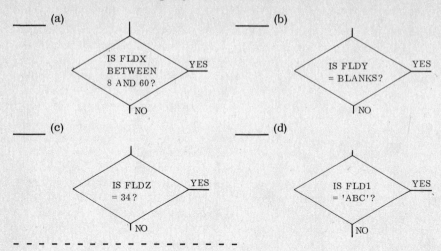

_____ (a)

IS FLDX
BETWEEN
8 AND 60?   YES

NO

_____ (b)

IS FLDY
= BLANKS?   YES

NO

_____ (c)

IS FLDZ
= 34?   YES

NO

_____ (d)

IS FLD1
= 'ABC'?   YES

NO

- - - - - - - - - - - - - - - - - -

(b), (c), and (d) are valid decisions—they each compare a field to specific
contents. (a) is invalid because it attempts to perform two tests in a single
decision; that is, to determine if FLDX is between 8 and 60, we must use
two tests, one which sees if FLDX is greater than 8 and one which sees if
FLDX is less than 60. This cannot be performed by a single decision. (More
about this later.)

32. The use of decisions is a critical aspect of flowcharting and of programming. Very frequently, we need to see if input or storage fields are equal to,
less than, or greater than specified contents. For example, we may need to
know if an AMOUNT field has zero contents, in which case special processing
is required. Or, we may need to know if an ACCT-NO field is equal to a pre-
viously read ACCT-NO field to determine if a duplicate record error has occurred.

   Thus, a decision test is performed to compare: (1) a given field with a
specified constant or literal, or (2) a given field with another field in storage.
The comparison of a given field with a specified constant or literal may be a
numeric comparison or a non-numeric comparison, depending upon whether
the literal is numeric or non-numeric. In (d) of frame 31, FLD1 is compared
to the non-numeric literal _____, while in (c) of that frame, FLDZ is
compared to the numeric constant, or literal _____.

- - - - - - - - - - - - - - - - - - -

ABC; 34

33. Look again at the numeric literal and the non-numeric literal. What dis-
tinguishes the way in which they are represented? _____
- - - - - - - - - - - - - - - - - - - -

'ABC'
Non-numeric literals have quotation marks while numeric literals merely
contain the required digits.   Thus, to compare the field CODE to SESAME,
we would have:

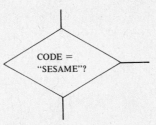

34. Any logical comparison to be programmed by the computer is flowcharted
as shown below.

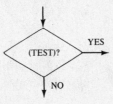

Note that in this diamond-shaped symbol, a question is asked. If the comparison to be performed by the computer yields a YES result, one course of ac-
tion is taken, indicated by the YES flowline. If a NO result is obtained, the
computer continues with the next sequential instruction, denoted by the NO
flowline. In the above, then, a YES result or answer causes a change in the
sequence of execution. We can also flowchart the following variation, where
the NO result or answer causes a change in the sequence of execution.

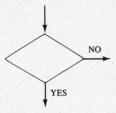

Most programming languages allow for a change in execution when a condition
is present or when a condition is not present.

A decision symbol has how many flowlines entering it? _____ Unlike any

other symbol, the decision symbol has how many flowlines leaving it? _____

The flowlines leaving a decision symbol contain notations.   What are these

notations? _____

- - - - - - - - - - - - - - - - - -

one; two; YES and NO

35. Concise wording is generally used in flowcharting symbols. For example, GREATER THAN is often abbreviated as G.T. or > in mathematical notation, and LESS THAN is often abbreviated as L.T. or < . So example (a) from frame 30 would be flowcharted as:

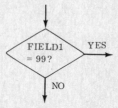

Now you try flowcharting examples (b), (c), (d), and (e), from frame 30.

- - - - - - - - - - - - - - - - -

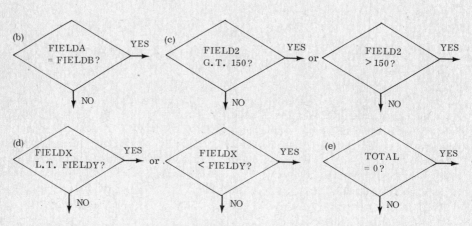

36. In most cases a YES result of a decision or comparison causes a <u>branch</u> to another sequence to be coded in the program. This is flowcharted as:

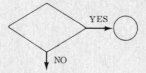

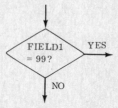 is called a <u>conditional</u> branch connector, which will cause a branch to another sequence only if the condition is met. Like the unconditional branch connector, the conditional branch connector must contain a label or name that corresponds to an entry connector elsewhere in the flowchart.

In the space provided on the next page, name the three kinds of connector symbols and give the symbol(s) for each.

- - - - - - - - - - - - - - - - -

unconditional branch connector:

conditional branch connector:

entry connector: or

37. Every unconditional branch or conditional branch connector must have a corresponding _____.

- - - - - - - - - - - - - - - - -

entry connector

38. Draw the symbols required to test FIELD1 for zeros. Branch to ERR-RTN if it is zeros; if not, proceed to the next sequential step. (ERR-RTN is an abbreviation for ERROR-ROUTINE.)

- - - - - - - - - - - - - - - - -

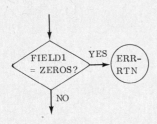

39. Draw the symbols required to branch to WRITE-RTN if FIELD1 = FIELD2.

- - - - - - - - - - - - - - - -

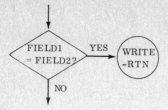

40. Now let's see how these decision symbols (logical comparisons) are used in flowchart sequences. Suppose we want to draw a flowchart for a program that:

    (1) reads in cards;
    (2) tests the amount field on each card for zero quantity;
    (3) moves the input fields to the output area and writes a line if
           the amount is not zero;
    (4) does no processing for a card if the amount field is zero.

Here is our flowchart. Study it carefully and then go on to the frames that follow.

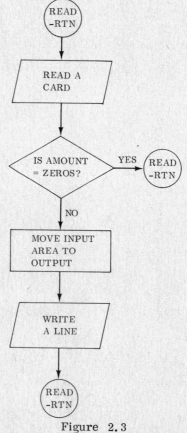

Figure 2.3

41. As we noted earlier, every entry connector must be unique. That is, there may be only <u>one</u> entry connector with a given name. We may, however, branch to that entry point from several different places in a given program. Therefore, it is common to have several branch connectors with the same label name.

Look at the flowchart in Figure 2.3. Which is the entry connector in this flowchart? _____ How many branch connectors are associated with it? _____

- - - - - - - - - - - - - - - - - -

  ; two

42. In Figure 2.3, separate paths may be taken in the flowchart. The paths depend on only one thing. What is the one element upon which the program's sequence of operations depends? _____

- - - - - - - - - - - - - - - - - -

the value of AMOUNT (If AMOUNT is equal to zero, one path will be taken; if AMOUNT is not equal to zero, another path will be taken.)

43. List the sequence of operations in each of the two paths that the computer will perform, depending upon AMOUNT. Use a separate sheet of paper to make your lists and to draw the simplified flowlines, if needed.

- - - - - - - - - - - - - - - - - -

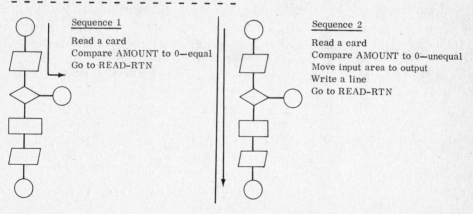

Sequence 1

Read a card
Compare AMOUNT to 0—equal
Go to READ–RTN

Sequence 2

Read a card
Compare AMOUNT to 0—unequal
Move input area to output
Write a line
Go to READ–RTN

The value of AMOUNT for any given input card will determine the path or sequence followed. Sequence 1 is considered a <u>minor</u> sequence because it follows a path that is not the normal or standard path. The standard path, which is followed for most input records, is the <u>major</u> sequence. Here Sequence 2 is the major sequence.

44. Suppose we wish to draw a flowchart for a routine to do the following, if
FIELDX = FIELDY.

    (1) Add AMT to TOTAL
    (2) Write a line
    (3) Branch to BEGIN

If FIELDX is not equal to FIELDY, we should proceed to the next sequential
step. That is, under normal circumstances FIELDX is not expected to be
equal to FIELDY. The flowchart excerpt for this routine is shown below.

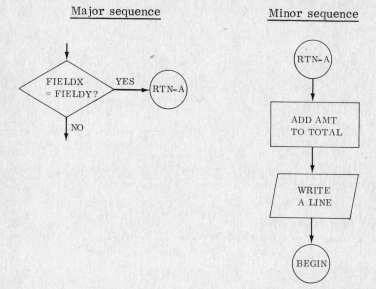

Major sequence   Minor sequence

From this flowchart, we see that a flowchart can consist of a main sequence
in addition to some minor sequences. How does processing reach these minor

sequences? _____

_____

- - - - - - - - - - - - - - - - - - -

by means of a decision which causes a conditional branch

45. In the flowchart in frame 44, the decision symbol that compares FIELDX
to FIELDY will have what kind of connector associated with the YES branch?

_____ The label of this connector will

correspond to the label of a(n) _____ connector which labels a three-
step sequence or routine that is not part of the main sequence.

- - - - - - - - - - - - - - - - - - -

conditional branch connector; entry

46. Draw a flowchart excerpt to read in cards and to print each card unless the field called CODE is zero for a particular card. For the card with zero in CODE, print NAME only.

- - - - - - - - - - - - - - - - - -

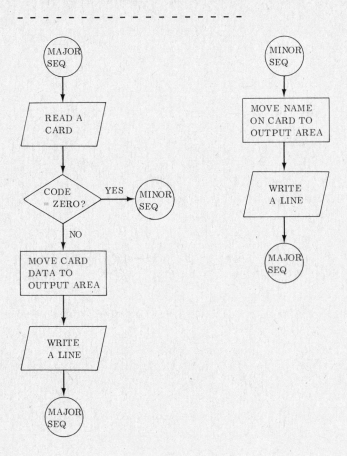

47. At this point, a review of terms and concepts might be helpful. A branch that occurs only if a specific condition is met is called _____

_____.

- - - - - - - - - - - - - - - - - -

a conditional branch

48. A branch that occurs regardless of any existing conditions is called ____

_____.

- - - - - - - - - - - - - - - - - -

an unconditional branch

49. Are decision symbols required to cause an unconditional branch? _____
A conditional branch? _____

- - - - - - - - - - - - - - - - - -
no; yes

50. A conditional branch connector is always associated with what kind of
symbol? _____ What is the purpose of a conditional
branch connector? _____

- - - - - - - - - - - - - - - - - -
a decision symbol; signifies to what step the program will branch, if the condition is met

51. If a sequence of steps has an unconditional branch connector in it, where
in the sequence must this connector be located? _____

- - - - - - - - - - - - - - - - - -
in the last step (Unconditional branch connectors always alter the flow of logic.
If a step were to follow the unconditional branch it would never be executed.)

52. Consider this flowchart excerpt, then answer the questions that follow.

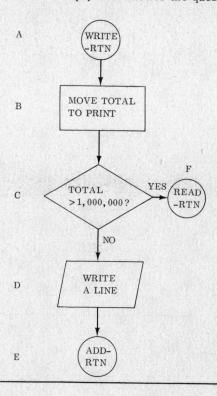

(a) The symbol > in the flowchart means _____.

(b) What letter is adjacent to (1) the unconditional branch connector? _____

(2) the conditional branch connector? _____

(3) the decision symbol? _____

(4) the entry connector? _____

- - - - - - - - - - - - - - - -

(a) greater than; (b) (1)—E; (2)—F; (3)—C; (4)—A

53. Examine the following flowchart. Then see if you can determine how many cards are read. _____

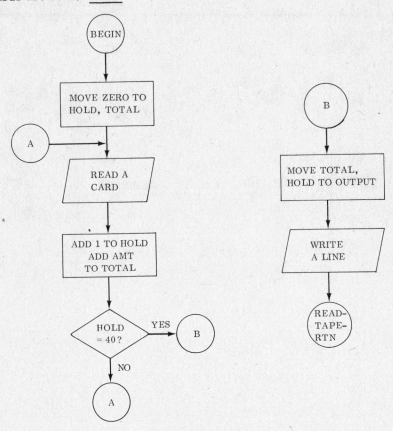

- - - - - - - - - - - - - - - -

40. Every time a card is read, one is added to HOLD; therefore when HOLD is equal to 40, there will have been 40 cards read.

54. Now, let's alter the sequence somewhat. Suppose every odd-numbered input card has a '1' in code and every even-numbered input card has a '0' in code. That is, the first card has a '1' in code, the second card has a '0' in code, the third card a '1', and so on. For the routine flowcharted below, what will be the number of cards read? _____

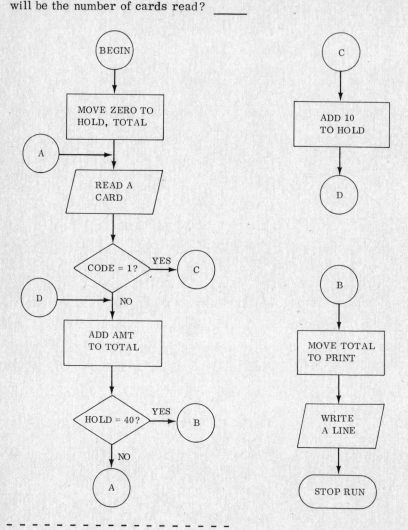

- - - - - - - - - - - - - - - -

If you said 7 cards, congratulate yourself! For the first card read, CODE is a '1' so HOLD is incremented by 10; HOLD equals 10, then. For the second card, HOLD is not incremented because CODE is not a '1'. For the third card, HOLD is incremented by 10 again which makes it equal to 20; it stays at 20 for the fourth card. For the fifth card, HOLD is again incremented by 10, to 30, and it remains at 30 for the sixth card. For the seventh card read, CODE is a '1' and HOLD is incremented to 40. Since HOLD is then compared to 40, a branch to B occurs, where the computer is told to stop.

Later in the book you'll see many applications for these card counting and coding techniques.   You'll also be introduced to STOP RUN later.

55. We want to draw a flowchart excerpt that reads in a card and determines the <u>absolute value</u> of the AMOUNT on the card. The absolute value is defined as the amount regardless of the sign. (For example, the absolute value of 15 is 15; the absolute value of –15 is 15; the absolute value of –3 is 3.) Once the absolute value has been determined, it will be printed.

Such a problem is normally flowcharted this way: For each card the a- mount is tested to see if it is less than zero. If it is less than zero, process- ing goes to a minor sequence where the amount is multiplied by –1. (In effect, that "cancels" the minus sign, leaving the absolute value.) Then the absolute value is printed.

Try drawing this flowchart excerpt. There are at least two good ways to do it.

- - - - - - - - - - - - - - - - - -

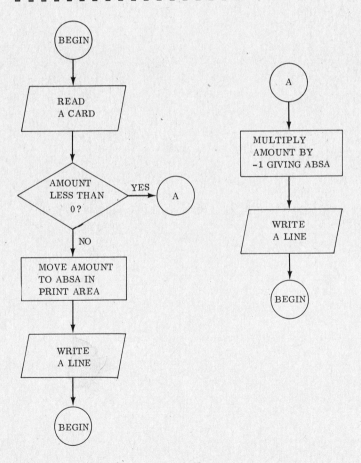

or, you could have done the following:

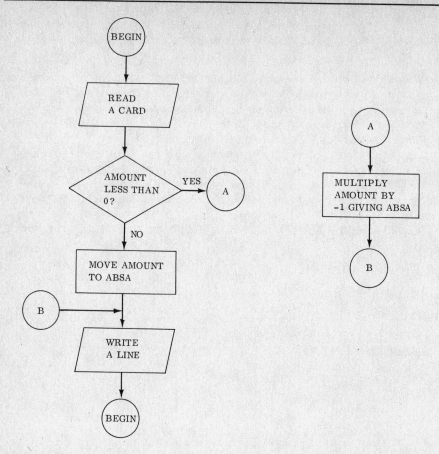

These flowcharts use the abbreviation ABSA for the absolute value. You could have used any other variable name. You could also have said WRITE ABSA instead of WRITE A LINE. In some of the entry connectors we used the single letter A or B instead of a name like BEGIN. Single letters are commonly used in connectors because there's little writing space in the connector symbol. The choice of name or letter is up to you, as long as the corresponding branch connectors and entry connectors match. Note that the second flowchart is more efficient because it has fewer steps; we've eliminated the need for two separate WRITE statements.

56. Now suppose we want to draw a flowchart that reads in cards and:

    (1) if CODE of a card is 1, AMT is added to TOTAL and TOTAL is printed;

    (2) if CODE of a card is 2, AMT is subtracted from TOTAL and TOTAL is printed;

    (3) if CODE is neither 1 nor 2, the error message 'INVALID CODE' is printed.

Examine our flowchart carefully and then answer the questions that follow.

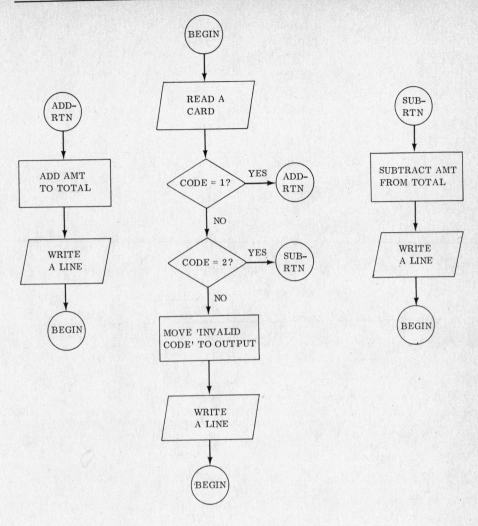

For the first time, this flowchart shows two decision symbols in succession. There's a special art to the order of logical comparisons; you'll learn more about that (and about codes) as we get into more complex decision-making. For now, let's just see how this flowchart works.

(a) A branch to ADD-RTN occurs only if what condition exists? _____

_____

(b) The test CODE = 2? is performed only if what condition exists? _____

_____

(c) An error message is printed only if what condition exists? _____

_____

- - - - - - - - - - - - - - - - - - - -

_____

(a) CODE =1

(b) CODE does not equal 1 (If CODE =1, a branch to ADD-RTN would have occurred and no further test would have been performed.)

(c) CODE is not equal to 1 or 2 (This is a good check for improper coding.)

57. ADD-RTN and SUB-RTN are common abbreviations for ADDITION ROUTINE and SUBTRACTION ROUTINE. Other labels might be used, of course. And the minor sequences or routines may be drawn anywhere on the page. In this flowchart, how many major sequences are there? _____ How many minor sequences? _____

- - - - - - - - - - - - - - - - - -

one; two

58. In your own words, describe the type of field that will result from the se-ries of operations shown in the flowchart. _____

_____

_____

- - - - - - - - - - - - - - - - - -

The result field TOTAL contains the cumulative total for each input record, with increments or decrements depending upon the value of CODE.

59. What do you think should be the initial value of TOTAL before the program begins processing data? _____

- - - - - - - - - - - - - - - - - -

Hope you said "zero"—otherwise we'd have no way of knowing the "true" value of the cumulative total field.

60. The flowchart in frame 56, then, is not complete because it has not de-fined TOTAL as a storage area with an initial value of zero. We generally define and initialize, or set, fields at the beginning of a program, so they must be specified at the start of a flowchart.

The following is a revised flowchart which defines TOTAL. Note that the unconditional branch to the start of the major sequence has been altered to a branch to the READ-RTN. Once TOTAL has been initialized we do not wish to branch back to this initializing operation again.

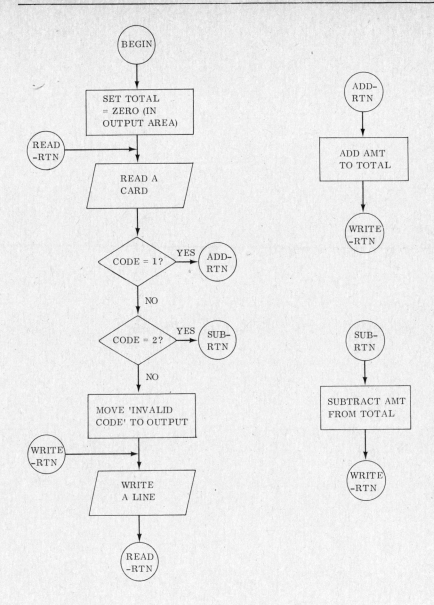

Notice that two other changes were made from the earlier version. What
are they? _____

_____

_____

- - - - - - - - - - - - - - - - - - -

(in either order) The ADD-RTN was moved to the right of the major sequence.
(That's okay; remember that minor sequences can appear anywhere on the

page.) The ADD-RTN and SUB-RTN no longer contain a WRITE instruction; instead, they branch back to the main sequence for the WRITE instruction, which is much more efficient.

61. Note that it is considered more efficient to branch to a series of steps, or a routine, from several points in a flowchart than to repeat the series of steps. The following flowchart contains some repetitive sequences. Using what you know so far, redraw the flowchart to make the flow of logic more efficient.

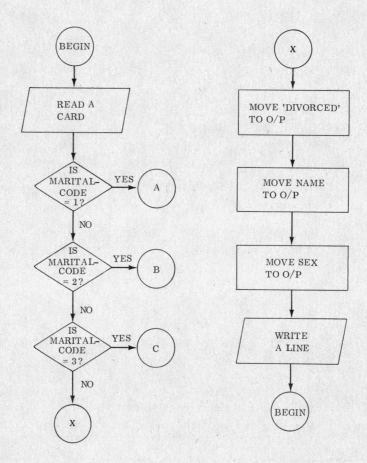

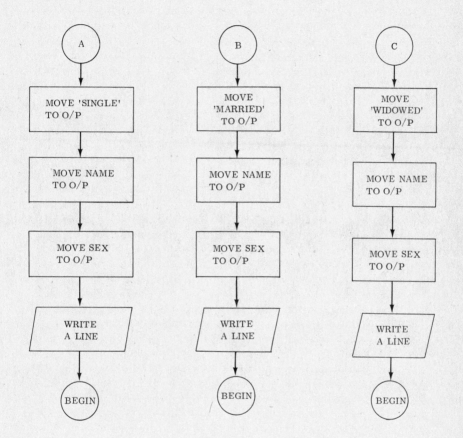

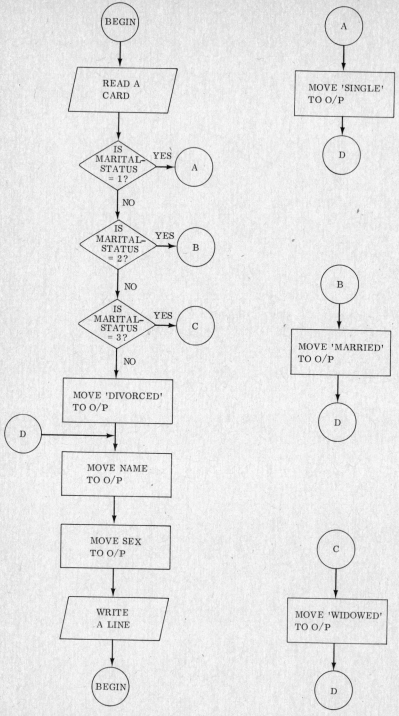

Note that a check for erroneous codes should have been included in this flow-chart but was left out for simplicity.

END OF FILE CONDITION

62. All the flowcharts drawn thus far, if coded precisely as drawn, would result in repetitive operations without any formal end to the program. That is, we would continue reading cards until there were no more to be read, at which point the computer would "hang up" or abort (abnormally terminate) the run, because it would not know what to do.

So, you must always instruct the computer what to do when there is no more input or when the program should be stopped or terminated.

When would we generally terminate a program? _____

_____

Do you recall what symbol we would use? (Draw it.)

- - - - - - - - - - - - - - - - -

when there is no more input to process; a terminal symbol

63. An instruction to stop the run, usually called an END OF JOB HALT, does not actually stop the computer; it merely instructs the computer to begin read-

ing the next program. Thus a (STOP RUN) instruction will cause the com-

puter to read in the next program with no pause at all.

·To provide for an end of job routine, we usually read data and then test to see if the last record has been processed. If it has, we instruct the computer to proceed to a routine labeled EOJ, which is an abbreviation for End of Job.

The last record of a file usually contains a special end of file indicator, and the test for last record is a comparison for that indicator. For flowcharting purposes, we can just ask WAS LAST CARD PROCESSED?, as in the example below.

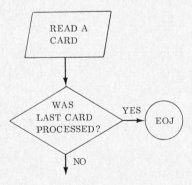

This end of file test can be written in many ways. For example, we might ask LAST CARD?, END OF FILE?, or any note that indicates an end of file test. The conditional branch connector labeled EOJ must correspond to an entry connector which contains a minor sequence or routine that results in a

- - - - - - - - - - - - - - - - - -

Stop Run—termination of the program.

64. Any summary or totalling functions are performed at EOJ after all records have been read and before the terminal symbol. If there are no summary or totalling functions to be performed at EOJ we can merely instruct the computer to stop, which results in the computer's reading of the next program. This simplest EOJ routine would be drawn as:

Now let's see how well you can put all these elements together. Code an entire flowchart to:

  (1) read a card;
  (2) if CODE is not equal to A, proceed; if CODE is equal to A, get another card;
  (3) add AMT to TOTAL;
  (4) continue getting cards;
  (5) after all cards have been read and processed, move TOTAL to print area and print TOTAL.

- - - - - - - - - - - - - - - - -

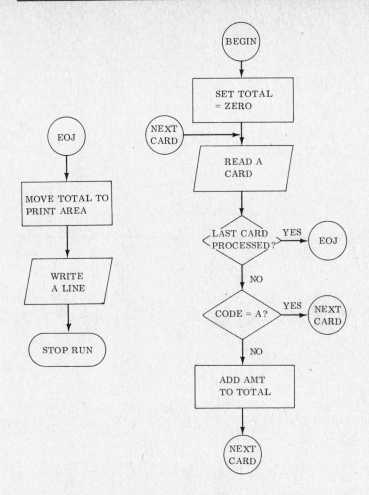

If you correctly flowcharted the above, you're on your way to becoming a top-notch programmer! Although the logic is not very complicated, the integration of all the elements requires good conceptual ability. If you do not understand the flowchart above, review the material in this chapter before proceeding.

65. The READ A CARD instruction causes the reading of data from a card reader. For most computers, the input deck must be directly followed by a card with a /* in the first two positions, usually called a slash-asterisk card. This /* card is the one which actually signals the computer that there are no more input cards to be read.

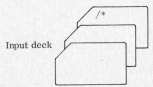

Input deck

Thus the end of job test could be coded as:

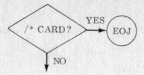

If there are ten input cards followed by a /* card, a branch to EOJ occurs when which card is tested? _____

- - - - - - - - - - - - - - - - - -

/* or eleven—that is, after all ten input cards have been processed

66. While we have confined our discussion to the reading of card input, the very same logic applies to all forms of input—magnetic tape, disk, and so on. Other forms of input would not use a /* card to signal the end of file, but would use other last record indicators. Is the following program excerpt valid? Explain your answer.

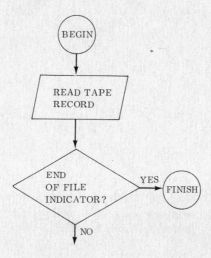

_____

_____

- - - - - - - - - - - - - - - - - -

Yes. END OF FILE INDICATOR? would apply to all last record indicators. And any label may be used to denote an end of file routine.

67. Interpret the following flowchart. That is, explain in your own words the type of processing that the program created from the flowchart will perform.

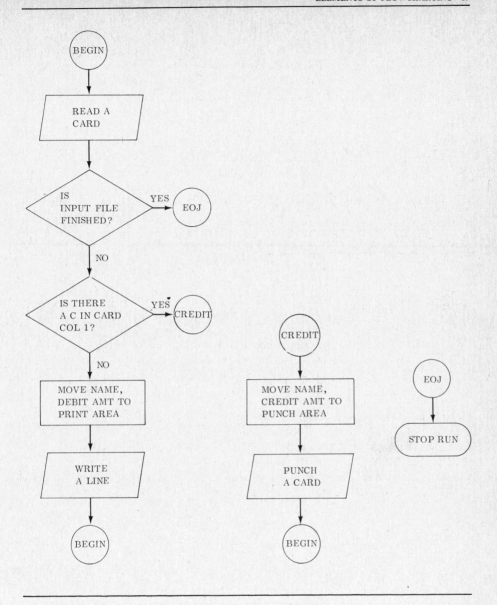

Cards are read. If there is a C in card column 1 then a branch to a CREDIT routine occurs. At CREDIT routine, an output card is punched. If there is not a C in card column 1, then output data, including a DEBIT AMOUNT, is printed. When the input file is finished the run is terminated.

68. A CODE field or position is an area of a record that is used to indicate which of two or more operations is to be performed. Depending upon the contents of a CODE field, different types of operations will be performed.

Coded fields are often used to make data more concise. The use of a code on computer storage media is an effective method of saving positions. For example, a CODE of 1, 2, 3, or 4 in a MARITAL–STATUS field can represent four different conditions, such as married, divorced, single, or widowed. Rather than requiring several positions, the field need be only one position long, to represent the actual status. If the MARITAL–STATUS field needs to be printed, the program, through the use of decision tests, can convert the code back into the actual representation.

Does the flowchart in frame 67 contain a CODE field? Explain your answer. _____

_____

- - - - - - - - - - - - - - - - - -

Yes. Card column 1 is used to indicate which of two sets of operations the computer is to perform.

69. Draw a flowchart which computes WAGES from the following input cards.

NAME	HOURLY RATE	HOURS WORKED	

For each card, print NAME and WAGES. WAGES is computed as HOURLY RATE x HOURS WORKED for hours worked not in excess of 40. If an employee works more than 40 hours, his wages are computed as (40 x HOURLY RATE) + (OVT–TIME HOURS x HOURLY RATE x 1.5), with time and a half for overtime. OVT–TIME HOURS = HOURS WORKED – 40

- - - - - - - - - - - - - - - - - -

Following are two possible answers. The first, which appears on the next page, is the most efficient. The second is less efficient, but still correct. You will recall from earlier in the chapter that several arithmetic operations can be coded in a single processing symbol if they all relate to a specific function, so your flowchart may look somewhat different from these. Just check to be sure that you have included all the operations in the proper symbols and in the right order.

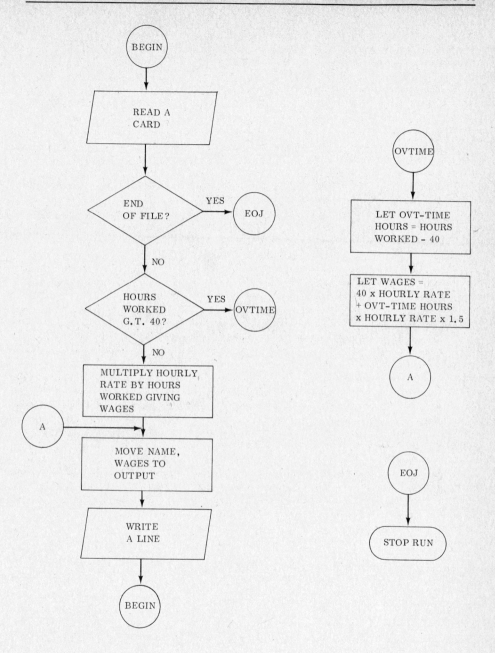

or, the following:

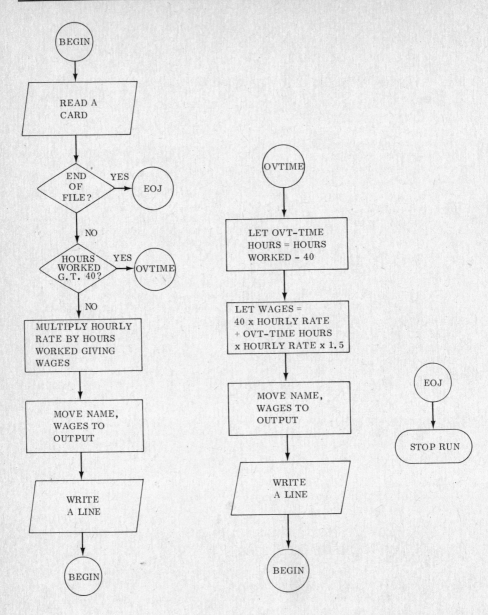

Parentheses may be included in the flowchart symbols as in the problem statement to clarify arithmetic functions.

70. Here are some fun questions to test the thoroughness of your understanding of branches. Use a simple English sentence to explain the logic in each of
the following routines. Follow the example in the first one, which we have
completed for you.

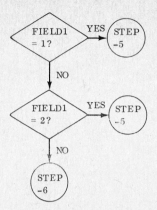

If FIELD1 is equal to 1 or 2 branch to STEP-5, otherwise branch to STEP-6. Got it? Try the following.

 a.

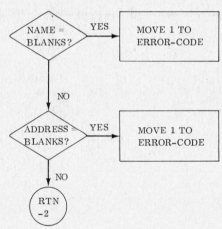

b.

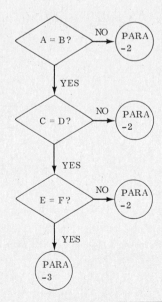

c.

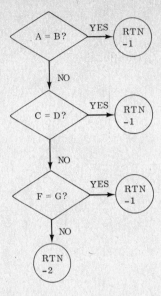

d.

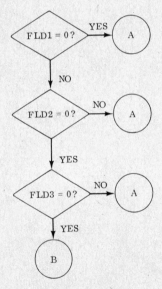

- - - - - - - - - - - - - - - - - -

(a) If NAME or ADDRESS is equal to blanks, move 1 to ERROR-CODE; otherwise, branch to RTN-2.

(b) If A = B, C = D, and E = F, branch to PARA-3; otherwise, branch to PARA-2. Or if A isn't equal to B, C isn't equal to D, or E isn't equal to F, branch to PARA-2; otherwise, branch to PARA-3.

(c) If A = B or C = D or F = G, branch to RTN-1; otherwise, branch to RTN-2.

(d) If FLD1 is zero or FLD2 isn't zero or FLD3 isn't zero, branch to A; otherwise, branch to B. Or if FLD1 isn't zero and FLD2 is zero and FLD3 is zero, branch to B; otherwise, branch to A.

SELF-TEST

1. Identify each of the following symbols.

(a)

(b)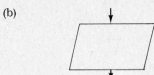

_____

(c)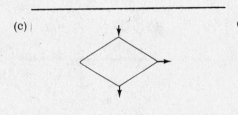

(d)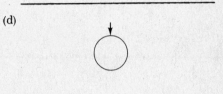

_____

(e)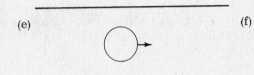

(f)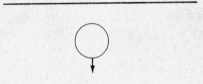

_____

(g)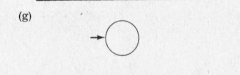

(h)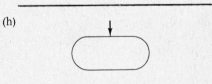

_____

2. Consider the following flowchart excerpt.

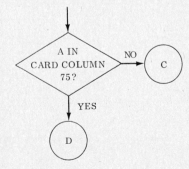

If there is not an A in card column 75, what will occur? _____

_____

3. Where in a sequence must an unconditional branch connector occur? ____

_____

4. To every branch connector, there must correspond a(n) _____

_____.

5. (True or False.) A branch to one entry point may occur from several different points in a flowchart. _____

6. Consider the flowchart in Figure 2.4. The flowchart depicts the logic in an automobile insurance company procedure. Column 18 denotes marital status (M = married, S = single, O = other, such as widowed, divorced, separated). Column 19 denotes sex (M = male, F = female, blank denotes that sex is unknown). The <u>routine</u> determines the total number of individuals who will receive discounts because they are either: (1) female, or (2) married and male.

It has been determined by several studies that female drivers and married male drivers have fewer accidents than other people. Because of this fact, this insurance company will issue discounts to those categories of people. With the following input cards, what will be the contents of TOTAL at the end of all operations? _____

Card No.	Contents of Column 18	Contents of Column 19
1	M	M
2	M	F
3	S	M
4	M	F
5	O	F
6	S	M
7	S	F
8	M	M

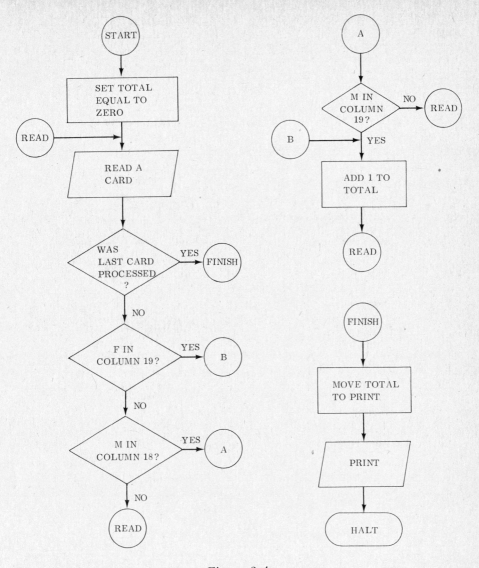

Figure 2.4.

(Note that HALT is a term sometimes used in place of STOP RUN.)

7. Draw a flowchart which reads in cards that have NAME, AMT, TAX, and CREDIT as input fields and prints, for each card, NAME and TOTAL where TOTAL = AMT + TAX - CREDIT.

8. Draw a flowchart which prints only the names of all employees who earn more than $5,000. Assume that the input consists of data cards with NAME and SALARY as the input fields.

9. What does the following flowchart excerpt accomplish?

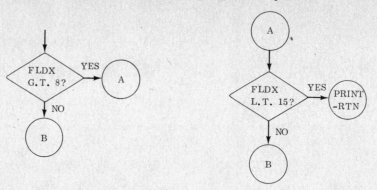

10. What is the purpose of the following flowchart excerpt?

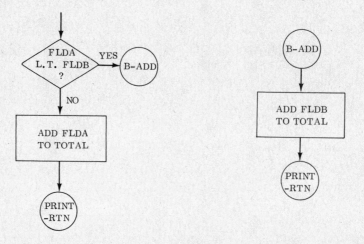

Answers to Self-Test

1. (a) processing; (b) input/output; (c) decision; (d) unconditional branch connector; (e) entry connector; (f) entry connector; (g) conditional branch connector; (h) terminal
(frames 8, 13, 17, 21, 28, 36)

2. a branch to C (frames 30, 31, 34-36)

3. at the end of the sequence (frames 13-17, 22, 23, 51)

4. entry connector (frames 17-20, 23, 28)

5. True (frames 41, 55)

6. 6 (frames 52–60)

7.
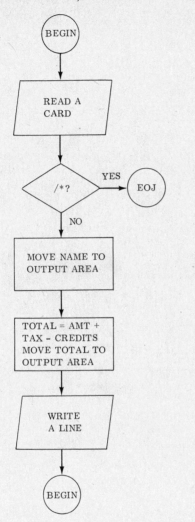
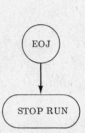

(frames 46–69)

8.

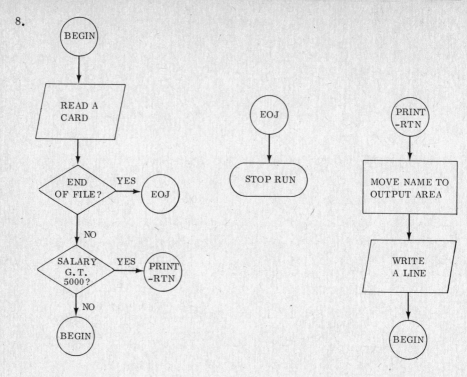

(frames 46–69)

9. If FLDX is <u>between</u> 8 and 15, a branch to PRINT-RTN occurs; if not, a branch to B occurs. (frames 34–69)

10. The larger of the two fields, FLDA or FLDB, gets added to TOTAL. (frames 34–69)

CHAPTER THREE
Problems with More Complex Processing

Now that you have learned to integrate the basic symbols of flowcharting into logical sequences and routines, you can draw more complex, useful, and challenging flowcharts. In this way, you will better understand how to communicate with a computer through programming. When you complete this chapter, you will be able to:

- interpret some important business applications of computer processing;

- draw simple and intermediate level flowcharts that enhance your knowledge of computer logic;

- flowchart common programming techniques including loops, counters, multiple decisions, and arithmetic routines of varying complexity;

- use appropriate terminology in flowcharts for business applications.

INTERMEDIATE-LEVEL FLOWCHART PROBLEMS

This section includes problems that will help integrate all material presented thus far and help you better understand the business applications of computer processing.

1. We want to draw a flowchart for a college bursar's office which will compute for each semester:

(1) Tuition for each student;
(2) Total tuition for all students.

Input: Student cards. The following represent card columns (often abbreviated cc) and the corresponding fields.

1-20 Student name
21-22 Number of credits
23-80 Not used

<u>Output</u>: Magnetic tape. Positions on the tape of the corresponding fields are as follows.

    1-20   Student name
    21-22   Number of credits
    23-25   Tuition
    26-40   Not used

Print the message TOTAL TUITION and the computed total figure. Tuition is $360 if the number of credits is over 12, and $30 per credit for 12 credits or less. This is a formalized problem with specific input and output. The problem is presented just as a similar one would be presented in a formal business environment. It is therefore important for you to learn how to interpret problems in this form. (You'll get lots of practice in this Self-Teaching Guide.)

Here is our flowchart for this problem. Study it carefully. Be sure you understand each step, so that you could flowchart a similar problem yourself. Then answer the questions in the frames that follow. Note that in some cases several instructions are condensed within a single processing symbol. For example, MOVE NAME, NO-OF-CREDITS, TUITION TO OUTPUT TAPE AREA really consists of <u>three</u> separate instructions—one moves NAME to the output tape area, one moves NO-OF-CREDITS to the output tape area, and one moves TUITION to the output tape area. The actual phraseology and the number of symbols used to represent processing functions is of minimal significance, because only the actual program instructions require a very specific notation.

Notice, too, that this flowchart, when programmed, produces <u>two</u> different forms of output, a printed line and tape records.

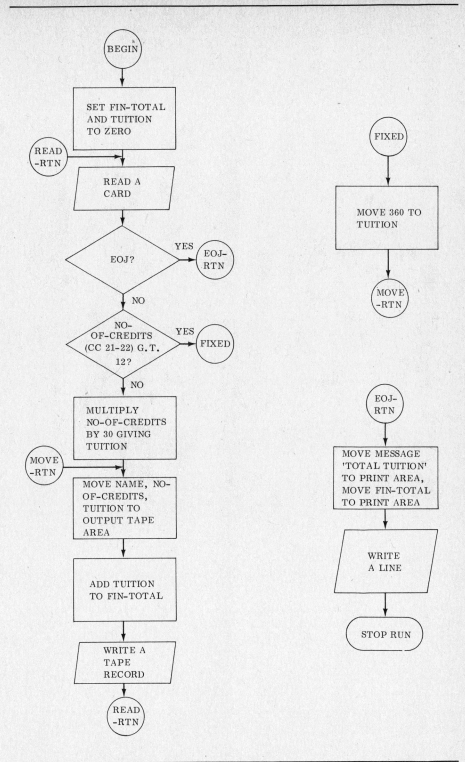

2. Why is the first instruction required? _____

_____

Why does the major routine or sequence branch back to READ-RTN instead of

BEGIN? _____

_____

- - - - - - - - - - - - - - - - - - - -

to establish and initialize the two storage fields of FIN-TOTAL and TUITION.
(Note that we can arbitrarily call these fields by any name—each programming
language has its own rules for forming data names.); because we need to initialize the storage fields only once, at the beginning of the program.

3. The test notation EOJ? really means _____

_____

- - - - - - - - - - - - - - - - - - - -

has the last data card been read and processed?

4. (True or False.) The procedures required to write tape records differ

substantially from the procedures required to print records? _____

- - - - - - - - - - - - - - - - - - - -

False. As indicated in the above flowchart, there is no difference.

5. Special marks are placed around a message or constant that is to be
printed along with a computed value. The flowchart includes an example of
a message. What marks are used to distinguish a message from an estab-

lished storage area? _____

- - - - - - - - - - - - - - - - - - - -

quotation marks

6. Draw a flowchart which prints the names of all employees whose salary
is less than $5,000 and creates a tape file of the names of all employees whose
salary is greater than $20,000. Assume that there are two input fields, NAME
and SALARY, for each input employee record.

- - - - - - - - - - - - - - - - - - - -

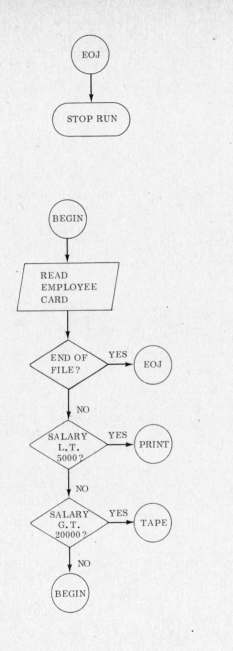

In your flowchart, you might have chosen different labels and different terms, and you might have written some operations in a slightly different order. That's okay, as long as you have included all of the operations in some form. For example, if you tested SALARY to determine if it is greater than $20,000 before comparing it to $5,000, that's fine. Be sure, however, that in the two output routines, labeled PRINT and TAPE, when NAME is moved, the two receiving fields are not the same. That is, if in both cases you said something like MOVE NAME TO OUTPUT, this would be incorrect because the problem requires two output areas, a tape and a print area. The computer must be told which one you are referencing.

7. Now we want to draw a flowchart to summarize accident records in order to obtain the following information.

> (1) Percentage of drivers under 25
> (2) Percentage of drivers who are female
> (3) Percentage of drivers from New York state

There is one tape record for each driver involved in an accident in the past year, as shown below.

> 1-4 Driver number
> 5   State code (1 for New York)
> 6-9 Birthdate of driver (month and year)
> 10   Sex (M for male, F for female)

Results should be printed with the following constants.

> % OF DRIVERS UNDER 25
> % OF FEMALE DRIVERS
> % OF DRIVERS FROM NY

Use a separate sheet of paper for your flowchart.

- - - - - - - - - - - - - - - - - - -

Our flowchart appears on the next page. Examine it carefully enough so that you could flowchart a similar problem. Then answer the questions in the frames that follow. (CTR is a common abbreviation for COUNTER.)

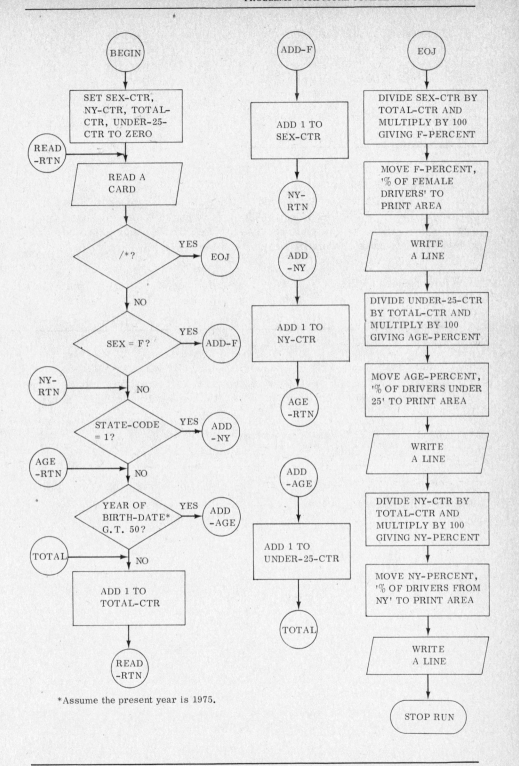

*Assume the present year is 1975.

8. The test notation /* is a test for _____ .

- - - - - - - - - - - - - - - - - -

last card (Did you remember?)

9. Why is a 1 added to TOTAL-CTR? _____

_____

- - - - - - - - - - - - - - - - - -

to compile a percentage, which is equal to the total number in a specified category (female, NY, under 25) divided by the total number of all accident cases.
A counter field, here called TOTAL-CTR, is required when we need to keep
track of the number of records processed. Each time a record is read, 1 is
added to the counter. (More about counters later.)

10. Each processing function in the EOJ routine performs the division and then
multiplies the result by 100. Why is the multiplication by 100 required?

_____

- - - - - - - - - - - - - - - - - -

to give the result in percentage form. (Example: Suppose NY-CTR = 50 and
TOTAL-CTR = 200. The division would yield .25. Since .25 is actually 25%,
we must multiply the result by 100 to obtain the answer in percentage form.)

11. The year of BIRTH-DATE is compared to 50 because _____

_____

- - - - - - - - - - - - - - - - - -

all people born after 1950 are under 25 years of age, assuming the present
year to be 1975

12. Each write instruction produces a single line of output. What would happen if the program had one write instruction at the end of all calculations,

rather than three separate write instructions? _____

_____

- - - - - - - - - - - - - - - - - -

all the results would be printed on one line, instead of three

13. Now draw a flowchart to create output tape records from the following
input tape.

1-5	Salesman number
6-33	Salesman name
34-38	Sales amount
39	Not used

The output record format is as follows.

1-5	Salesman number
6-33	Salesman name
34-38	Sales amount
39-41	Discount percent
42-46	Discount amount
47-51	Net
52-75	Not used

Use a separate sheet of paper for your flowchart. The flowchart should allow for the following.

(1) If SALES-AMOUNT exceeds $100.00, allow 3% discount;

(2) If SALES-AMOUNT is $100.00 or less, 2% discount is allowed;

(3) DISCOUNT-AMOUNT = SALES-AMOUNT x DISCOUNT-PERCENT

(4) NET = SALES-AMOUNT - DISCOUNT-AMOUNT

- - - - - - - - - - - - - - - - - - -

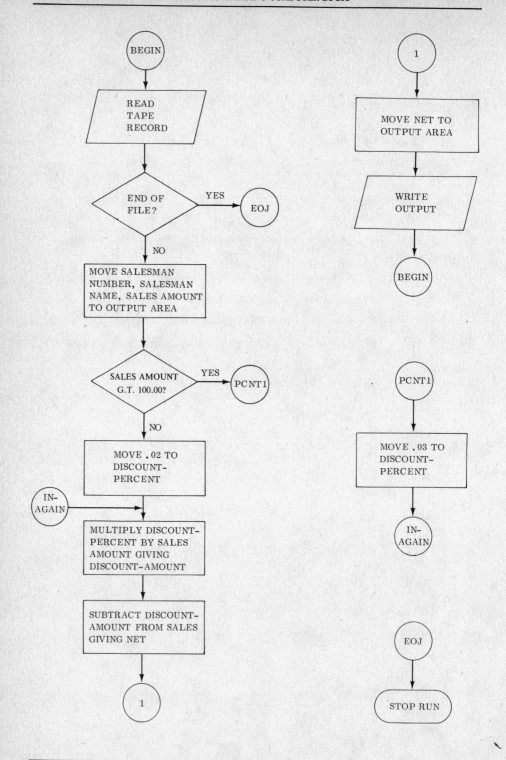

Note that the field called NET could be assigned, in the program, as part of the output area. If this is done, the instruction MOVE NET TO OUTPUT AREA would be unnecessary. As a general rule, however, we create numeric fields such as NET in some area separate from the output area so that they can be edited before printing. In such cases, our MOVE NET TO OUTPUT AREA is really an abbreviation for MOVE AND EDIT NET TO OUTPUT AREA. Note also that in the preceding flowchart, the output instruction was WRITE OUTPUT. Here, again, the actual note could have been WRITE TAPE or WRITE OUTPUT TAPE.

14. Let's try another common application. Draw a flowchart to print each student's class average. The input records are student class cards with the following format.

1-20	Student name
21-23	Exam 1 score
24-26	Exam 2 score
27-29	Exam 3 score
30-32	Exam 4 score
33-80	Not used

Each output line should contain NAME and AVERAGE for each input card. The very first line of the report should include the heading CLASS GRADES. (In case you don't remember how to calculate an average, here's how: total the scores and divide the total by the number of scores:

$$\text{Average} = \frac{\text{Total of Scores}}{\text{Number of Scores}}$$

- - - - - - - - - - - - - - - - - -

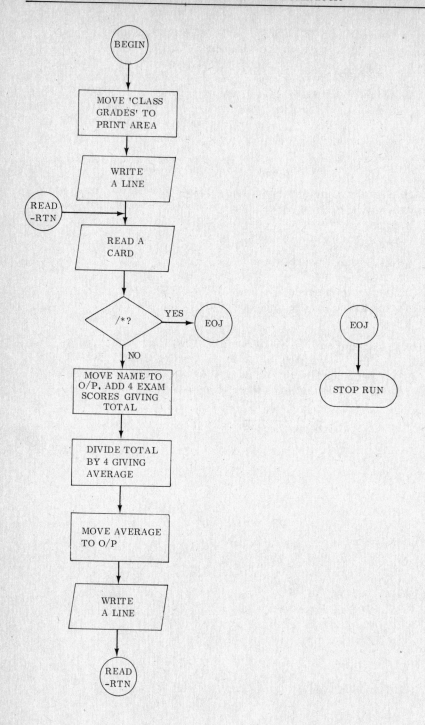

ILLUSTRATION OF A PAYROLL PROCEDURE

15. A primary use of the computer in most installations is the computing of payroll figures. An employee's salary is read into the computer and the basic net pay is determined. Net pay is the amount of money the employee is to receive after all the necessary deductions and taxes are subtracted from his or her gross pay.

The usual deductions from an employee's gross pay include state income tax, federal income tax, municipal income tax, social security tax, insurance payments (such as health, life, and disability), savings or investment plan payments, pension payments, and union dues. State and federal income tax deductions involve more complex flowcharts than we are ready for, so we will save that discussion until Chapter 6. Most union dues, insurance, savings, and investment plan payments are fixed and thus result in the same deductions every pay period.

If an employee earns $5.50 per hour and works 40 hours per week, his or her gross weekly wages (that is, before deductions) would be _____. If the fixed deductions totalling $22 per week are subtracted, the resulting net pay would be _____.

- - - - - - - - - - - - - - - - - -

$220 ($40 x $5.50); $198 ($220-$22)

16. The deduction for social security tax is commonly referred to as FICA, an acronym for Federal Insurance Compensation Act, which created the social security tax. This tax is currently 5.85% of the first $13,200 earned by an employee each year. Earnings in excess of $13,200 are not taxed. Since we cannot use percents in calculations, we must change the percents to normal decimal form. For calculations, we must change 5.85% to _____.

- - - - - - - - - - - - - - - - - -

.0585 (Divide by 100.)

17. In our flowchart we will test to see if an employee's salary is over $13,200. Rather than calculate the tax each time for these employees, we can apply a constant FICA, since the tax will be the same for all salaries of $13,200 or more. Calculate this constant FICA tax for salaries over $13,200.

_____

- - - - - - - - - - - - - - - - - -

$772.20 ($13,200 x .0585)

18. The payroll tape to be read contains the following fields of information for each employee.

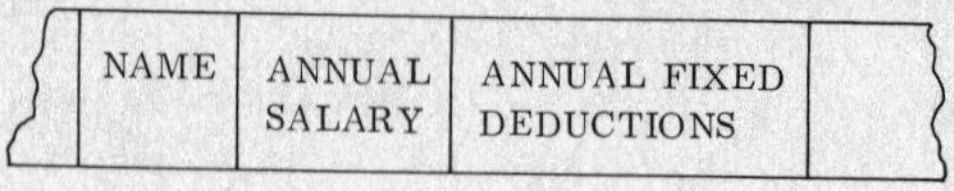

NAME	ANNUAL SALARY	ANNUAL FIXED DEDUCTIONS

Suppose, for the moment, that there are no other deductions. How would you determine the gross weekly salary? _____

_____

The net weekly salary? _____

_____

- - - - - - - - - - - - - - - - - - - -

divide annual salary by 52; subtract annual fixed deductions from annual salary and then divide by 52

19. Now let's look just at annual pay. We wish to compute net pay as:

net pay = annual salary – annual fixed deductions – FICA,

where FICA is 5.85% of the first $13,200 earned.

Draw a flowchart to accomplish this for each input tape record and to print the results.

- - - - - - - - - - - - - - - - - - - -

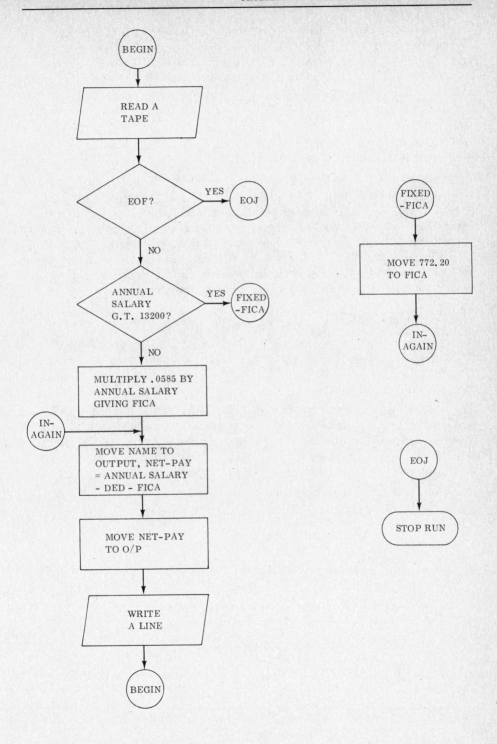

20. Although $13, 200 is the current ceiling upon which FICA tax is computed, this number can change from time to time, depending on Congressional legislation. If the constant 13200 is used in the program (as in the flowchart of frame 19), would you need to alter the program every time the ceiling changed?

_____

- - - - - - - - - - - - - - - - - - -

yes (Incidentally, notice that the 13200, as a numeric constant, does not contain a dollar sign or a comma.)

21. To alleviate the problem of alterations, a data card could be read into the computer which contains the appropriate upper limit, or ceiling. Prior to normal processing, we could read the number from the card into a field called STORE, for example, and then compare ANNUAL SALARY to STORE instead of to a numeric constant such as 13200. STORE is then said to contain variable data since it may change each time the program is run. Using this procedure, would you need alter the program each time Congress set a new upper limit? _____

- - - - - - - - - - - - - - - - - - -

No, you would only need to change one data card to reflect the change in the ceiling.

21. Redraw the flowchart from frame 19, using STORE as a storage area which will hold the variable upper limit. This number is to be read in on a punched card as the first procedure of the program. (Notice that, since the upper limit varies, we cannot use a constant FICA tax for salaries over the limit, but must instruct the computer to calculate the tax.)

- - - - - - - - - - - - - - - - - - -

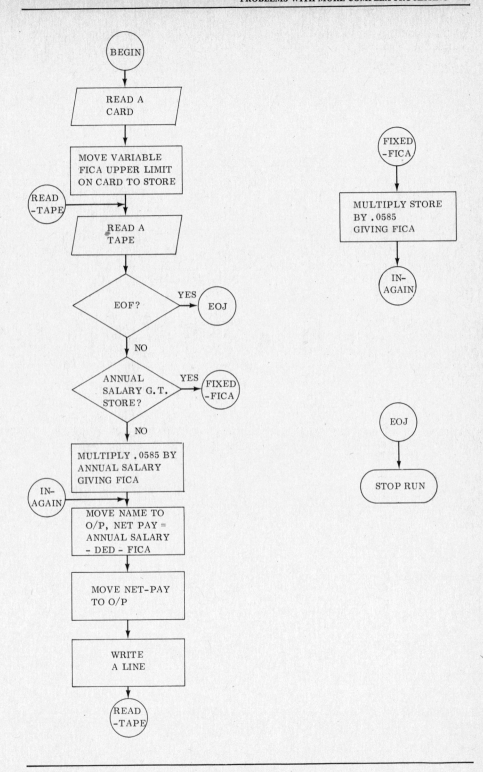

23. In addition to frequent changes to the upper taxable limit, the actual percentage sometimes fluctuates. Suppose we read in a single data card with the following variable data items.

CURRENT PERCENT	CURRENT UPPER LIMIT	

Draw a flowchart to compute FICA and NET PAY.

— — — — — — — — — — — — — — — — — —

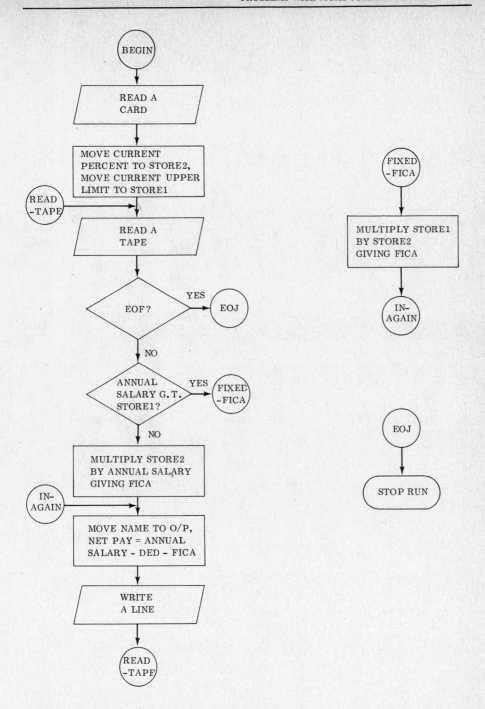

You should have used two variables (we called ours STORE1 and STORE2), rather than constants, for storing FICA limits. To eliminate repeating the multiplications at the routine called FIXED-FICA, it is possible to perform it just _once_, prior to the READ-TAPE routine. That is, after the data has been moved into STORE1 and STORE2, we could have flowcharted the operation MULTIPLY STORE1 BY STORE2 GIVING HOLD. In this way, at FIXED-FICA it would only be necessary to move HOLD to FICA, rather than perform the multiplication. This procedure is more efficient because it takes the computer less time to move data in storage than to perform repeated multiplications.

24. Let us now make our FICA illustration more realistic and, by doing so, more complex. The following represents a concise Master Employee Payroll Record:

	NAME	YEAR-TO-DATE EARNINGS	WEEKLY GROSS PAY	

The problem is to compute weekly net pay from weekly gross pay. Assume that FICA is 5.85% of the first $13,200 earned. If year-to-date (YTD) earnings exceeds $13,200, will FICA be deducted from weekly gross pay? _____

- - - - - - - - - - - - - - - - - -

no

25. Suppose that YTD earnings equal $12,950 and that weekly gross pay equals $300. How much of weekly gross pay would be taxable for FICA tax? _____

- - - - - - - - - - - - - - - - - -

only the first $250   ($13,200 - YTD earnings)

26. Thus, if YTD earnings are less than $13,200 but YTD earnings plus weekly gross pay exceeds $13,200, the formula for computing FICA for that week is _____.

- - - - - - - - - - - - - - - - - -

FICA = .0585 x ($13,200 - YTD earnings)

27. If YTD earnings plus weekly gross pay are less than $13,200, the formula for computing FICA tax is _____.

- - - - - - - - - - - - - - - - - -

.0585 x weekly gross pay

28. Determine FICA tax for each of the following master records.

Name	YTD earnings	Weekly gross pay	FICA tax
THOMAS	$13,900	$300	(a) _____
JONES	7,500	500	(b) _____
SMITH	13,000	300	(c) _____
WAYNE	12,900	350	(d) _____

- - - - - - - - - - - - - - - - - - -

(a) 0;   (b) $29.25;   (c) $11.70;   (d) $17.55

29. Draw a comprehensive flowchart to read in the tape records and to print NAME and FICA for each master tape record.

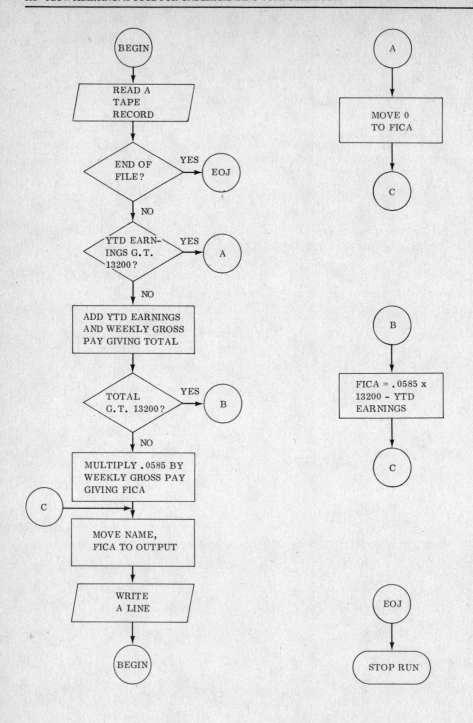

MORE COMPLEX DECISION PROBLEMS

From the previous illustration of payroll procedures, you have learned to flowchart for some specific applications. Hopefully, you better understand the importance of precise programming in all computational work. In addition, you are now more aware than decisions can become somewhat complex.

The skill of a programmer is often measured by his or her ability to solve difficult logic problems. And the proper use of decisions is basic to the solving of these logic problems. This section shows how to use decisions in order to develop more skillful programming techniques.

30. Consider the following input card.

NAME	ANNUAL SALARY	

Suppose we want to draw a flowchart that will print the names of all employees whose annual salary is between $50,000 and $100,000. The flowchart below illustrates the logic involved. Study it carefully and then answer the questions in the frames that follow.

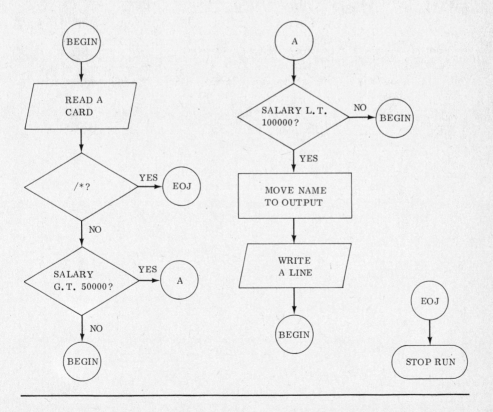

31. The sequence labeled (A) is reached only if _____

_____.

In all other cases, _____.

- - - - - - - - - - - - - - - - - -

an employee's salary exceeds $50,000; the program will call for another
input card (branch to BEGIN)

32. Thus, if the test to determine if SALARY is less than $100,000 results in

a YES answer, the salary must fall within the range of _____

and _____.

- - - - - - - - - - - - - - - - - -

$50,000 and $100,000 (Remember that the test is not performed at all unless
salary exceeds $50,000.)

33. According to the logic flow in the flowchart, an employee whose salary is

exactly $50,000 (will, will not) _____ print. An employee whose

salary is $100,000 (will, will not) _____ print.

- - - - - - - - - - - - - - - - - -

will not—only salaries in excess of $50,000 result in a branch to A; will—
$100,000 is not less than $100,000 (it's equal), thus a branch does not occur
since the result of the comparison is a YES. Since no branch occurs, the
name is printed.

34. The flowcharted interpretation of a salary between $50,000 and $100,000
exclusive of endpoints can be represented as:

$$50,000 < \text{SALARY} < 100,000$$

That is, $50,000 must be less than (<) SALARY at the same time that SALARY
is less than $100,000. The following symbols are often used in business. On-
ly the first three are permitted in flowcharts because they are the symbols
which can be employed in most programming languages.

Symbol	Meaning
$<$	less than
$=$	equal to
$>$	greater than
$\leq$	less than or equal to
$\geq$	greater than or equal to
$\neq$	not equal to

It is important to note that the word "between" can mean <u>exclusive</u> of endpoints, or it can mean <u>inclusive</u> of endpoints. That is, if a job description called for printing an error message when a field called CODE is between 1 and 5, we must ask, "Should the values of 1 or 5 yield an error message, or does the error message only apply for values <u>greater than</u> 1 and <u>less than</u> 5?" The ambiguous term "between" can lead to different interpretations of the required coding. For example:

Branch to ERR–MESS–RTN if $1 \leq CODE \leq 5$ (inclusive of endpoints)
or
Branch to ERR–MESS–RTN if $1 < CODE < 5$ (exclusive of endpoints)

Clearly the results produced will be different, depending upon which interpretation is used. So when you are given a job description that involves ranges of values, it is critical that you, as the programmer, find out if one, both, or neither endpoint is to be included within that range.

35. The notation $300 \leq AMT \leq 1000$ means that AMT must be _____

- - - - - - - - - - - - - - - - - -

between 300 and 1,000—AMT could be equal to 300, equal to 1,000, or equal to any quantity between these endpoints.

36. The above notation is sometimes interpreted as: AMT must be between 300 and 1,000 inclusive of endpoints. The phrase "inclusive of endpoints"

means _____.

- - - - - - - - - - - - - - - - - -

if AMT is equal to either of the endpoints (300 or 1,000) it "passes the test."

37. Note that in a flowchart only the $<$, $=$, and $>$ symbols will be used. We use the others only for ease of presenting job descriptions. Since $\leq$, $\neq$, and $\geq$ are not permitted in all programming languages, we will not use them in flowcharting.

Thus, to flowchart a branch to ERR–RTN if $FLD1 \leq 6$, we can use two flowcharting symbols as follows.

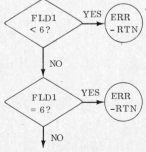

Or we can use one symbol.

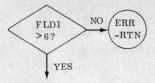

That is, a branch to ERR-RTN is to occur if FLD1 is <u>not</u> greater than 6. To say that a field is not greater than a specific value means that it is less than or equal to that value.

Note that the second flowchart method results in a conditional branch for the NO path rather than the YES path. Although this is acceptable flowcharting form, it is sometimes more difficult to code this type of routine, because of the programming language employed. Because of this possible complication, we shall avoid using such NO path branches unless the advantages are clearly evident.

Draw a flowchart to read input cards and to print the names of all salesmen whose total AMT OF SALES is between $300 and $1,000, inclusive of endpoints. Assume that the input cards have two fields, NAME and AMT OF SALES.

- - - - - - - - - - - - - - - - - -

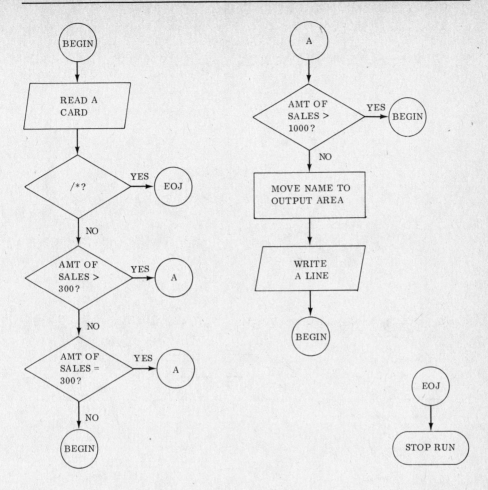

Or you might have incorporated the two AMT OF SALES tests into a single test.

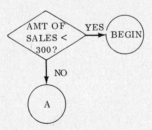

Because such decision problems may be correctly flowcharted in alternate ways, we will devote little extra space to such problems.

38. Sometimes it is important to know the exact representation of the input fields. For example, if, in the problem of frame 37, we assume that AMT OF SALES is a five-position <u>integer</u> field (integer meaning whole numbers only, no decimals), we can draw a single operation to accomplish the following.

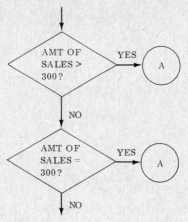

Code this single operation and state why it would not be accurate if AMT OF SALES were not an integer field. _____

_____

_____

- - - - - - - - - - - - - - - - - - -

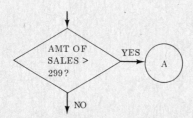

If AMT OF SALES were not an integer field, then 299.95 would pass the test while, in reality, the problem calls for the printing of fields greater than or equal to 300.

39. Assume that FLD1 is a three-position integer field. Draw a single decision symbol that will cause a branch to RTN1 to occur if FLD1 is greater than or equal to 450.

- - - - - - - - - - - - - - - - - - -

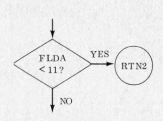

FLD1 > 449? YES → RTN1
NO

40. Assume that FLDA is a two-position integer field. Draw a single decision symbol that will cause a branch to RTN2 to occur if FLDA is less than or equal to 10.

- - - - - - - - - - - - - - - - - -

FLDA < 11? YES → RTN2
NO

41. Interpret the following flowchart. That is, explain in your own words what the flowchart does.

Input

SALESMAN NAME	SALARY	SALES

Output: Salesmen checks

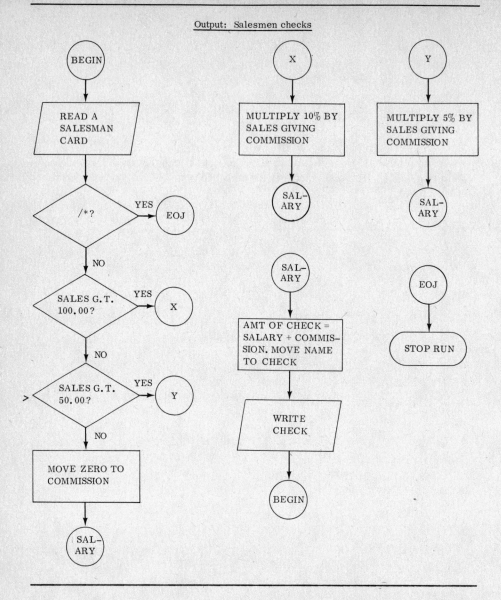

The flowchart reads salesman cards as input, determines salesman commission, and prints a salary check which includes the commission. COMMISSION is 10% of SALES when SALES exceeds $100. COMMISSION is 5% of SALES when 50 < SALES ≤ 100. For SALES less than or equal to $50, no commission is paid. The salary check is equal to salary plus the computed commission. Note that, when comparing fields to constants such as 100.00 or 50.00, decimal points may be used.

42. From the following card format, we wish to print the names of all blue-eyed, blonde males and all brown-eyed, brunette females.

       Card format

       1-20   NAME
       21   SEX (M = male, F = female)
       22   COLOR OF EYES (1 = blue, 2 = brown, 3 = other)
       23   COLOR OF HAIR (1 = brunette, 2 = blonde, 3 = other)
       24-80 Not used

The numbers represent columns of the card. A 2 in position 22 indicates that

_____. Can you remember what types of

fields COLOR OF EYES and COLOR OF HAIR are called? (Hint: What are

fields called that contain a single digit in place of a word such as BLUE or

BROWN that would require more card columns to represent?) _____

- - - - - - - - - - - - - - - - - -

the person has brown eyes; CODE

43. Draw a flowchart to print the names of all blue-eyed, blonde males and all brown-eyed, brunette females. Assume that this program would be used by a dating service.

- - - - - - - - - - - - - - - - - -

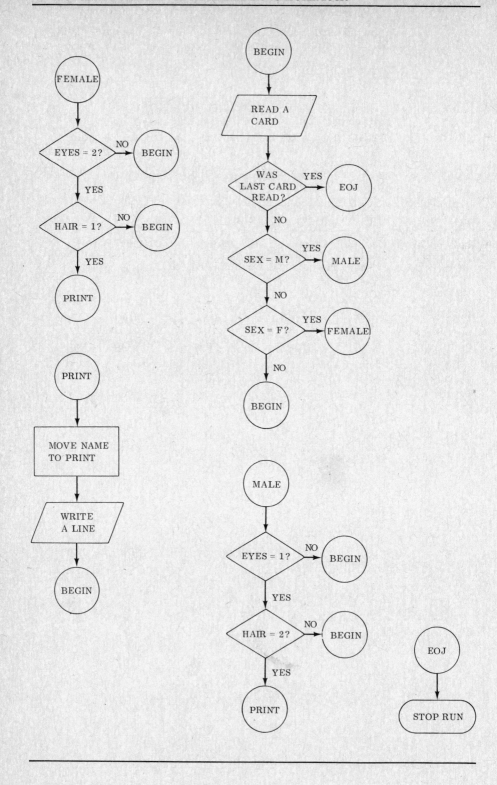

44. Let us modify the preceding dating service procedure so that it is somewhat more realistic (and thus more complex). Draw a flowchart for a dating
service that uses the following format for its input data.

Card input

1-20	NAME
21-23	WEIGHT (in lbs.)
24-25	HEIGHT (in inches)
26	COLOR OF EYES (1 = blue, 2 = brown, 3 = other)
27	COLOR OF HAIR (1 = blonde, 2 = brunette, 3 = other)
28-79	Not used
80	Sex (M = male, F = female)

Note that in the flowchart you need only the assigned field names and not the
card columns. But you need to plan card input layout very carefully because,
when you write the actual program, the field names must be equated to corresponding card columns. (You must know, for example, that all the fields
will fit onto one card!)

Output is punched cards with the names of all: (1) Blue-eyed, blonde
males over 6 feet (72 inches) tall and weighing between 185 and 200 lbs., inclusive; (2) Brown-eyed, brunette females between 5 feet 2 inches (62 inches)
and 5 feet 6 inches (66 inches), inclusive, and weighing less than 120 lbs. All
other combinations should not be printed.

- - - - - - - - - - - - - - - - - -

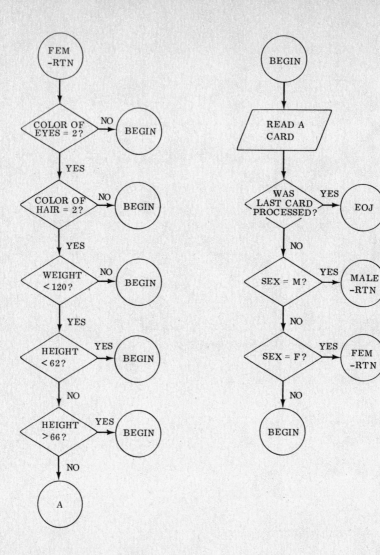

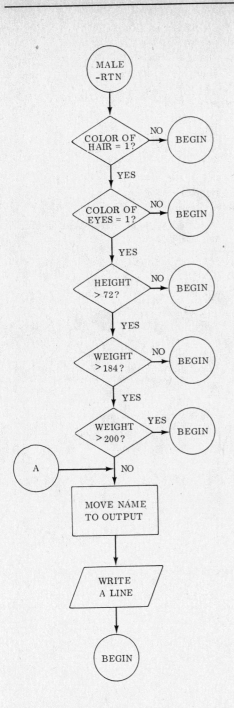

Note that the preceding flowchart could be written in various ways. For example, the sequence of tests performed is not crucial, as long as all tests are adequately performed. The actual program from which this flowchart is coded can be simplified if the programming language used allows for compound conditionals. COBOL and PL/I, for example, are two programming languages which can incorporate many tests into a single statement. Note also that the order in which sequences are flowcharted (from left to right) will not be deemed significant, for purposes of this text.

The branch to BEGIN at the end of the major sequence (the one which has an entry connector of BEGIN) is only performed if the tests for an M in SEX and for an F in SEX produce NO results. This would only happen if the SEX field were erroneously coded. Thus the branch to BEGIN in the major sequence is a protective measure which prevents erroneous data from being processed. How extensively you use such error procedures will depend upon the type of input, the degree of manual handling, and cost.

45. Suppose we wish to branch to RTN1 if ACCT = 2 and branch to RTN2 if ACCT = 0. In that case, would the following routine accomplish the desired processing? _____

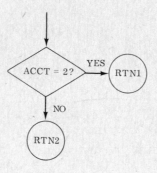

- -

Assuming that ACCT can contain only a 0 or 2, the above is logical. It can, however, lead to inaccurate processing in the event that ACCT were accidentally miscoded as a 3, for example. In such a case, a branch to RTN2 would occur. To learn how to prevent such inaccurate processing, read on.

46. In frame 45, no provision was made for possible errors in the ACCT field. That is, if ACCT did not equal 2, it was automatically assumed that it equaled 0. This assumption is often erroneous, especially in the case of card processing, because keypunching errors are fairly common. To insure that a branch to RTN2 occurs only if ACCT equals 0, we would add another decision symbol to test whether ACCT equals 0. If ACCT equals neither a 2 or a 0, this would be an error condition and we would branch to ERR-RTN (error routine).

Modify the flowchart segment from frame 45 to branch to ERR-RTN if ACCT is improperly coded.

- - - - - - - - - - - - - - - - - - - -

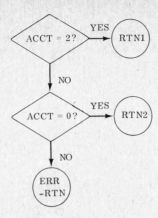

47. Draw a flowchart to print out patient name and preliminary diagnosis for each of the following input medical cards.

1-20	Patient name
21	Lung infection (1 if found, 0 if not found)
22	Temperature (1 if high, 0 if normal)
23	Sniffles (1 if present, 0 if absent)

Specifications

(1) If patient has a lung infection and temperature, the preliminary diagnosis is PNEUMONIA.

(2) If patient has a combination of two symptoms (other than the combination of lung infection and temperature), the preliminary diagnosis is COLD.

(3) If patient has any single symptom, the preliminary diagnosis is POTENTIAL COLD.

(4) If patient has no symptoms, the preliminary diagnosis is OK.

- - - - - - - - - - - - - - - - - -

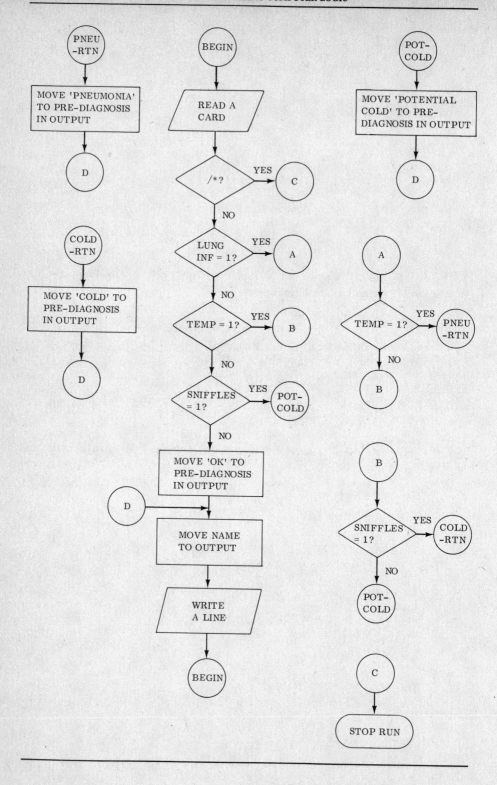

Note that in the preceding flowchart, we moved NAME to output <u>after</u> the diagnosis was moved. We did this to save additional steps by having all diag-
nostic routines branch back to a single point where the NAME is moved to the
output area and the output record is written. It is important to realize that it
doesn't matter whether NAME is moved before or after any other data, because
nothing is printed until the write instruction is given.

48. We might have simplified the flowchart in frame 47 by using a CTR to
store the sum of all symptoms. That is, if we add the symptom fields to
SYMP-CTR, we can then determine whether a patient has a single symptom
by comparing SYMP-CTR to 1, whether a patient has two symptoms by comparing SYMP-CTR to 2, and so on. This technique is particularly useful when
the number of combinations is great. Note that this technique only works because the symptom fields have values of 0 or 1 <u>only</u>. If these fields had different values, their sum would not produce a true count of symptoms.

Consider the following problem, which has an additional symptom field.
If the above SYMP-CTR technique were not employed, the number of decision
symbols required would be excessive. In this flowchart we will be using the
counter technique.

Draw a flowchart to print out patient name and preliminary diagnosis for
each of the following input medical cards.

1-20	Patient name
21	Lung infection (1 if found, 0 if not found)
22	Temperature (1 if high, 0 if normal)
23	Sniffles (1 if present, 0 if absent)
24	Sore throat (1 if present, 0 if absent)
25-80	Not used

<u>Specifications</u>

(1) If patient has a lung infection and temperature, the preliminary
diagnosis is PNEUMONIA.
(2) If patient has a combination of two or more symptoms (excluding
the combination of lung infection and temperature), the preliminary
diagnosis is COLD.
(3) If patient has any single symptom, the preliminary diagnosis is
POTENTIAL COLD.
(4) If patient has no symptoms, the preliminary diagnosis is OK.

- - - - - - - - - - - - - - - - - - - -

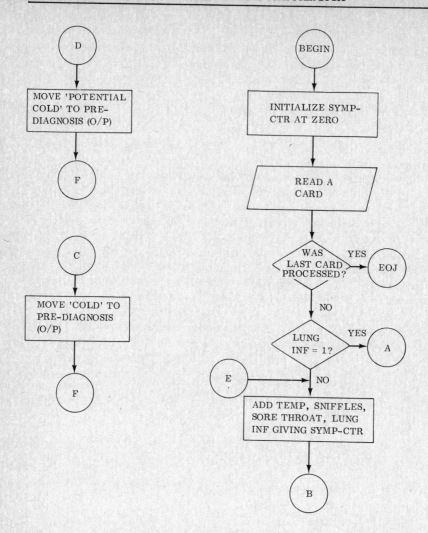

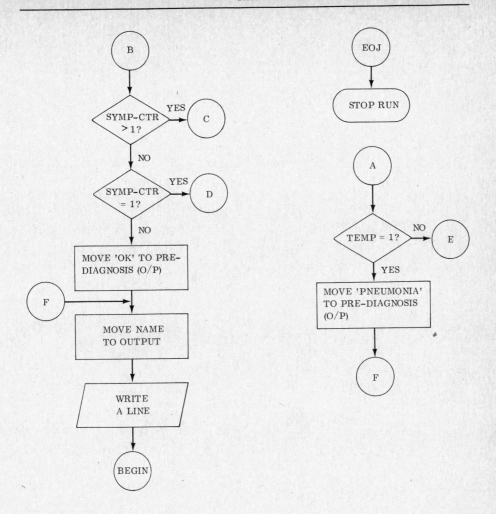

The branch to B in the preceding flowchart is needed simply because there was no more room for the additional entries required.

49. SYMP-CTR is used for _____.

- - - - - - - - - - - - - - - - - -

determining the number of symptoms present. To code this flowchart with individual decisions would be very cumbersome, so the counter SYMP-CTR represents a far simpler method for obtaining the required results.

50. The following is a flowchart which, when programmed, will read in three numbers, A, B, and C, and print one of these. Which one does it print?

_____

_____

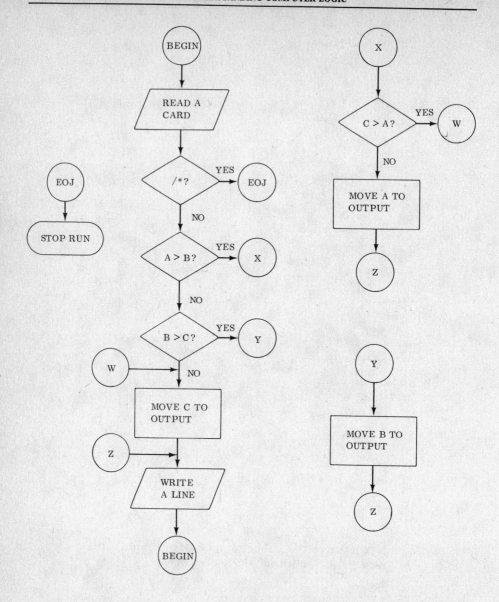

the largest

51. Suppose A = 20, B = 30, and C = 25. With the use of arrows, show the path that will be followed in the flowchart in frame 50.

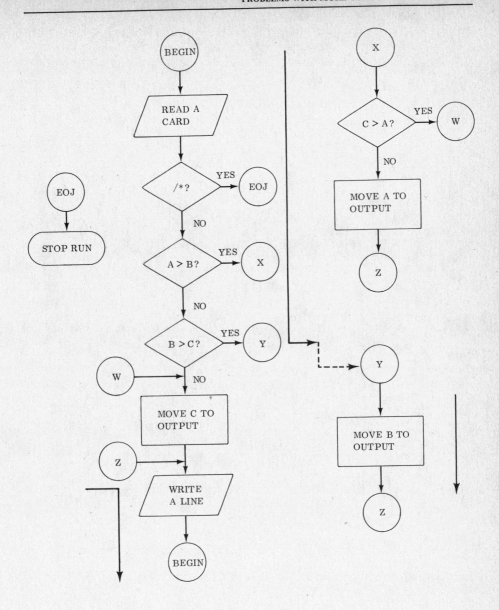

Note that the routine in frames 50–51 for printing the largest of three numbers could be drawn in various ways; our representation is only one possibility. Draw a flowchart to print the smallest of three numbers, X, Y, and Z.

- - - - - - - - - - - - - - - - - -

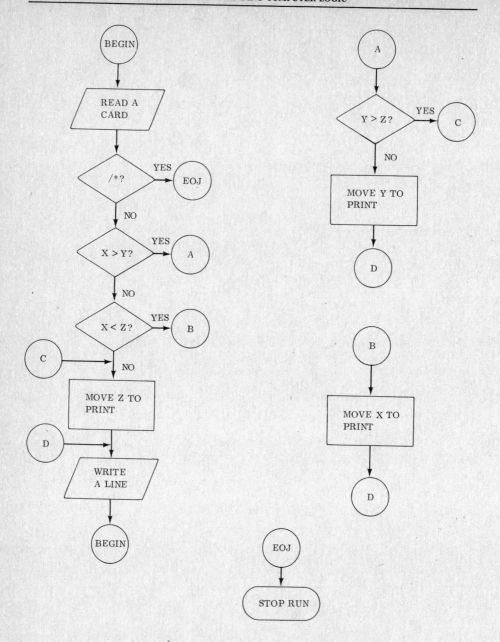

This flowchart, too, could be drawn in various ways. Here is one. If yours is different, and you're not sure it's correct, choose some sample numbers and follow their path through the flowchart to see if it produces the smallest number.

LOOPS

We've been using loops for a while now (whether you knew it or not).   Let's examine them more closely to see how they operate.   A loop is a procedure which results in the repetition of a series of operations until a specified condition occurs.   Through the use of a loop, the computer can be instructed to repeat a series of instructions a specified number of times.

53. Suppose we wish to read a card and punch five output cards containing the same information.   Given what you know so far (that is, without using loops), draw a flowchart that will perform these operations.   Have the flowchart branch to a routine labeled OUT when the cards have been punched.   When you are finished, check our flowchart on the following page.

- - - - - - - - - - - - - - - - - -

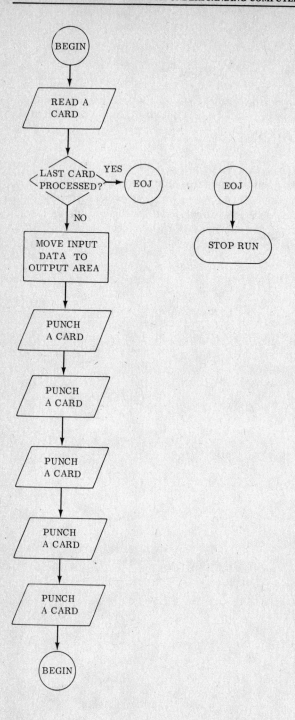

54. To draw a flowchart that has five successive punch commands may not seem excessively cumbersome, but suppose that the problem required the punching of 100 cards rather than just five! There is a less cumbersome method for coding repetitive operations that must be performed a fixed number of times. This method is called looping.

Rules for looping

(1) Establish a field in storage that is to be used as a counter.

(2) Initialize this counter field at zero.

(3) Perform operation.

(4) Every time the required operation or operations are performed, add 1 to the counter.

(5) Test the counter, after each operation, to determine if it was performed the required number of times.

(6) If the required number has been reached, branch to the next routine.

(7) If the required number has not been reached, branch back to the routine which performs the operation (branch to 3 above).

Using the above rules for looping, carefully draw a flowchart excerpt which will punch 100 cards from a single input card, and then branch to OUT (a separate routine).

- - - - - - - - - - - - - - - - - -

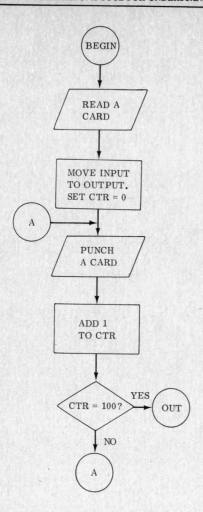

55. Using the loop procedure, draw a flowchart to read in cards and print the total number of cards read.

- - - - - - - - - - - - - - - - - - -

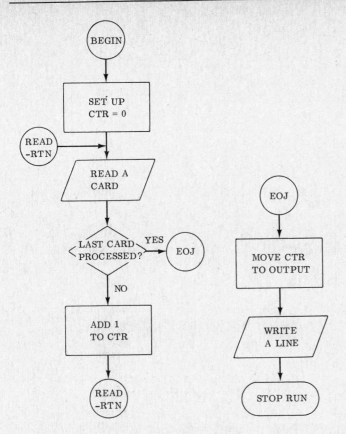

Notice that, in the above, a single number will print without any reference to the meaning of that number. To prevent any misinterpretation of output, it is considered good programming form to include a literal explaining the meaning of the printed number. Thus, the following would represent a somewhat more meaningful flowchart.

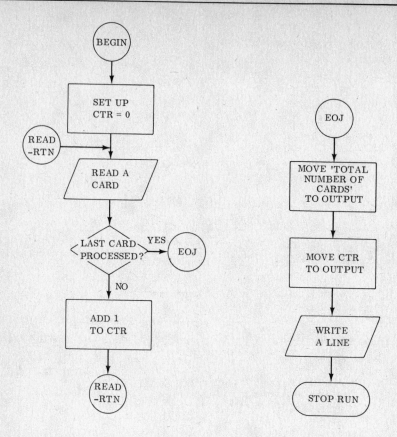

56. Printed forms produced by the computer must have adequate margins on both top and bottom. Sometimes we arbitrarily allow the printing of 50 lines per page. After 50 lines have been printed, we usually advance to a new page and continue printing until we have 50 more lines, and so on. Draw a flowchart using the loop procedure that reads input cards and prints them, but prints exactly 50 lines on a page.

- - - - - - - - - - - - - - - - - -

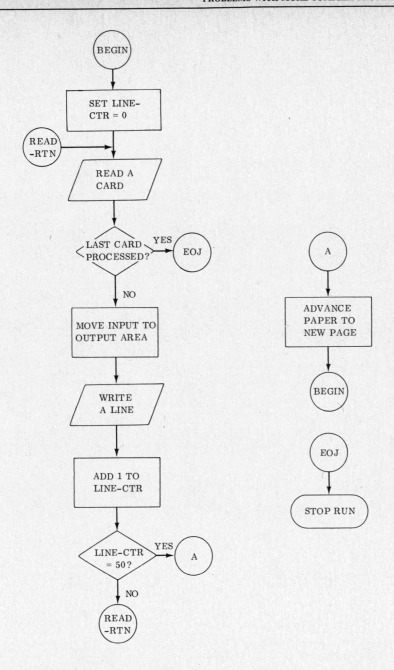

57. In the flowchart of frame 56, the sequence labeled A branches back to BEGIN, rather than to READ-RTN, in order to re-initialize LINE-CTR. If the sequence labeled A branched back to READ-RTN, what would happen?

_____

_____

- - - - - - - - - - - - - - - - - -

_____

After the first page was printed, line after line would keep printing. The test for LINE-CTR = 50 would never be met since LINE-CTR would be 51, 52, 53, and so on. And after the first page, no top and bottom margins would result.

58. Draw a flowchart which will sum the first 100 integers.

- - - - - - - - - - - - - - - - - - -

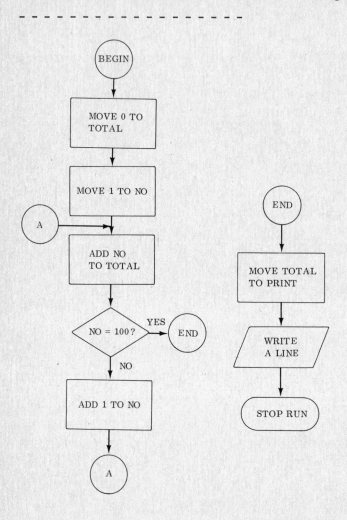

The storage areas in this flowchart are called TOTAL and NO, with NO acting as the counter. Whatever you called your storage areas, be sure that you defined and initialized them at the beginning of the flowchart.

59. Draw a flowchart which will sum the odd numbers from 1 to 101. (Hint: start CTR at 1 and add 2 each time.)

- - - - - - - - - - - - - - - - - - -

60. Draw a flowchart that will sum the first 50 even numbers, from 2 to 100.

- - - - - - - - - - - - - - - - - -

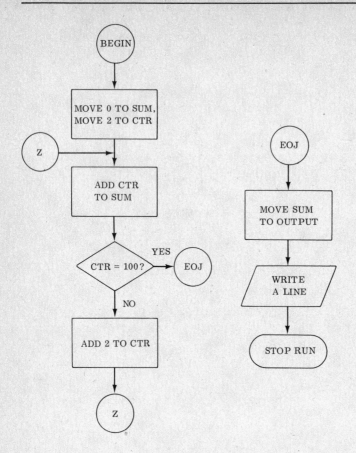

SELF-TEST

1.   Write an instruction inside a decision symbol to determine if an employee is under 30 years of age.   Assume that the present year is 1975 and that the input contains a field called BIRTH DATE which consists of a month and a year.

2.   Draw a single flowcharting decision symbol which causes a branch to STEP5 if AMT,   a three-position integer field, is greater than or equal to 250.

3.   Write a routine to branch to PATH1 if FIELD1 is between 20 and 30, inclusive of the endpoints. If not, branch to PATH2.

4.   Write a routine to branch to PATH1 if FIELD1 is between 20 and 30, exclusive of the endpoints. If not, branch to PATH2.

5.   Examine the flowchart below and then answer the questions that follow.

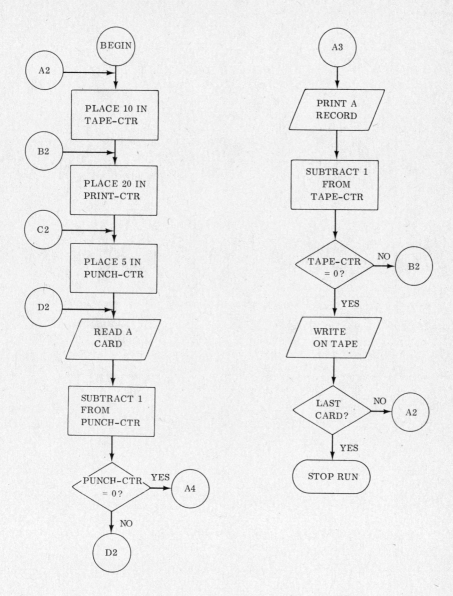

Note: flowchart is continued on the next page.

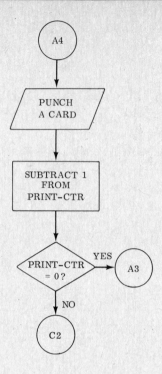

(a) In the preceding system, a record is punched after reading how many cards? Explain. _____

_____

(b) The system is printing a record after reading how many cards? Explain.

_____

_____

(c) The system is writing on tape after reading how many cards? Explain.

_____

_____

6. Questions (a) through (d) refer to the flowchart on the next page. Input used is on 15 cards. Codes on 15 cards (in column 1) are:

        1, 2, 3, 2, 1, 1, 2, 2, 3, 3, 1, 2, 3, 1, 2

(a) How many cards will be read?

(b) What is the value of SWITCH when a branch to EOJ occurs? _____

(c) What is the value of ACCUM when a branch to EOJ occurs? _____

(d) How many cards would have been read if ACCUM were originally set to 1 instead of 0? _____

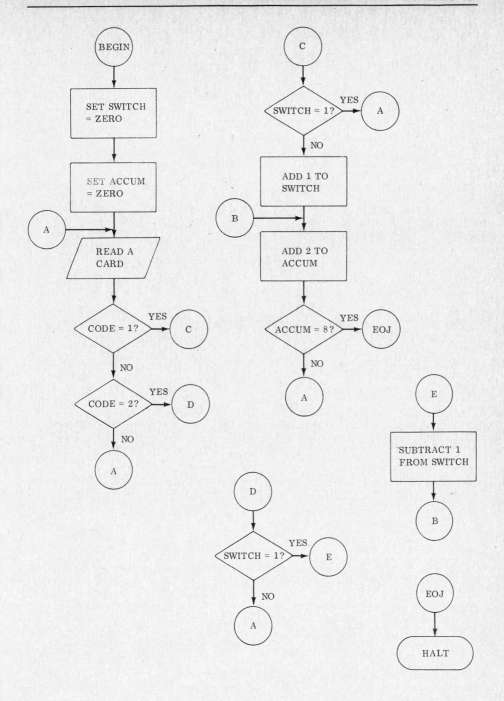

7. Draw a flowchart to read in groups of 100 cards and print a total of all AMT fields on each card, for each group. Assume that the number of cards in the deck is an even multiple of 100.

8. Explain what the following flowchart does.

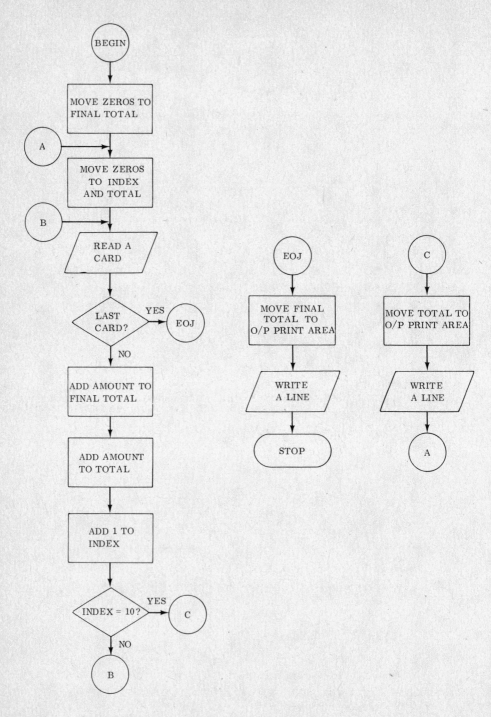

9. Draw a flowchart which reads in cards with the following format.

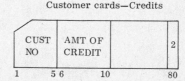

Customer cards—Charges

| CUST NO | AMT | | 1 |
| 1 | 5 6 | 10 | 80 |

Customer cards—Credits

| CUST NO | AMT OF CREDIT | | 2 |
| 1 | 5 6 | 10 | 80 |

The cards will not arrive in any specific sequence; that is, cards with a 1 in column 80 may be preceded or followed by cards with a 2 in column 80.

The problem is to print two totals, one total of all charges (all cards with a 1 in column 80) and one total of all credits (cards with a 2 in column 80). If an input card has neither a 1 nor a 2 in column 80, print an error message.

10. Draw a flowchart which reads in cards with the following format.

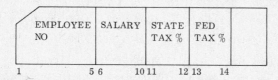

| EMPLOYEE NO | SALARY | STATE TAX % | FED TAX % | |
| 1 | 5 6 | 10 11 | 12 13 | 14 |

The problem is to print for each employee:

(1) EMPLOYEE NO.
(2) NET SALARY = SALARY - STATE TAX - FED TAX, where STATE TAX = SALARY x STATE TAX %, and FEDERAL TAX = SALARY x FED TAX %. (If STATE TAX % or FEDERAL TAX % is blank on the card, denoting an error, NET SALARY = 00000.00.)
(3) LEVEL, where LEVEL = 1 if NET SALARY < $5000.00; LEVEL = 2 if NET SALARY is between $5,000.00 and $10,000.00, inclusive; and LEVEL = 3 if NET SALARY > $10,000.00.

Answers to Self-Test

1.

YEAR OF BIRTH DATE G.T. 45?

(frame 7)

2.

(frames 30–40)

3.

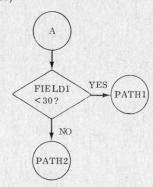

(frames 30–40)

4.

(frames 30–40)

5.   (a) 5; PUNCH-CTR decreases from 5 to 0 while 5 cards are read.
(b) 100; After 5 cards are read, one card is punched and PRINT-CTR
decreases by 1. In order for PRINT-CTR to be decreased by 20, the
reading of groups of five cards must be repeated 20 times. Thus, 100
cards are read.
(c) 1,000; After 100 cards have been read, a record is printed, and
TAPE-CTR is decreased by 1. In order for TAPE-CTR to be decreased
by 10, the reading of 100 cards must be repeated 10 times. Thus, 1,000
cards must be read.
(frames 41–44)

6.   (a) 7
(b) 0
(c) 8

(d) All of them   (ACCUM would never be equal to 8 since it began at 1 and was incremented by 2, resulting in 1, 3, 5, 7, 9, and so on. (frames 41-44)

7.

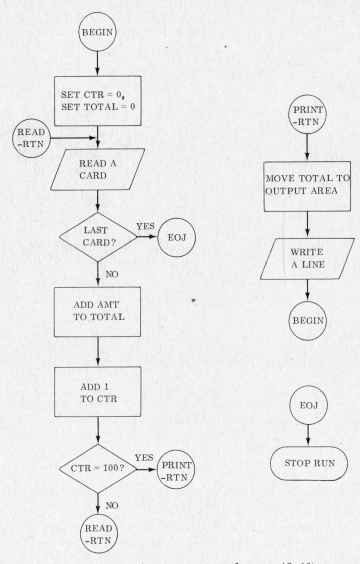

(frames 45-60)

8.   The TOTAL of ten AMOUNT fields from ten separate cards is printed, then the TOTAL of ten AMOUNT fields from 10 more cards is printed, and so on.   At the end of the run a final total of all cards is printed. (frames 41-44)

9.

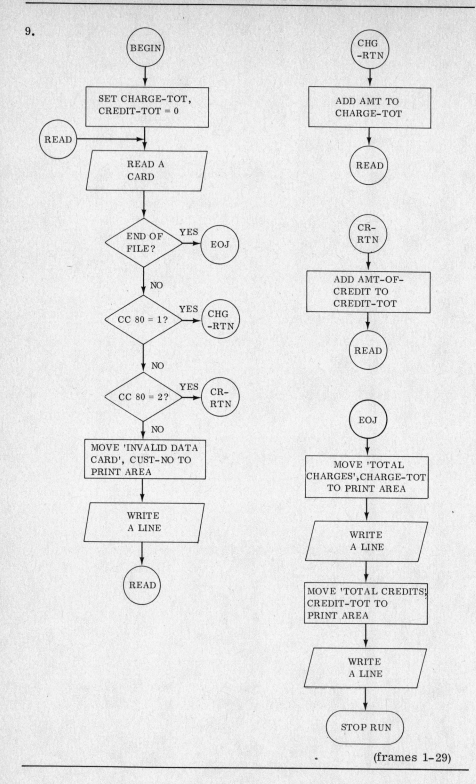

(frames 1–29)

10.

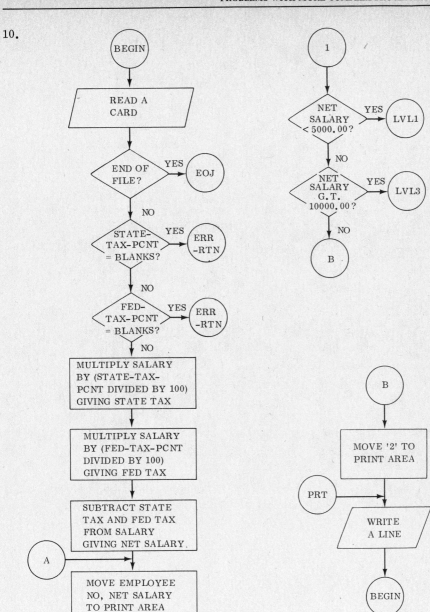

Note: flowchart is continued on the next page.

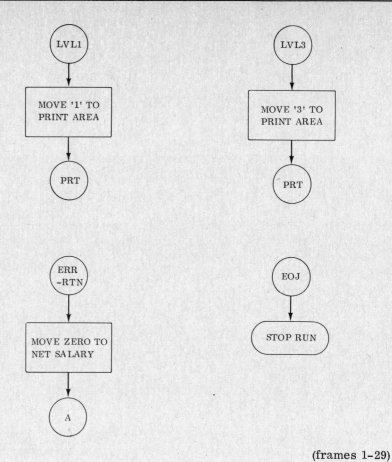

(frames 1–29)

CHAPTER FOUR
Complex Arithmetic

In Chapters 2 and 3 you learned the basic flowcharting symbols and the logical technique you can use to integrate them. Chapters 4 and 5 will familiarize you with some additional applications of computer processing through the use of flowcharting and will teach you how to flowchart more complex and precise arithmetic procedures.

In this chapter you will learn how to:

- write instructions more precisely by using formula notation;

- flowchart rounding procedures;

- flowchart sequence-checking procedures;

- use switches in flowcharting.

FLOWCHARTING ARITHMETIC PROBLEMS

1. So far we have drawn arithmetic problems in separate steps, as in Example A following. Or we have combined the steps into one symbol, as in Example B.

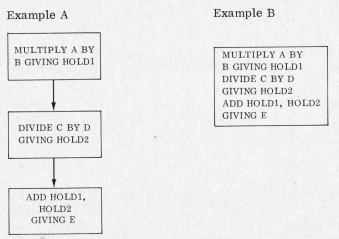

Example A

MULTIPLY A BY
B GIVING HOLD1

DIVIDE C BY D
GIVING HOLD2

ADD HOLD1,
HOLD2
GIVING E

Example B

MULTIPLY A BY
B GIVING HOLD1
DIVIDE C BY D
GIVING HOLD2
ADD HOLD1, HOLD2
GIVING E

However, for more complex arithmetic problems, both of these methods of flowcharting can be cumbersome. To make complex arithmetic easier to flowchart, and easier to code, we can use formula notation. For example, to obtain the same results as the above flowchart segments, we could write: $E = A \times B + C/D$. This formula can then be shown in a single step.

```
SET E =
A x B + C/D
```

In this case, E is made equal to the value of $A \times B + C/D$. Words such as SET, LET, COMPUTE, or CALCULATE are optional to indicate that a formula is being used.

Suppose that A = 4, B = 8, C = 9, D = 3, and E = 6 at the beginning of the run. What would be the result if the formula $E = A \times B + C/D$ were executed?

_____   Where would the answer be placed? _____

- -

35; E (Note that the original content of E did not take part in the arithmetic calculation. In the flowchart, as in the corresponding program that would be coded from it, E <u>is set equal</u> to the result of the computation. The original content of E would then be lost, unless it were stored somewhere else.)

2.   In every major programming language, the following operator symbols are used to represent arithmetic operations.

Operation	Symbol
Addition	+
Subtraction	−
Multiplication	*
Division	/
Exponentiation (raising a number to a power, e.g. 4^2)	**

Rewrite the formula $E = A \times B + C/D$ in a flowcharting symbol, using the appropriate computer operators.

- - - - - - - - - - - - - - - - - - -

```
SET E =
A * B + C/D
```

3. Using the appropriate computer operator symbols, flowchart a step which finds $C = A + \dfrac{B}{3}$

- - - - - - - - - - - - - - - - -

```
┌─────────────────────┐
│   SET C =           │
│   A + B/3           │
└─────────────────────┘
```

4. Now suppose that we wish to find $C = \dfrac{A + B}{3}$. Note that this is a different operation from the one in frame 3. Suppose that $A = 6$ and $B = 9$. What would be the result at C for $C = A + \dfrac{B}{3}$? _____

For $C = \dfrac{A + B}{3}$? _____

- - - - - - - - - - - - - - - - -

for $C = A + \dfrac{B}{3}$, $C = 9$; for $C = \dfrac{A + B}{3}$, $C = 5$

5. We use parentheses to surround variables that are to be treated as a unit. Draw the flowchart for finding $C = \dfrac{A + B}{3}$, using computer symbols. Group A and B in parentheses, so they will be treated together.

- - - - - - - - - - - - - - - - -

```
┌─────────────────────┐
│   SET C =           │
│   (A + B)/3         │
└─────────────────────┘
```

Without parentheses here, only B would be divided by 3.

6. Using a single statement, find the average of A, B, and C and place the result in a field called AVERAGE.

- - - - - - - - - - - - - - - - -

```
┌─────────────────────┐
│   SET AVERAGE       │
│   = (A + B + C)/3   │
└─────────────────────┘
```

Here, again, you must include the parentheses; otherwise only the last variable would be divided by three, instead of the whole expression.

7. Find NET = GROSS - DISCOUNT, where DISCOUNT = .03 x GROSS.
Draw the flowchart steps required, and try to write the operations in as few
steps as possible.

— — — — — — — — — — — — — — — — — —

This is a correct answer.   This is a simpler, more efficient answer.

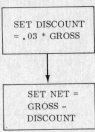

SET DISCOUNT
= .03 * GROSS

SET NET =
.97 * GROSS

SET NET =
GROSS –
DISCOUNT

NET = GROSS - DISCOUNT,
where DISCOUNT = .03 * GROSS.
So NET = GROSS - (.03 * GROSS),
NET = 1.00 GROSS - .03 GROSS,
and NET = .97 GROSS. Thus, we
can eliminate the extra step.

8. Unlike formulas, the type of arithmetic statements discussed here makes
the calculated right side of the expression equal to the left variable. Thus,
to add 1 to A, we can say: A = A + 1. That is, 1 is added to A and the result
is placed back into A. (Notice that we can have only a single variable on the
left side of the expression, so A + 1 = A is an invalid flowcharting statement.)
Indicate whether the following pairs of statements are equivalent.

(a)
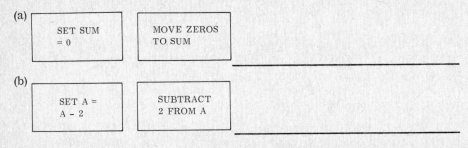

SET SUM
= 0

MOVE ZEROS
TO SUM

(b)

SET A =
A – 2

SUBTRACT
2 FROM A

— — — — — — — — — — — — — — — —

(a) equivalent; (b) equivalent

9. Note that in our list of operations, there is a symbol for exponentiation.
For those of you who have forgotten some of your intermediate algebra, we
will review the meaning of exponentiation. If you remember how to raise
numbers to any power with no difficulty, you may skim quickly or skip to
frame 18.
The term exponentiation refers to the process of raising a number to a
power. A ** 2, in computer terminology, is the same as the mathematical
expression A^2, which is the same as A x A, or A "taken twice, or A squared."

(a) What is the value of A ** 2 where A = 3? _____

(b) What is the value of B^2 where B = 5? Represent B^2 using computer symbols. _____

- - - - - - - - - - - - - - - - -

(a) A ** 2 = A^2 = A x A = 3 x 3 = 9; (b) B^2 = B x B = 5 x 5 = 25; B^2 = B ** 2

10. The expression A ** 3 corresponds to the mathematical expression A^3, A x A x A, or A "cubed." What, then, is the value of B ** 3 where B = 5?

_____

- - - - - - - - - - - - - - - - -

B ** 3 = B^3 = B x B x B = 5 x 5 x 5 = 125

11. What is the value of A^3 where A = 3? Represent A^3 using computer symbols. _____

- - - - - - - - - - - - - - - - -

A^3 = A x A x A = 3 x 3 x 3 = 27; A^3 = A ** 3

12. Now let's see how well you can generalize. What is the value of A^4 where A = 3? Represent A^4 using computer symbols. _____

_____

- - - - - - - - - - - - - - - - -

A^4 = A x A x A x A = 3 x 3 x 3 x 3 = 81; A^4 = A ** 4

13. What is the value of C ** 5 where C = 2? _____

_____

- - - - - - - - - - - - - - - - -

C ** 5 = C^5 = C x C x C x C x C = 2 x 2 x 2 x 2 x 2 = 32

14. The area of a circle corresponds to the formula A = πr^2, where π = 3.14 and r is the radius.

   Using the computer symbols for arithmetic operations, write a flowchart operation that will compute A. (Assume that r is read into the computer as input elsewhere in the program.)

- - - - - - - - - - - - - - - - -

| SET A = |
| 3.14 * R ** 2 |

Note: The expressions 3.14 * (r ** 2) and 3.14 * (r * r) would be equally correct.

15. If the formula in frame 14 is used, what will be the value of A if r = 3?

A = 3.14 x 3 x 3 = 3.14 x 9 = 28.26

16. Draw a flowchart operation that will compute $C = A^2 + B^2$.

```
SET C =
A ** 2 + B ** 2
```

17. Is the following a correct statement of $C = A^2 + B^2$? _____

```
ADD A, B GIVING
C.  MULTIPLY
C BY C
```

No, because it yields $(A + B)^2$ which is not the same as $A^2 + B^2$.

Hierarchy of Operations

18. Rather than writing out each step of a program's basic arithmetic operations, as we've been doing, we can use the computer operator symbols discussed in this chapter to facilitate our programming. Most computer languages permit the use of the operator symbols we have discussed. Now let's see how they work in practice.

The computer operates on arithmetic expressions essentially in accordance with the following priorities.

Operation	Hierarchy
Exponentiation (**)	1st
Multiplication (*) and Division (/)	2nd
Addition (+) and Subtraction (-)	3rd

When we have several operations of the same priority level or hierarchy, they are evaluated in order from left to right. Thus, in statement X = B * C * D, the computer first multiplies B by C and then multiplies that product by D. The more complex statement A = B - C * D + E ** 2 is evaluated by the computer in the following manner.

(1) E ** 2

Since the highest level of priority in this expression is the exponentiation operation, E is squared first.

(2) C * D

(3) B – C * D

After C is multiplied by D, the product is subtracted from B since subtraction has a lower level of priority than multiplication. Since the subtraction and addition operations in the illustration have the same level, the subtraction, as the leftmost operation, is performed first.

(4) A = B – C * D + E ** 2

The result B – C * D is added to E ** 2 and that result is set equal to A.

Now you try some. Indicate the manner in which the following operations are evaluated.

(a) X = A + B / C ** 3 _____

_____

(b) Y = A / E + B – C ** 2 _____

_____

– – – – – – – – – – – – – – – – – – – –

(a) (1) C ** 3; (2) B / C ** 3; (3) X = A + B / C ** 3
(b) (1) C ** 2; (2) A / E; (3) A / E + B; (4) Y = A / E + B – C ** 2

19. Sometimes, however, we want to override the priority rules. To change the normal hierarchy of operations, we use <u>parentheses</u>, which have top priority. Suppose that in the illustration in frame 18 we really wanted the computer to multiply the difference between B and C by D (instead of subtracting the product of C and D from B), then adding E squared. We have just seen that we cannot write the statement A = B – C * D + E ** 2 to accomplish that. But by using parentheses to change the priority operations, we can write our desired formula as A = (B – C) * D + E ** 2. The computer now does the following.

(1) (B – C) is evaluated first because it is in parentheses. Operations within parentheses are performed in accordance with the rules of the hierarchy (that is, first exponentiation, then multiplication and division, last addition and subtraction). In this case, C is subtracted from B.

(2) E ** 2 is evaluated next since, in the absence of parentheses, normal hierarchy rules are followed.

(3) (B – C) * D is evaluated next. Essentially, the computer looks for the highest symbol remaining, in this case *. Thus, the difference of B – C is multiplied by D.

(4) A = (B – C) * D + E ** 2

Since there are no operations left to be performed, the computer finally stores the answer in the field to the left of the equal sign, here A.

Indicate the order in which the following are evaluated.

(a)   X = (A + B – C) * E + (F ** 2) / G _____

_____

(b)   Y = (A * B) ** 3 + (E – F) / G _____

_____

– – – – – – – – – – – – – – – – –

(a)   (1) A + B;   (2) (A + B – C);   (3) (F ** 2);   (4) (A + B – C) * E;
      (5) (F ** 2) / G;   (6) X = (A + B – C) * E + (F ** 2) / G
(b)   (1) A * B;   (2) (E – F);   (3) (A * B) ** 3;   (4) (E – F) / G;
      (5) Y = (A * B) ** 3 + (E – F) / G

20. Now here's some practice in translating from computer symbols to algebraic symbols, and back again. (You'll notice that, by convention, algebraic formulas are usually written in lower case letters and computer statements are usually written in capital letters.) Draw the computer flowchart symbols and statements corresponding to the following algebraic expressions.

(a) $x = \dfrac{1}{\left(b - \dfrac{c}{2}\right)^2}$

(b) $y = \dfrac{(c - d)^3}{2} - (1 - c)$

(c) $x = 1 + \dfrac{\dfrac{b}{2} + b^3}{c^2 - 2}$

– – – – – – – – – – – – – – – – – –

(a)

```
CALCULATE X
= 1/(B – C/2) ** 2
```

(b)

```
CALCULATE Y =
(C – D) ** 3/2
– (1 – C)
```

(c)

```
CALCULATE X =
1 + (B/2 + B ** 3)/
(C ** 2 – 2)
```

You might have said SET, LET, COMPUTE, or anything similar for CALCULATE—or you might have omitted this verbal instruction altogether. Such instructions are optional. Note also in the answers provided that some of the expressions have been "closed up," or written without spacing. Spacing is optional, and may be used to clarify operations, but has no significance to the operations themselves.

21. Now write the mathematical formulas that correspond to the following computer statements.

(a)
```
VALUE = 1.5 * C
* AMT/TOTAL
- 25.5
```

(b)
```
I = (AMT1 + AMT2)
** 4/2 - AMT3
```

(c)
```
RESULT =
A/(B + C) ** D
* 2.5
```

- -

(a) $\text{VALUE} = 1.5 \times c \times \dfrac{\text{AMT}}{\text{TOTAL}} - 25.5$

(b) $I = \dfrac{(\text{AMT1} + \text{AMT2})^4}{2} - \text{AMT3}$

(c) $\text{RESULT} = \dfrac{2.5 \times A}{(B + C)^D}$

ROUNDING RESULTS

22. As you may have noticed, we've generally used integers rather than decimal numbers so far in this book. That's because integers are easier to work with and decimals sometimes require special procedures, one of which we'll discuss now.

When data is stored in the computer, the programmer must indicate the specifications of the data fields. That is, he or she must indicate the length of these fields, the type of data they contain (alphabetic, numeric, or alphanumeric) and, if numeric, how many decimal positions they contain. These specifications are part of all programs but are rarely represented in a flowchart, since they are assignments that do not reflect the logic of the program.

In this section, we will be concerned with numeric fields, in which arithmetic operations are to be performed on various data fields with differing specifications.

Consider the following:

```
SET C
= A + B
```
where A = 12.857 and B = 25.142

Suppose that C is in storage and has a specification of two integer positions and two decimal positions. What do you think the result of the addition will be? _____

- -

If you said 37.99, you're right!

23. In the absence of additional instructions, the computer truncates (or "chops off") excess digits when the results of arithmetic operations specify fewer decimal positions than do the operating fields. So, in our example of frame 22, although A and B both have three decimal positions, the last digit of the answer is dropped because C specifies only two decimal positions.

   To be sure you understand how this works, try this problem.

SET X = Y + Z	Y = 37.245 Z = 12.694

What result would be placed in X for each of the following cases, if X has a specification of:

(a) 2 integer positions and no decimal positions? _____

(b) 2 integer positions and 2 decimal positions? _____

(c) 2 integer positions and 4 decimal positions? _____

- -

(a) 49; (b) 49.93; (c) 49.9390 (This last one is tricky, since we haven't discussed this case; when the result field exceeds the operations field, the computer normally "fills in" the result field with blanks or zeros.)

24. Note that a more accurate result for frame 22 would be 38.00. That is, the true total 37.999 is closer to 38.00 than it is to the truncated result 37.99. Rather than truncating <u>all</u> excess digits, the technique of <u>rounding</u> allows us to express the result that is closest to the actual value. That is, if the first excess digit is 5 or more, we round to the higher value; if the first excess digit is less than 5, we drop the excess digits. Thus, it is more reliable to round results to the nearest decimal position than to truncate. If you don't remember the technique of rounding, stick with us for a review. If you do, you may skim quickly or skip to frame 27.

25. In rounding, if the first excess digit is 5 or more, we round to the higher value; if the first excess digit is less than 5, we drop all excess digits. For example, if we want to round 18.786 to two decimal positions, we look at the third decimal position. The third decimal position contains a 6, which is more than 5, so we add 1 to the second decimal position, giving a rounded result of 18.79.

The following example should show the process clearly. Suppose the "true" result of the operation X = Y * Z is 748.679848.

If X is rounded to:	the rounded result is:
6 decimal positions	748.679848
5 decimal positions	748.67985
4 decimal positions	748.6799
3 decimal positions	748.680
2 decimal positions	748.68
1 decimal position	748.7
0 decimal positions	749.

Now you try one. The operation C = A + B is performed and the "true" result obtained is 37.923. Round this to two decimal positions. _____

- - - - - - - - - - - - - - - - - - - -

37.92 (Because the third decimal position is less than 5, it is truncated.)

26. Suppose the operation C = A - B is performed and the "true" result obtained is 37.49268. The field C has specifications for two integer positions and three decimal positions. The rounded result in C should be _____.

- - - - - - - - - - - - - - - - - - -

37.493 (Because the 4th position is 5 or more, we increment the 3rd position by 1; the 5th position, and any other excess digits, would be dropped.)

27. Now try the following.

(a) 43.677   rounded to 2 decimal positions _____   truncated _____

(b) 43.3655 rounded to 3 decimal positions _____   truncated _____

(c) 43.27611 rounded to 4 decimal positions _____   truncated _____

(d) 43.100   rounded to 2 decimal positions _____   truncated _____

- - - - - - - - - - - - - - - - - - -

	Rounded	Truncated
(a)	43.68	43.67
(b)	43.366	43.365
(c)	43.2761	43.2761
(d)	43.10	43.10

28. The above technique is most often used for rounding a result by hand. The computer, however, uses a more efficient method. In computer processing, 5 must be added to the decimal position to the right of the decimal position to be rounded. The number is then truncated, and the result is the same as if we had rounded it by hand. For example, we wish to round 56.3677 to two decimal positions. We add 5 to the third decimal position, giving 56.3727, which is then truncated to give the rounded result of 56.37.

$$\begin{array}{r} 56.3677 \\ + \quad .005 \\ \hline 56.3727 \end{array} \quad \text{truncated to } 56.37$$

Notice that this is the same result we would get if we rounded 56.3727 by hand to two positions.

We want to round 69.782 to one decimal position using the computer technique of rounding. We would add 5 to which digit? _____

- - - - - - - - - - - - - - - - - -

the second decimal digit, 8 (because we want to round to the first digit)

29. Complete the rounding problem in frame 28. _____

- - - - - - - - - - - - - - - - - -

$$\begin{array}{r} 69.782 \\ + \quad .05 \\ \hline 69.832 \end{array} \quad \text{truncated to } 69.8$$

30. Notice, in frame 29, that adding 5 to the second digit causes the first digit (the digit to be rounded) to be incremented by 1. Suppose we were rounding 69.742 to one decimal position. If we added 5 to the second position what would happen to the first decimal positions? _____

- - - - - - - - - - - - - - - - - -

nothing—it would be unchanged:
$$\begin{array}{r} 69.742 \\ + \quad .05 \\ \hline 69.792 \end{array} \quad \text{truncated to } 69.7$$

Notice that this is the same result you would get if you rounded 69.742 manually.

31. Some computer programming languages allow the programmer to just say ROUNDED when he or she wants the results rounded to field specifications. But you should know how the computer carries out the rounding procedure in any case. Here's some more practice in the computer method of rounding. If you think you understand how it works, go on to frame 32 where we'll show you how to flowchart this rounding procedure.

Add 5 to the appropriate digit and complete the rounding for each of the following.

(a) 43.677 to two decimal positions

(b) 93.2655 to three decimal positions

(c)   27.8911 to one decimal position

(d)   36.30908 to four decimal positions

- - - - - - - - - - - - - - -

(a)   43.68   43.677
                 +   .005
                   43.682   truncated to 43.68

(b)   93.266   93.2655
                 +   .0005
                   93.2660   truncated to 93.266

(c)   27.9   27.8911
                 +   .05
                   27.9411   truncated to 27.9

(d)   36.3091   36.30908
                 +   .00005
                   36.30913   truncated to 36.3091

32. Here is an example of a rounding operation as it might appear in a flow-chart.

```
SET C =
A + B + .005
```

How many decimal positions will be in the resultant field, C? _____

- - - - - - - - - - - - - - - - -

two (If you're not sure why, review the previous few frames.)

33. Consider the following addition:

```
SET D
= E + F
```

where E and F have specifications of two decimal positions and D has a specification of one decimal position. Suppose that E = 2.34 and F = 3.65. What would be the result in D, if no provision is made for rounding? _____

- - - - - - - - - - - - - - - - - -

5.9 (The last position would merely be truncated.)

34. If we wish to round a result to one decimal position, what should be added to the flowchart symbol in order to be able to do so? _____

- - - - - - - - - - - - - - - - - - -

.05 (To round to one decimal position, we add .05; that is, we add 5 to the
second decimal position.)

35. Given the values from frame 33, what would be the result in D from the
following operation? _____

```
SET D =
E + F + .05
```

- - - - - - - - - - - - - - - - -

6.0

Now that we have considered the rounding option, let's proceed to some
problems involving more complex logic. From now on, the use of rounding
with arithmetic statements will be optional and will no longer be stressed.

36. Now let us integrate some complex logic with our complex arithmetic.
Job description: A teacher would like to have the computer determine
the average grade for each student in his class at the end of the semester.
In addition, he would like to know the overall class average. Each student
has taken four exams which have the following weights associated with them.

Exam	Weight
EXAM1	10%
EXAM2	30%
EXAM3	20%
FINAL	40%
	100%

The input consists of each student's identification number and the four grades
as shown below.

STUDENT NAME	EXAM1	EXAM2	EXAM3	FINAL	
1 20	21 23	24 26	27 29	30 32	

The output will consist of the average for each student and, at the end of the
report, the overall class average. Draw the flowchart to perform the required operations. (Hint: It is necessary to count the number of cards processed to obtain the overall class average.)

- - - - - - - - - - - - - - - - -

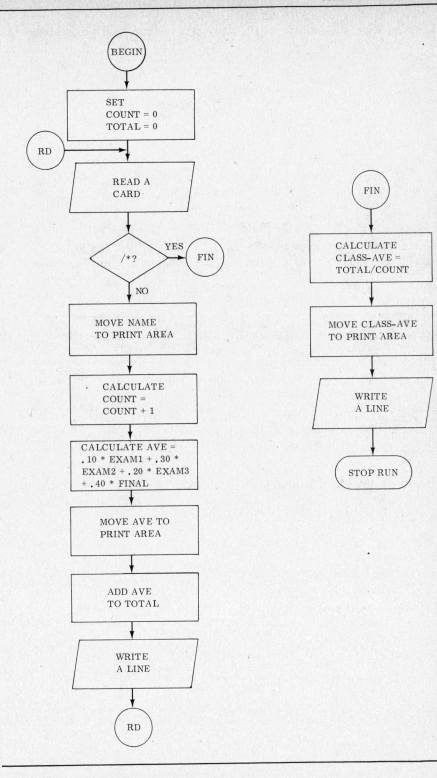

37. In the next frame we will draw a flowchart to read in cards with the following format.

The purpose of the program will be to print each salesman's name and corresponding bonus. The bonus is determined as follows.

>5% of the first $50,000 of sales
>10% of the next $25,000 of sales
>20% of any amount over $75,000

Notice that if the sales are greater than $75,000, the formula for the bonus is simply 5000 + .20 * (SALES - 75000). Try to figure out how that amount was

determined. _____

_____

_____

_____

- - - - - - - - - - - - - - - - - - -

5% of the first 50,000 = 25000
10% of the next 25,000 = 25000
20% of SALES   75,000 = .20 * (SALES - 75000)
Total Bonus = 2500 + 2500 + .20 * (SALES - 75000)
         = 5000 + .20 * (SALES - 75000)

Always look for ways to simplify arithmetic operations. Remember, the fewer the steps, the more efficient the program.

38. With these figures in mind, now construct a flowchart for the required operations.

- - - - - - - - - - - - - - - - - - -

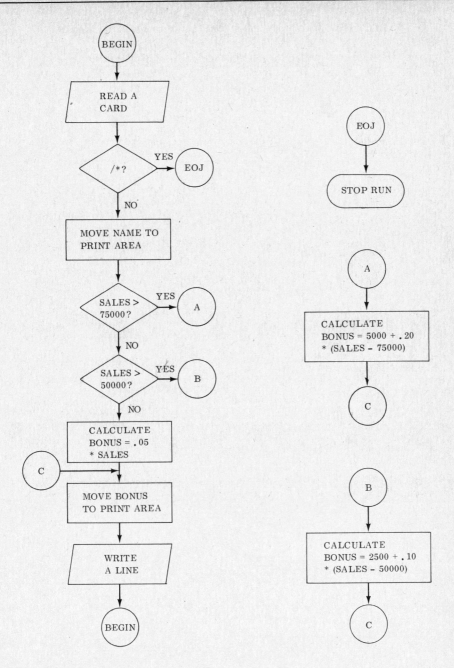

39. An attorney wishes to computerize his billing procedure. We will assume that his fees are fixed, so a computer can easily be used to calculate the required fees for each client. Draw a flowchart to read in cards with the following format.

TYPE OF FEE: 1 = 1/3 of amount recovered for client.
2 = sliding scale as follows:
50% of the first $1,000 recovered;
40% of the next $2,000 recovered;
35% of the next $22,000 recovered;
25% of any amount recovered over $25,000.
If TYPE OF FEE is not 1 or 2, print 'INCORRECT DATA.'

The output will be a listing of each client's name and the corresponding attorney's fee to be charged for handling the case.

- - - - - - - - - - - - - - - - - - - -

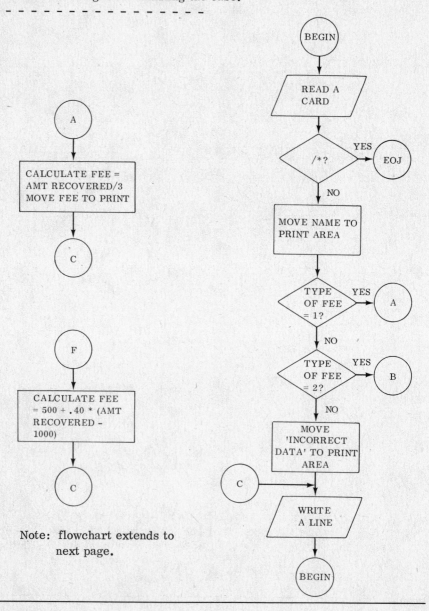

Note: flowchart extends to
next page.

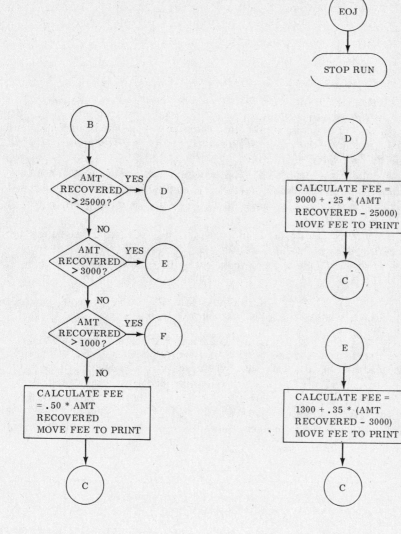

SEQUENCE-CHECKING

40. Sequence-checking is a routine commonly performed in computer programs. If output data is required in a specific sequence, the most efficient
method is to first sort the input data into the required order. That is, if an
output payroll report, created from payroll cards, is to be in Social Security
number sequence, then the input cards should be sorted into Social Security
number sequence.

    The sorting of input cards can be performed by an electronic accounting
machine called a <u>sorter</u>. The sorting of magnetic tape records and disk records can be performed by a computer using a special program called a utility
or sort program. The programmer only needs to supply specifications, called
parameters, indicating the fields to be sorted and whether they are in ascending or descending sequence.

    While special machines and special programs may be used to sort all
forms of input, the programmer must still check the sequence of the incoming
data on cards. Operators can cause mistakes by accidentally dropping or
shuffling cards, and if the computer output is to be as free from error as possible, the sequence of the input should be verified in programs where a specific sequence is required.

    Suppose that cards are used as input, with the following format.

DISTRICT OFFICE NUMBER	SALESMAN NAME	SALARY	

We will write a routine to determine if the cards are arranged by district office number in ascending sequence. If they are not, an error message is to
print and the run is to be terminated. This type of routine is often incorporated in higher level computer programs.

    After the first data card is read into the computer, its district office

number must be stored. Can you guess why? _____

_____

_____

_____

- - - - - - - - - - - - - - - - - - -

In order to compare it to the district office number on the next input card.
If the district office number on the first card were not stored, it would be
replaced with data from the second card, and there would be no basis for
comparison.

41. Here, on the following page, are the first few steps necessary to process
the first card.

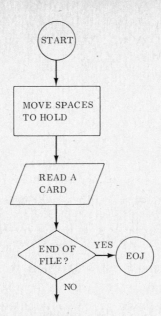

We must move blanks or spaces to HOLD because the content of HOLD is un-known. If HOLD were not cleared initially, the result of any comparison with HOLD would be unpredictable. A blank field automatically compares <u>low</u> on any sort of comparison. That is, any district office number read in on the first card would be considered by the computer to be higher than a field of blanks or spaces. (Also, notice that an end of file test has been included; an end of file test should accompany <u>every</u> read command, even for the first card.) Note that in some programming languages, the MOVE SPACES in-struction will be unnecessary because the machine is already cleared.

After the second card is read, a comparison should be performed. Can

you guess what that comparison should be? _____

_____

- - - - - - - - - - - - - - - - - - -

compare the district office number in the second card with the one stored at HOLD

42. The type of comparison we will make depends on: (1) whether the re-quired sequence is ascending or descending; and (2) whether we will accept multiple district office numbers (that is, the same sequence number on more than one input card).

"Ascending sequence by district office number" means that the district office numbers get higher as succeeding cards are read. Descending sequence means that the deck begins with the highest number and, as additional cards are read, the numbers get smaller. Gaps between numbers, such as 1, 2, 6, 9, . . . , are fine, as long as the numbers are in sequence.

Suppose that a deck of cards is to be in ascending sequence by district office number. The sixth card read has a district office number of 675 and the seventh card has a number of 727. Is this okay, or does it indicate an

error condition? _____

- - - - - - - - - - - - - - - - - - -

It is okay—the numbers are getting higher, which is the meaning of ascending sequence.

43. Suppose that a deck of cards is to be in descending sequence by district office number. The eighth card has a number of 726 and the ninth card has

a number of 823. Is this okay, or does it indicate.an error? _____

_____

- - - - - - - - - - - - - - - - - - -

It is an error—the numbers should be decreasing.

44. We must also indicate whether multiple numbers are acceptable. That is, do we wish to accept the same sequence number on more than one input card, or should that be considered an error?

    Our answer to that question will depend on the specific application. For a master file or summary report, we would often wish to accept only one card for a number (for example, one account number or one district office number). But with detail files, we might accept multiple cards with the same number (indicating, for example, several transactions in a month or several salespeople in a district office).

    If we accept only one card with a sequence number, an equal condition on a sequence check should indicate an error condition. If we accept multiple cards, an equal condition would not yield an error condition.

    Suppose we are checking for ascending sequence. We will not accept multiple district office numbers. Should the following sequence of input data cards be considered okay, or should it signal an error condition?

        542, 567, 568, 568, 573

_____

- - - - - - - - - - - - - - - - - - -

It should yield an error condition, because we accept only one card for each number in sequence.

45. Suppose we are checking for descending sequence. We will accept multiple district office numbers. Is the following sequence okay, or erroneous?

        682, 645, 645, 648, 632

_____

- - - - - - - - - - - - - - - - - - -

It is erroneous—648 is higher than 645, so it is out of order in this descending sequence. It is okay, however, to have 645 appear more than once in this sequence.

46. Assume that we are checking for ascending sequence of district office numbers. We will accept only one card for any sequence number. Multiple sequence numbers should indicate an error condition. Write the decision symbol to perform this comparison of HOLD and DIST OFF NO. (Try to write the test with just one instruction, rather than two.)

- - - - - - - - - - - - - - - - - - -

This is the most efficient answer.

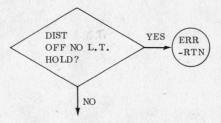

Notice that you could have asked two questions: HOLD G.T. DIST OFF NO? and HOLD = DIST OFF NO? But that would have been far less efficient.

47. Now suppose we are checking for ascending sequence of district office numbers and we <u>will</u> accept multiple cards. Write the decision symbol to perform this comparison. (Hint: In this case, an equal condition would <u>not</u> yield an error condition.)

- - - - - - - - - - - - - - - - - - -

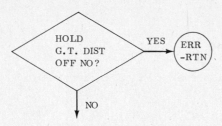

48. After the comparison has been made, what operation should be performed before the next card is read? (Assume that no sequence error has been found.)

_____

- - - - - - - - - - - - - - - - - - -

DIST OFF NO must be moved to HOLD, to be stored for comparison with the district office number on the next card read.

49. Now, putting together what you have learned, draw a flowchart routine which checks the sequence of the input cards described in frame 40 to see that they are in ascending order by district office number. Multiple district office numbers are okay. In case of a sequence error, print INVALID SEQUENCE and stop the run. Try to make your flowchart as efficient as possible.

- - - - - - - - - - - - - - - - -

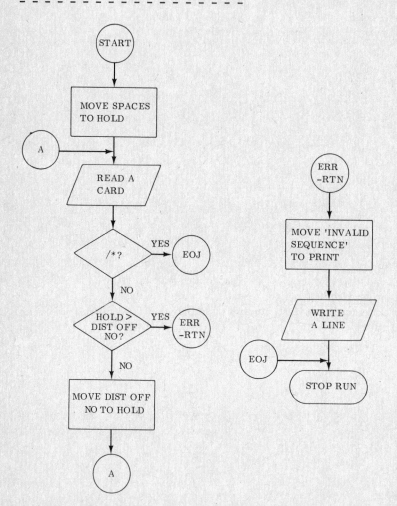

The above flowchart is probably the most efficient for this problem. The flowchart which follows is logically correct, but not as efficient, because it contains extra steps. It contains two READ routines where only one is necessary. Also, since a STOP-RUN instruction is included as part of the sequence in ERR-RTN, a separate STOP RUN at EOJ is not necessary. By integrating ERR-RTN and EOJ, we can save an extra step. Try to eliminate unnecessary duplication of instructions, for the most efficient flowcharts.

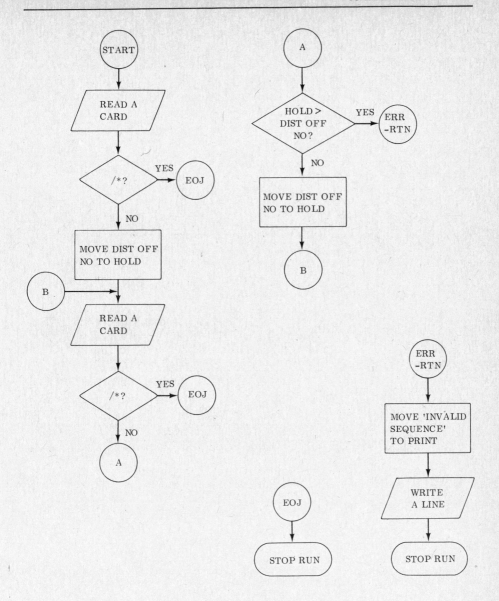

50. In programs that operate on large volumes of input, it is often inefficient to abort a run in the event of a <u>single</u> sequence error. That is, it is often more important to process all the data, including the one error, than to abort and restart the job, a costly and time-consuming operation. In such cases, the run is stopped only if a sizable number of sequence errors occurs.

Modify the first flowchart given in frame 49 so that: (1) it prints all data from each erroneous card; and (2) if there are more than ten sequence errors the run is aborted and a MORE THAN 10 ERRORS—RUN ABORTED message is printed.

- - - - - - - - - - - - - - - - - - - -

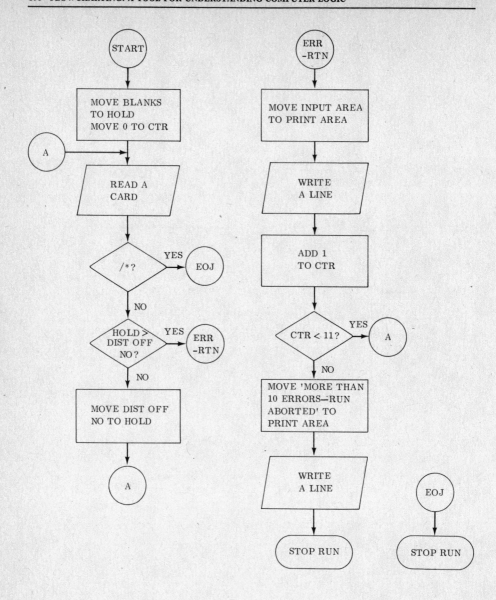

51. It is extremely important to ascertain whether duplicate sequence numbers are valid or invalid for a particular job. As a programmer, you are responsible for obtaining a complete job description, and checking on just such details as these. If these details are disregarded, the resulting erroneous programs may require extensive and costly revisions.

Suppose that multiple sequence numbers are <u>not</u> acceptable. Alter the flowchart in frame 49 so that more than one card with a particular sequence number signals an error condition.

_ _ _ _ _ _ _ _ _ _ _ _ _ _ _ _ _ _ _

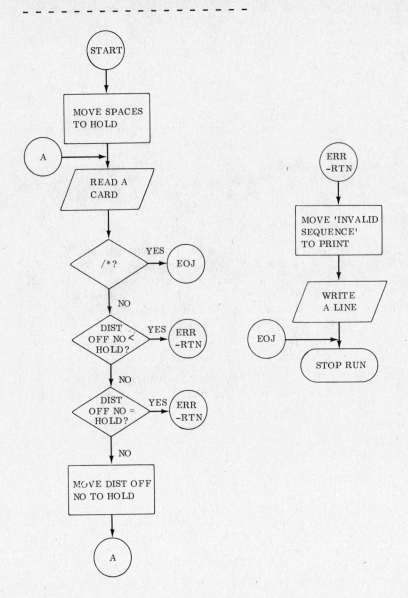

52. The field that is used for sorting is often called the <u>sequence</u> or <u>control</u> <u>field</u>. In our example, the sequence field has been the district office number, though it could be any convenient field.

For descending sequence checks, each succeeding card should contain a

sequence field that is (less/greater) _____ than the preceding one.

_ _ _ _ _ _ _ _ _ _ _ _ _ _ _ _ _ _

less

53. You have seen that, for ascending sequence checks, we must initialize HOLD at blanks so that the first card's sequence field will be considered higher than HOLD, because HOLD might have previous, unknown contents. For descending sequence checks, however, we cannot initialize HOLD at blanks.

Can you guess why? _____

_____

_____

- -

For descending sequence checks, each card's sequence field should compare lower than the preceding one, which is stored at HOLD. But if HOLD contained blanks, the first card would compare high, which would immediately yield an error.

54. Because we cannot initialize HOLD at blanks for descending checks, we must find another way to insure that the first card compares low or at least equal when compared to HOLD. The highest value in any numeric field is all 9's. Thus, we will initialize HOLD with all 9's. This will insure that the first card's sequence field will be taken by the computer as (lower/higher)

_____ than HOLD.

- - - - - - - - - - - - - - - - - - - -

Lower (or equal, if the sequence field happened to contain all 9's). Notice that initializing at 9's would <u>not</u> work for ascending checks, because the first comparison would yield an error.

55. Now consider the following tape format.

EMPLOYEE NUMBER	SALARY	POSITION	TERR	DEPT	

We want to draw a flowchart routine to ascertain that the records (not cards) are in correct descending sequence by employee number. Multiple employee numbers are considered errors. Write the appropriate decision so that only a NO result under either of <u>two</u> conditions will indicate a valid record—when HOLD is (not) less than EMP NO and when HOLD is (not) equal to EMP NO.

- - - - - - - - - - - - - - - - - - - -

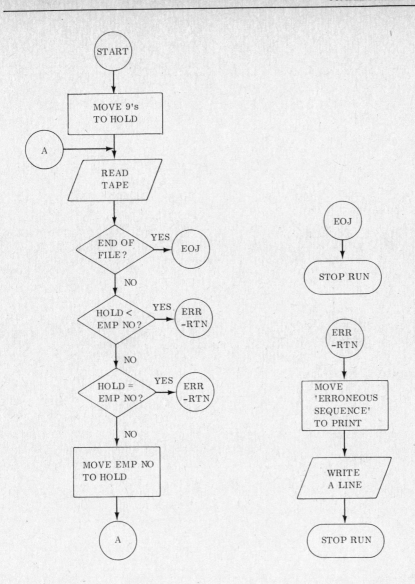

56. Now try to draw the same flowchart routine (to check descending sequence by EMP NO with multiple employee numbers considered errors), but this time use one less decision symbol. In case of a sequence error, print ERRONEOUS SEQUENCE and stop the run.

- - - - - - - - - - - - - - - - - -

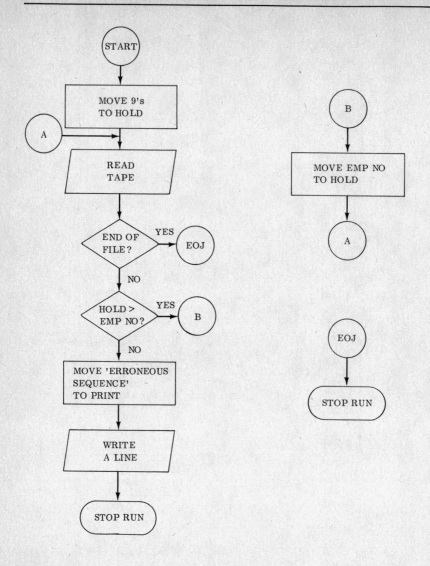

or, the following:

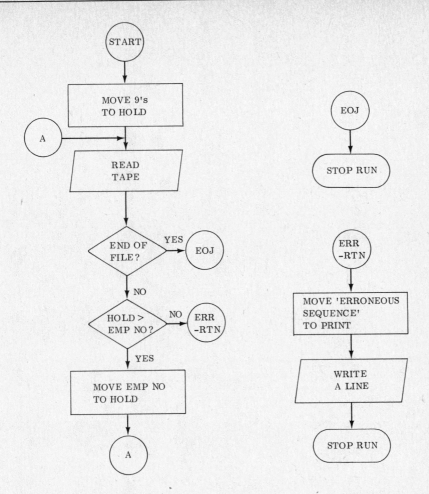

While the conditional branch is usually the result of a YES decision, it can also be the result of a NO decision, as in the preceding illustration. For the sake of uniformity, most of our examples will use conditional branches as YES decisions. The preceding example has been included just to remind you that NO decisions can also be used to yield conditional branches. The first flowcharted solution has the advantage of specifying only YES branches, thereby making it relatively easy to depict the logic required. The advantage of the second solution is that the major sequence, labeled START, depicts the normal path that will be followed for the predominant number of cases. Thus, in the second illustration, branches are the exception rather than the rule.

57. Now alter the flowchart in frame 56 so that duplicate sequence numbers do not yield an error. Try to make your flowchart as efficient as possible, incorporating either YES or NO branches.

- - - - - - - - - - - - - - - - - - - -

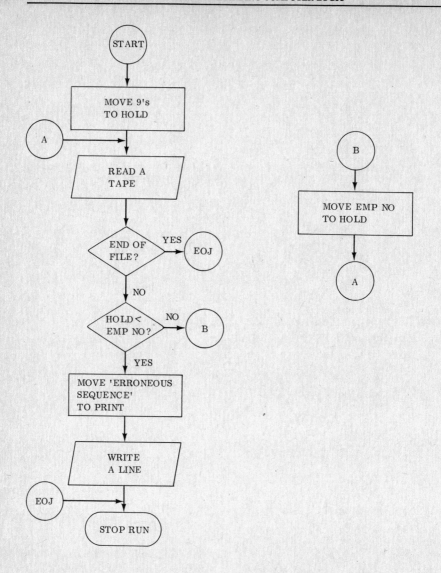

or, the following:

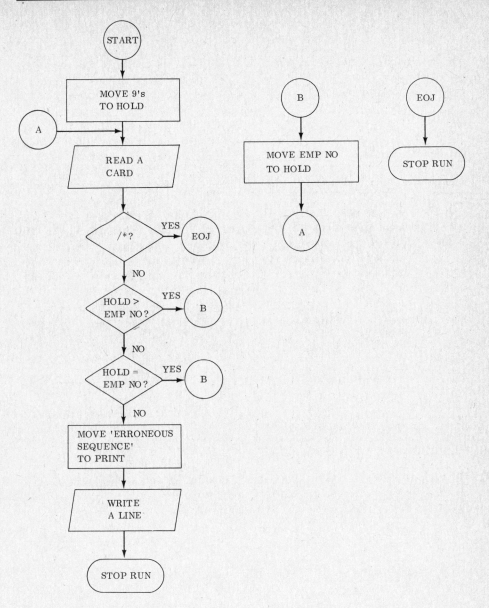

In our sequence checks, we have been dealing with numeric fields. Now, a word about alphabetic sequence fields. The computer treats alphabetic fields exactly the same as numeric fields, with B considered greater than A and less than C. Note also that if, by chance, an alphabetic field were compared to a numeric one, the alphabetic field would always be considered less than any number. Thus we would have

$$A < B < C \ldots < Z < 0 < 1 \ldots < 9$$

SWITCHES

58. As we have seen, sometimes we wish to have the computer perform certain operations when a specific condition exists and other operations when the condition does not exist. If the condition is dependent upon the value of input, we merely use a decision symbol to test for the condition.

Sometimes, however, the condition to be tested is internal, that is, independent of input values. For example, we may need to test if a card being processed is the first card, or if the output produced is of a certain type. For such conditions, we can have the program signal the computer to indicate which operations to perform. Such a signal is usually coded with the use of a switch.

Beware! The term "switch" is a deceptive one. We use it only because it is the conventional term. The word "switch" usually brings to mind a "flip-flop" mechanical apparatus; this is not its meaning in computer terminology. A switch is generally a one-position storage area called by the field name SWITCH which the program sets equal to 1 when a specific condition is present, but equal to 0 when the condition is not present. Note that SWITCH is the name we will use, but any programmer-supplied name would serve just as well. Thus, it is meant to serve as a "flip-flop" concept—but it is not a mechanical apparatus.

A switch is a one-position storage area that simulates a "flip-flop" by containing a _____ when a specific condition is present and a _____ when the condition is not present.

- - - - - - - - - - - - - - - - - - -

1; 0

59. Suppose that we wish to avoid extra steps in our sequence-checking flowchart. In the previous illustrations, the first card (for ascending sequence checks) is always compared to a field containing blanks, whereas succeeding cards are compared against previous sequence fields. For descending sequences, the first card is compared to a field of 9's. But these first card comparisons are not really necessary (and can be time-consuming in more complex flowcharts where the comparison routines are lengthy). The conventional method for avoiding an unnecessary comparison is with the use of a switch. The following flowchart, which checks for ascending sequence, illustrates the use of the switch.

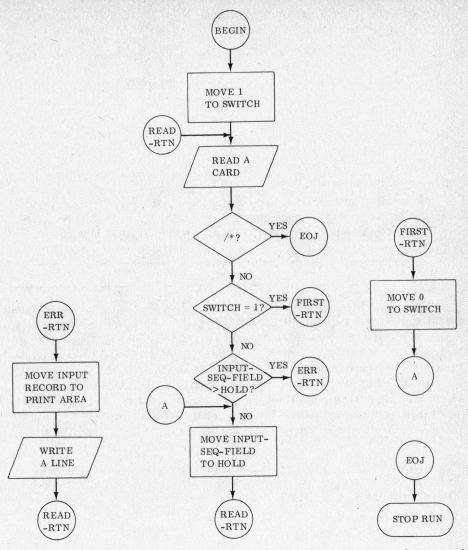

The switch is initialized at 1 prior to the first READ. Then, after a card is read, the switch is compared to 1 in order to determine if the card read is indeed the first card. A YES result causes a branch to a routine where SWITCH is reset to zero and a branch around the comparison to HOLD. This may seem more, rather than less, complicated. But bear with it, because you'll see later how switches can give a program extra flexibility. Right now, let's just understand how they work.

Study the flowchart above. How many times is FIRST-RTN executed?

Explain why. _____

_____

- - - - - - - - - - - - - - - -

_____

One time—it is only required for the first card. After that, SWITCH is set equal to, and remains, 0; we no longer wish to avoid the comparison with HOLD.

60. (True or False.) The switch used in the flowchart of frame 59 is a one-position storage area that contains either a 0 or a 1, depending on when it is tested. _____

- - - - - - - - - - - - - - - - - - -

True

61. In our other sequence-checking flowcharts, HOLD was set equal to blanks when ascending sequences were checked or equal to 9's when descending sequences were checks. Why is this not performed in the flowchart of frame 59? _____

_____

- - - - - - - - - - - - - - - - - - -

We initialized HOLD precisely because of the first card comparison. That is, if the first were compared to HOLD, then HOLD must contain some value that would not make the first card appear to be in an erroneous sequence. (Thus, in an ascending sequence, the first card will have the lowest sequence field, so it must be compared to the lowest possible quantity, which is a blank field. In a descending sequence, the first card will have the highest sequence field, so it must be compared to the highest quantity, which is all 9's.) Without the need for a first card comparison, we no longer need to initialize HOLD.

62. As indicated, the flowchart in frame 59 uses a switch to avoid unnecessary steps for the first card processing. But the price to pay for this seeming advantage is a sacrifice in efficiency. Try to determine what is inefficient in that flowchart. _____

_____

- - - - - - - - - - - - - - - - - - -

Because a SWITCH field is used, it is necessary to test (unproductively) SWITCH for all cards after the first one. So if there were 500 cards to be processed, there would be 499 extra comparisons of SWITCH to 1—all of which will yield a NO result since SWITCH remains at zero after the first card is processed. This is, indeed, a heavy price to pay. You ask, then, why bother with switches? Because in many situations, switches have a direct and obvious advantage: the extra test for SWITCH is far more convenient than the additional processing that would otherwise be performed. We illustrated switches with the sequence-checking procedure because it was relatively simple and easy to follow, <u>not</u> because switches were necessarily desirable in sequence checking!

63. Draw a flowchart which prints the total number of data cards read, along with the date of the run. The date is read in on the first card, which is <u>not</u> to be counted in the total. That is, the first card is a date card only and not considered a data card. (Hint: Use a switch to handle first card processing, so you need only a <u>single</u> read statement.)

- - - - - - - - - - - - - - - - - - -

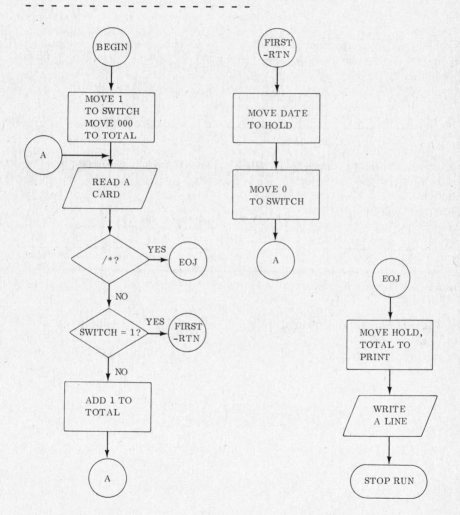

Was your flowchart fairly similar to this one? If not, study this carefully. Following are a few questions about the flowchart, to be sure you understand some fine points about switches.

64. What is the purpose of SWITCH in this flowchart? _____

_____

- - - - - - - - - - - - - - - - - -

to avoid a separate READ instruction to handle the first card

65. SWITCH is initialized at 1. What would happen if SWITCH were <u>not</u> initialized? _____

- - - - - - - - - - - - - - - - - -

The result of the comparison of SWITCH to 1 would be unknown since the content of SWITCH would be unknown.

66. Suppose at FIRST-RTN you forgot to set SWITCH to zero. What would happen? _____

- - - - - - - - - - - - - - - - - -

The computer would proceed to FIRST-RTN for all cards, since SWITCH would remain at 1.

67. What would be printed if SWITCH were not set to zero at FIRST-RTN?

_____

_____

- - - - - - - - - - - - - - - - - -

HOLD would contain whatever value was in the so-called DATE field and TOTAL would still contain zero.

In the flowchart of frame 63, the value of using SWITCH is more justifiable. Although we still have extra comparisons of SWITCH to 1, we have saved a separate READ instruction. READ instructions require far more computer time and effort to process than simple comparisons. Often, it is preferable to include a switch routine which saves separate input/output operations even though the switch will necessitate extra comparisons. This point will be made clearer in the next chapter.

SELF-TEST

1. Draw a single flowchart step to compute: $X = \dfrac{B}{C} + E^2$.

2. Draw a single flowchart step to compute: $Y = (B + C)^3$.

3. Are the following sets of statements equivalent?

(a)

| MOVE 3 TO SUM | SUM = 3 |

(b)

| SUBTRACT 5 FROM B | B = B - 5 |

(c)

| COMPUTE Z = B + C/D | COMPUTE Z = (B + C)/D |

(d)

| MULTIPLY A BY A GIVING B | COMPUTE B = A ** 2 |

4. Consider this statement:

| SET C = A + B |

where A and B have three decimal positions. Suppose that the following are the results of the addition as performed by the computer. Indicate what the results would be in C, where the specifications of C are as noted.

Addition result	C decimal positions	Final result
(a) 43.263	1	
(b) 43.682	0	
(c) 43.687	2	
(d) 43.685	1	

5. Suppose that the following operation were performed.

SET C =
A + B • ROUNDED

The addition results in (a) through (d) of problem 4 indicate the total of A + B. In each case, what would be the result in C after .005 is added?

(a) _____ (b) _____ (c) _____ (d) _____

6. Suppose that C were a field with one decimal position, and A and B had two decimal positions. Draw a flowchart step that will add A and B to give C, with the results rounded.

7. A deck of input cards should be in ascending sequence by ACCT - NO. Draw a flowchart to ascertain that the sequence is correct. Multiple cards are not acceptable. Print any card that is in error. If there are more than ten sequence errors, stop the run. (Hint: No output is produced except for an error run.)

8. TAPE1 and TAPE2 are two separate tapes with the following format.

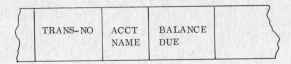

Both files are in sequence by TRANS-NO. That is, TAPE1 has all its records in ascending sequence by TRANS-NO and, similarly, TAPE2 has all its records in ascending sequence by TRANS-NO. Draw a flowchart which will merge the two files into a single file that is in sequence by TRANS-NO. Assume that the sequence of each file has already been ascertained to be correct, and that there are no two records with the same TRANS-NO.

9. Draw a flowchart to compute compound interest from the following input tape records.

> 1-20   Name of depositor
> 21-25 Amount of principal (p_0)
> 26-27 Interest rate (e.g., 25 in these two columns is interpreted
>   as .25)
> 28-29 Number of periods (n)

Output is a punched card with NAME and amount of principal after n periods of investment (p_n)—this last shall be printed as N-PER-PRINCIPAL. The formula for the principal amount is $p_n = p_0 (1 + r)^n$.

Restriction: Assume that the exponentiation feature of the computer language you are working with is not available. Therefore, you will need to include a loop for obtaining $(1 + r)^n$. This computation is clearer if you understand that:

$$(1 + r)^n = \frac{\overbrace{(1 + r)(1 + r) \ldots \ldots (1 + r)}}{n \text{ times}}$$

Answers to Self-Test

1.

```
COMPUTE X =
B/C + E ** 2
```

(frames 1-21)

2.

```
SET Y =
(B + C) ** 3
```

(frames 1-21)

3. (a) equivalent; (b) equivalent; (c) not equivalent; (d) equivalent
(frames 1-21)

4. (a) 43.2; (b) 43; (c) 43.68; (d) 43.6
(frames 22-35)

5. (a) 43.3; (b) 44; (c) 43.69; (d) 43.7
(frames 22-35)

6.

```
COMPUTE C
= A + B + .05
```

(frames 22-35)

7.

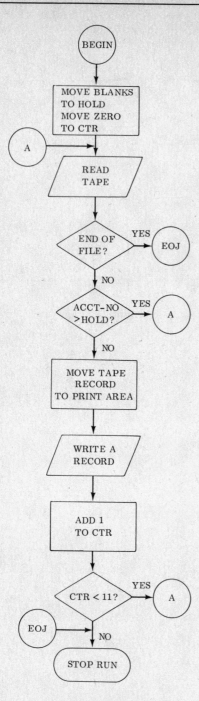

(frames 40–57)

8.

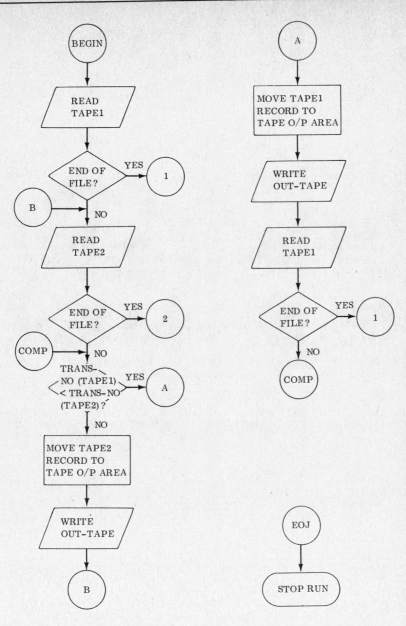

Note: The READ TAPE instruction is performed in exactly the same way as the READ CARD instruction.

Note: this flowchart is continued on the following page.

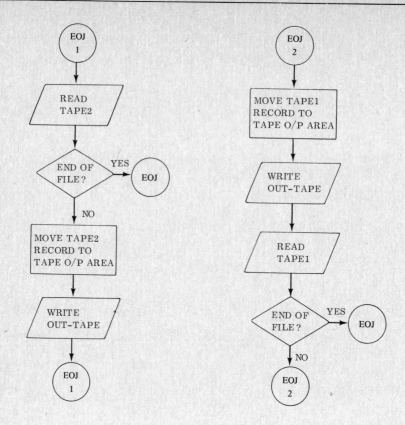

(frames 40–57)

9.

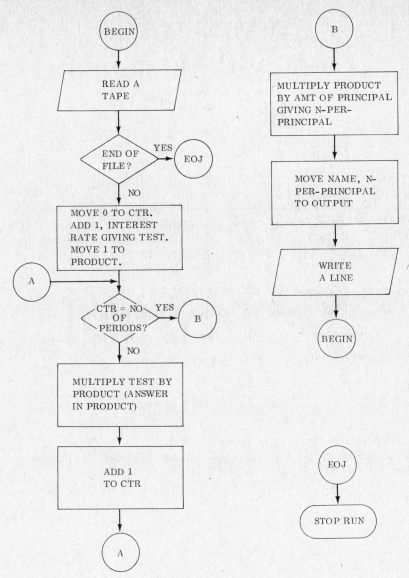

(frames 36–39)

CHAPTER FIVE
Common Programming Procedures

Thus far, our flowcharts have concentrated on various techniques and routines that illustrate computer logic. This chapter will present some common programming applications in complete flowchart form. While these programming applications must be adapted to specific job requirements, the procedures used are basically similar. In this chapter, you will learn how to:

- perform an update with the computer;
- merge two or more data files into a single output file;
- flowchart some common inventory and banking procedures;
- flowchart problems requiring control breaks.

UPDATE ILLUSTRATION

1. An update is a procedure to make a data file current. The updating of files is an essential and widely used application of computers. A master payroll file, for example, must be updated (usually weekly) with information on new employees (often called new hires), separations (employees who left the company), promotions, and salary increases.

An accounts receivable file contains all pertinent information on money owed to the company by its customers. The type of data that might be used to update an accounts receivable file includes new transactions (charges incurred by the customers), new accounts, payments, and credits (merchandise returned by the customers).

An inventory file contains information on items stocked in the warehouse of a company. The type of data that would be used to update an inventory file includes new items on order (as noted on purchase orders), additional items received by the warehouse (as noted on receiving reports), and items shipped from the warehouse.

At this point, you need not understand the intricacies of specific types of business files and their processing. It is important, however, for you to understand that a major file of information must be updated periodically in order to remain current.

Data processing files that are updated by computer are either <u>direct-access</u> files or <u>sequential</u> files. Direct-access files, such as magnetic disk, require more complex input/output processing. Most often, however, updates are performed on sequential files, such as magnetic tape files. Our examples will use sequential updating, with magnetic tape files as the primary files; the same rules would apply to card files which are also sequential.

A typical update procedure that uses sequential processing consists of three files: the input master file, the input detail file, and the output master file. We will discuss these one by one.

The <u>input</u> master file contains all the data except the most current data. That is, it contains master information that is current only up to the previous updating cycle. To standardize our references, we will call this file OLD-MASTER.

What must we do to an input master file to keep the information on the

file complete and current? _____

- - - - - - - - - - - - - - - - - - -

We must update it. (It is important that you understand the concept of updating a file. If you did not answer this question correctly, reread this frame before you go on.)

2. The <u>input detail file</u> (also called the transaction file) contains data for the present updating cycle only. If updates are performed weekly, for example, the detail file will contain only data on the present week's activity. We will call this file DETAIL.

A master payroll file contains all pertinent information on all employees within a company. Typical fields of information on such a file might include name, social security number, birth date, salary, federal income tax withheld, state income tax withheld, FICA, and various other deductions. Detail records used to update such a master payroll file might contain what types of

records? _____

_____

- - - - - - - - - - - - - - - - - - -

records of new employees (new hires), separations, promotions, raises, transfers, changes in tax deductions, and so on.

3. The <u>output master file</u> incorporates the current data and the previous master information. That is, data from OLD-MASTER and DETAIL will be combined so that an updated output master file is obtained. We will call this file NEW-MASTER.

The NEW-MASTER file obtained at the end of one updating cycle becomes the OLD-MASTER file for the next updating cycle, as illustrated on the following page. (The illustration is a pictorial representation of an update procedure—it is <u>not</u> a flowchart.)

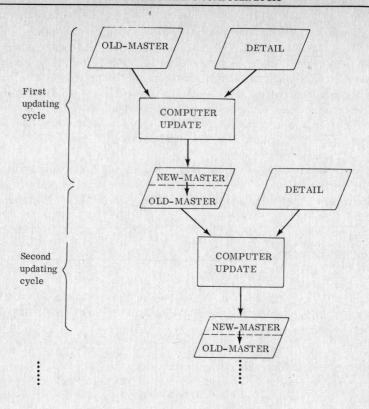

Suppose an accounts receivable file is updated weekly. At the end of Week 1, the two input files OLD-MASTER and DETAIL are used to produce an updated file called _____ . At the end of Week 2, the up-dated master file from Week 1, now called _____, is com-bined with the current DETAIL file to produce a new master file called _____ . This process is said to be <u>cyclical</u>.

- - - - - - - - - - - - - - - - - -

NEW-MASTER; OLD-MASTER; NEW-MASTER

4. To update files, data must be read into the computer in a specific se-quence. Since we wish to update particular master records with correspond-ing detail records, we must insure that each file is in the same sequence. As we saw in Chapter 4, files are checked for sequence according to a sequence field, also called the <u>control field</u>. The master file and the detail file must each be in sequence according to the same control field, such as ACCT-NO, PAYROLL-NO, or SALES-NO. During the update procedure, master records are matched with detail records according to this control field.

Not all master records will have a corresponding detail record. For records on the master file which need no alteration or update, there will be no corresponding detail record. For example, in updating an accounts receivable file, when no transactions have occurred for a particular record, the DETAIL file will not contain a record with that account number. In such cases, the master data from that OLD-MASTER record will simply be rewritten, as is, onto the NEW-MASTER file. This seeming duplication of effort is required for sequential processing because changes to an existing sequential tape file cannot be made if the tape is being used as input. Thus a new tape must be created, called NEW-MASTER, which incorporates unchanged master records along with appropriate updates.

Those master records for which there are corresponding detail records will require some form of updating. On some types of updates, there may be detail records for which there are no corresponding master records. This may be entirely appropriate where a detail record may denote a new account for an accounts receivable file, or a new employee for a payroll file. For some updates, however, every detail record must have a corresponding master record; otherwise, it signifies an error.

For an update procedure, what two input files should be used? _____

How should the files be organized? _____

- - - - - - - - - - - - - - - - - -

a detail file, here called DETAIL, and a master file, here called OLD-MASTER; in sequence according to the same control field

5. If a master record with ACCT-NO 800 is read and there is no detail record for that account, what type of processing should be performed? _____

- - - - - - - - - - - - - - - - - -

The master record with ACCT-NO 800 should be rewritten on NEW-MASTER, as is. (Since there is no detail record, the master record 800 requires no updating.)

6. If a detail record with ACCT-NO 900 is read and there is no master record for that account, what type of processing should be performed? _____

- - - - - - - - - - - - - - - - - -

This condition signifies either a new account or an error, depending upon the type of update performed. If the condition signifies a new account, the detail record is written on NEW-MASTER, as is; if the condition signifies an error, an appropriate error routine is required.

7.   In order for an updating procedure to be performed in which the NEW-MASTER record contains data from both the detail and master record, the detail and master records must have the same _____.

- - - - - - - - - - - - - - - - - -

control field, such as ACCT-NO

8.   Describe briefly the types of records contained on the OLD-MASTER, DETAIL, and NEW-MASTER files. _____

_____

_____

- - - - - - - - - - - - - - - - - -

OLD-MASTER contains records current through the previous updating cycle; DETAIL contains records from the current updating cycle only; NEW-MASTER contains all updated and current records

9.   Let us assume that we are performing an accounts receivable operation, in which we update a master transaction file with detail transaction records. A broadly defined <u>systems</u> flowchart of the procedure is shown below. (Chapter 7 discusses the difference between a systems flowchart and a program flowchart, such as those we have been working with.   You need not be concerned about that now.)

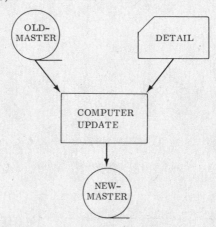

The OLD-MASTER is a tape file, DETAIL is a card file, and NEW-MASTER, which incorporates information from both, is also a tape file. The OLD-MASTER and NEW-MASTER files have the format depicted on the following page.

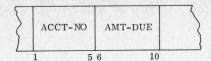

Note that when actually programming this problem, the programmer must know the actual number of positions used for each field. Thus ACCT-NO is a five-position field, occupying the first five positions of the tape record. AMT-DUE is also five positions long, occupying positions 6 through 10 on the tape. For purposes of flowcharting, the actual positioning of fields within a record is not terribly important, since we reference the fields by their names. Hence, we have not paid particular attention to field delineations. However, because programmers need to know these field delineations in order to code the problems, we will begin to include them with more frequency.

The DETAIL file has the following format.

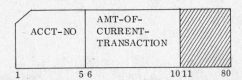

The update program will read data from cards and tape, both of which will be in ACCT-NO sequence. For each ACCT-NO that is on both the DETAIL and OLD-MASTER files, that record will be updated.

Here's a question that requires some insight: We update an OLD-MASTER record by adding AMT-OF-CURRENT-TRANSACTION from the

_____ file to the AMT-DUE from the _____

file to obtain a new AMT-DUE on the _____ file. In addition, what else must be moved to the NEW-MASTER record before it can be written? _____

- - - - - - - - - - - - - - - - - -

DETAIL; OLD-MASTER; NEW-MASTER; ACCT-NO—obtained from either the DETAIL or OLD-MASTER record, since both account numbers will be the same

10. If you answered the questions in frame 9 correctly, you are understanding the elements of updating. Note that the combination of detail card records and master tape records is a very common one.

If an OLD-MASTER record has an ACCT-NO which does not correspond to an ACCT-NO on a DETAIL record, this signifies that _____

_____.

- - - - - - - - - - - - - - - - -

_____

no updating is necessary—no business was transacted for that account during the current updating cycle

11. In such a case, the NEW–MASTER record will merely contain OLD–MASTER data. That is, no updating of the master record is necessary. Write a flowchart sequence to obtain OLD–MASTER data in the NEW–MASTER file.

‒ ‒ ‒ ‒ ‒ ‒ ‒ ‒ ‒ ‒ ‒ ‒ ‒ ‒ ‒ ‒ ‒ ‒

12. If a DETAIL record has an ACCT–NO which does not correspond to an ACCT–NO on the OLD–MASTER file, this signifies a new account which has been added during the current updating cycle. The corresponding NEW–MASTER record will then contain only data from the DETAIL file. Write a flowchart sequence to obtain DETAIL data on the NEW–MASTER file.

‒ ‒ ‒ ‒ ‒ ‒ ‒ ‒ ‒ ‒ ‒ ‒ ‒ ‒ ‒ ‒ ‒ ‒

13. The sequence control field on the two input files is ACCT–NO. The detail cards and the input master tape will both be in sequence by ACCT–NO. In what sequence will the output NEW–MASTER be created? _____

_____

‒ ‒ ‒ ‒ ‒ ‒ ‒ ‒ ‒ ‒ ‒ ‒ ‒ ‒ ‒ ‒ ‒ ‒

also in ACCT–NO sequence—if input files are in a specific sequence and output is created from that input as it is read, the output will be in the same sequence

14. After reading a single card and a single tape record, we will test for three possible conditions. The first test is:

Does ACCT-NO of DETAIL = ACCT-NO of OLD-MASTER?
When the account numbers are equal, what information will be contained

in the output record with that ACCT-NO? _____

_____

- - - - - - - - - - - - - - - - - - -

input information from OLD-MASTER updated by the corresponding DETAIL
record

15. When the account numbers are equal on both the OLD-MASTER and DE-
TAIL records, the card amount is added to the OLD-MASTER amount to obtain a NEW-MASTER amount. The NEW-MASTER record is created with the
appropriate ACCT-NO. Draw a flowchart sequence that performs the test indicated in frame 14 and then performs the required operations.

- - - - - - - - - - - - - - - - - - -

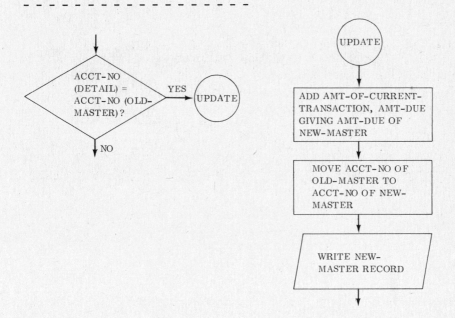

We could have moved ACCT-NO of DETAIL to ACCT-NO of NEW-MASTER.

16. After a record is written onto the new tape, another DETAIL card and
OLD-MASTER tape record are read. The second condition to be tested is:
Is ACCT-NO of DETAIL greater than ACCT-NO of OLD-MASTER?
This is the case where an OLD-MASTER record has an ACCT-NO for
which there is no corresponding DETAIL record. As an example, suppose
that the first DETAIL record has ACCT-NO 80503 and the first OLD-MASTER
record has an ACCT-NO of 80500. Since both files are in sequence by ACCT-
NO, this indicates that there is no ACCT-NO 80500 on the DETAIL file. That

is, ACCT–NO of DETAIL (80503) is greater than ACCT–NO of OLD–MASTER (80500). Thus, there were no transactions for ACCT–NO 80500 during the current updating cycle.

In this case, the NEW–MASTER record is created directly from what

record? _____

- - - - - - - - - - - - - - - - - -

OLD–MASTER

17. Draw a flowchart sequence to determine a "no update" condition and to process the required record accordingly.

- - - - - - - - - - - - - - - - - -

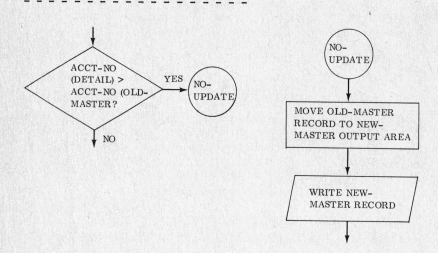

You would be correct, but much less efficient, if you moved each field separately, as in the flowchart sequence on the following page.

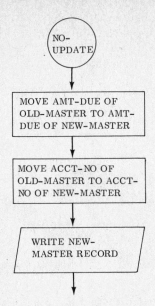

18. After a NEW-MASTER record is created from OLD-MASTER, we read only another OLD-MASTER record; we do not read another DETAIL card. Using the example of frame 16 (OLD-MASTER ACCT-NO = 80500, DETAIL ACCT-NO - 80503), after we have written the record with ACCT-NO 80500 onto the new file, we still have not processed DETAIL record 80503. Thus, we must read another OLD-MASTER record and determine if the ACCT-NO is the same as the one on the DETAIL record (80503).

Complete the sequence in frame 17 at NO-UPDATE. Read another OLD-MASTER record and branch to COMP-RTN at the end of the sequence. COMP-RTN is the name of the comparison routine where the account numbers on the input record are compared. Don't forget the end of file test after reading OLD-MASTER. Remember that every READ command should be directly followed by an end of file condition. Branch to EOJ1 if the end of file condition is reached. (We need separate end of job routines, depending upon which input file is finished first. This will be explained in more depth later.)

- - - - - - - - - - - - - - - - - - - -

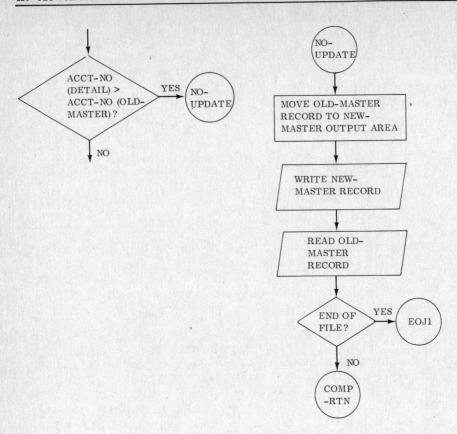

19. The third and last condition to be tested is:

Is ACCT-NO of DETAIL less than ACCT-NO of OLD-MASTER?

In this case, a DETAIL card record exists for which there is no corresponding OLD-MASTER record. We will consider this to be a new account. The NEW-MASTER tape record, then, will be created directly from the

_____ record.

- - - - - - - - - - - - - - - - - -

DETAIL

20. Note that we read only another DETAIL record after the new account has been processed; we do not read another OLD-MASTER record since the previous tape record has not been processed.

Consider the flowchart sequence on the following page to be the first few instructions necessary for the update flowchart.

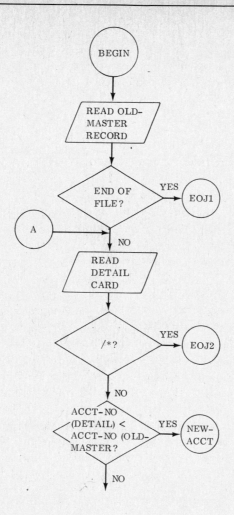

Draw, as best you can, the flowchart steps required at NEW–ACCT.

- - - - - - - - - - - - - - - - - -

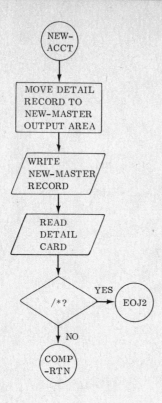

21. COMP-RTN is the name of the comparison routine where the account numbers on the input records are compared. If you are really "with it," you may
be able to see that in place of the READ command and its associated end of file

test at NEW-ACCT, we could have saved some steps by branching to _____.

- - - - - - - - - - - - - - - - - - -

A (If you're confused over this point, fear not—it will become much clearer
to you shortly.)

22. Before integrating all of the above procedures to form a complete update
flowchart, let's try some sample inputs and determine if you can create the
desired output, by hand, to be sure you understand the required processing.
    Suppose the following represents the first four input OLD-MASTER and
DETAIL records. Create the desired NEW-MASTER records from them.

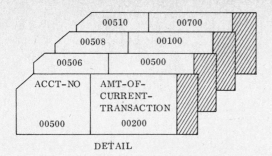

DETAIL

ACCT-NO	AMT-DUE	ACCT-NO	AMT-DUE	ACCT-NO	AMT-DUE	ACCT-NO	AMT-DUE
00500	08000	00504	09000	00506	11000	00510	00700

OLD-MASTER

- - - - - - - - - - - - - - - - - - - -

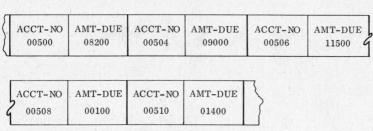

ACCT-NO	AMT-DUE	ACCT-NO	AMT-DUE	ACCT-NO	AMT-DUE
00500	08200	00504	09000	00506	11500

ACCT-NO	AMT-DUE	ACCT-NO	AMT-DUE
00508	00100	00510	01400

NEW-MASTER

23. The flowchart for this update procedure, exclusive of the end of job rou-
times, is illustrated in Figure 5.1. Before you study this flowchart, make an
attempt at drawing the flowchart yourself. Use the names assigned throughout this section. Do not attempt, as yet, to flowchart the end of job routine.

- - - - - - - - - - - - - - - - - - -

See Figure 5.1.

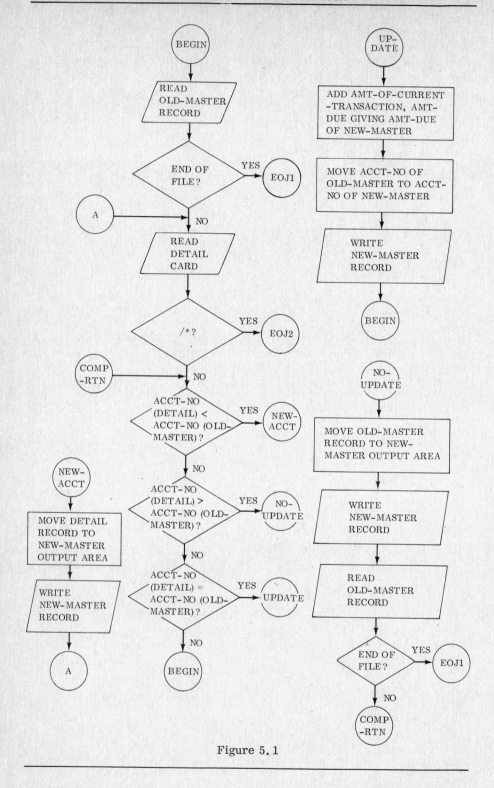

Figure 5.1

If your flowchart is essentially the same as the one in Figure 5.1, congratulations! You have proven your capabilities with computer logic. Don't be
discouraged, however, if your flowchart differs from the illustration. The
update technique must be learned, and you will be given more illustrations to
help you master the required procedures.

If you eliminated the test ACCT-NO (DETAIL) = ACCT-NO (OLD-
MASTER)?, you're being super-efficient. We do not always need all three
tests; sometimes the three tests in the COMP-RTN of Figure 5.1 can be reduced to two tests, as shown below.

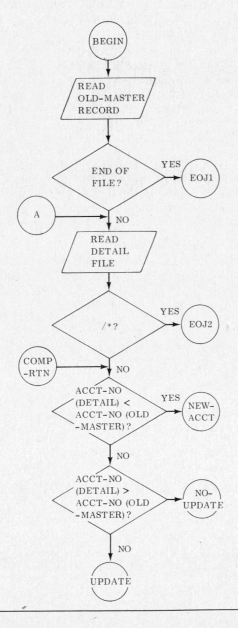

Notice that if ACCT-NO of DETAIL is not less than ACCT-NO of OLD-MASTER nor greater than ACCT-NO of OLD-MASTER, it must be equal to ACCT-NO of OLD-MASTER. Thus the last test in Figure 5.1 is unnecessary.

24. Before considering the end of job functions, let's modify the update flow-chart, to demonstrate the similarities between all types of update procedures.

Modify figure 5.1 so that DETAIL records with no corresponding OLD-MASTER records are considered errors. In such cases print an error message, ERRONEOUS DETAIL RECORD, along with the ACCT-NO of the DE-TAIL record. Here, again, don't try to write the end of file routines.

- - - - - - - - - - - - - - - - - - -

See Figure 5.2. If you used Figure 5.1 but had trouble modifying the routine, then reread this section on updates.

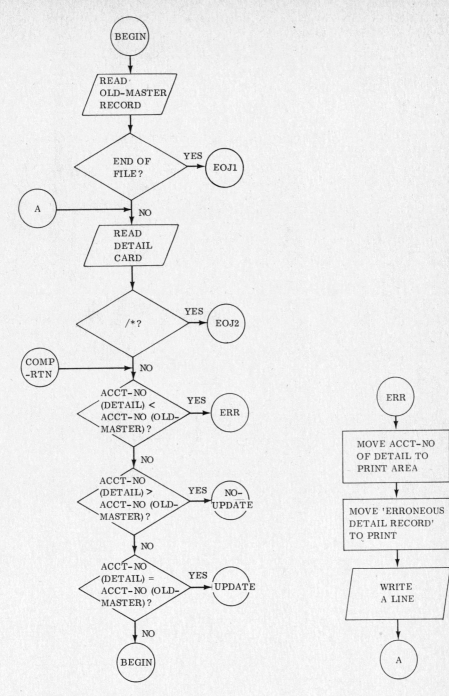

Note: the routines called NO-UPDATE and
UPDATE are prescribed in Figure 5.1.

Figure 5.2

25. Now let's consider the end of file routines for the flowchart in Figure 5.1. According to the illustration, when there are no more input master tape records to process, a branch to _____ occurs.

- - - - - - - - - - - - - - - - - - -

EOJ1

26. When there are no more OLD-MASTER records to process, there may <u>still</u> be DETAIL cards, representing new accounts, which must be added to the NEW-MASTER file. That is, at EOJ1, we must read DETAIL records and process them until we reach the end of the DETAIL file. When this happens, both the OLD-MASTER and the DETAIL files will be completed and the computer run can be terminated.

    Code the routine required at EOJ1

- - - - - - - - - - - - - - - - - - -

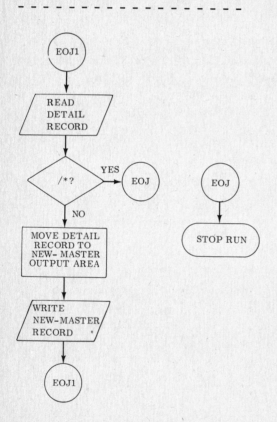

27. Similarly, according to Figure 5.1, when there are no more OLD-MASTER records to process, a branch to _____ occurs.

- - - - - - - - - - - - - - - - - - -

EOJ2

28. Note that a branch to EOJ2 would occur only after an OLD-MASTER record has been read and is in storage. Thus, when we reach EOJ2, an OLD-MASTER tape record still needs to be processed. There may also be additional OLD-MASTER records, which do not require updating but which must be rewritten onto the NEW-MASTER file. When these OLD-MASTER tape records have all been read and processed, the computer run can be terminated.

Code the routine required at EOJ2.

- - - - - - - - - - - - - - - - -

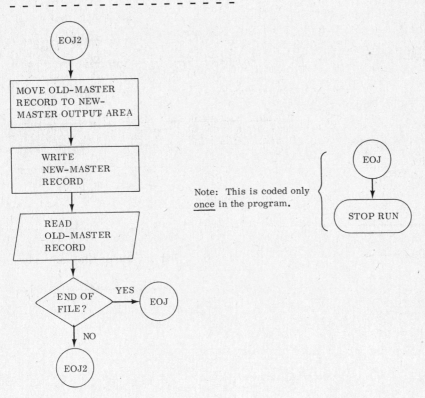

Note: This is coded only once in the program.

Be sure that, unlike the routine at EOJ1, a record is written before a new record is read because there is an OLD-MASTER record in the input area which has not yet been processed.

29. Either the EOJ1 routine or the EOJ2 routine will be performed for any given run of the program, but not both. Because for any given run we do not know which file will be terminated first, both routines are required, even though only one will be executed. If there are more OLD-MASTER records than DETAIL records, which routine will be performed? _____ If there

are more DETAIL records than OLD-MASTER records, new accounts are added at the end of the program at which routine? _____

– – – – – – – – – – – – – – – – – –

EOJ2; EOJ1

Before proceeding, a short review might be useful. Answer the following questions.

Review

A. What is the purpose of an update procedure? _____

_____

B. In a typical sequential update procedure, what files are involved and what information does each contain? _____

_____

_____

C. Why must the input files in an update procedure be in sequence? _____

_____

D. After records are read from the input files and the end of file tests have been performed, what routine usually follows? _____

_____

E. If a record is to be updated, information is written onto the output file from which input file? _____ After this, what is read? _____

F. If a master record does not need to be updated, what is written onto the output file? _____ After this, what is read?

_____

G. Describe two routines that are commonly performed if there is no master record for a corresponding detail record. _____

_____

In either case, what is read after processing? _____

H.   If the input master file is completely processed before the detail file has been completely processed, what must be done? _____

_____

I.   If the detail file is completely processed before the input master file, what must be done? _____

_____

J.   Is it possible to execute <u>both</u> end of file conditions during a single run of an update program?   Explain your answer. _____

_____

Answers to Review

A.   to make a file of data (usually a master file) current

B.   There are typically three files in an update procedure: an input master file, containing information current through the previous update cycle;   an input detail file, containing information for the current update period only;   and an output master file, containing the master data modified to include the current information.

C.   so the detail records and master records can be matched

D.   A comparison routine (which we've called COMP-RTN).   The control fields used for sequencing on both the input master and the detail files are compared to determine (1) if an update procedure is required (equal control fields), (2) if a no-update procedure is required (control field on detail is greater than control field on input master), or (3) if a new account or error procedure is required (control field on detail is less than control field on input master).

E.   both the input master and the detail files;   another record from each input file

F.   input master information;   another record from the input master file

G.   an error routine or a new account routine;   in either case, just another detail record is read

H.   Detail records must be read and processed, until that file is exhausted, signifying an end of job condition.

I.   The master input record in storage must be processed, and any succeeding input master records are read and processed as "no-updates," until there are no more input master records, signifying an end of job condition.

J. No. In any given run of an update program, we will complete either the input master file or the detail file first, at which point the program will branch to one of the two end of file routines.

31. As a potential programmer, you should know that some instructions require more "work" on the computer's part than others. Input and output instructions fall into this category. Thus it is important to minimize the number of input/output instructions in your program.

In the preceding update procedures, notice that the NO-UPDATE routines require the reading of OLD-MASTER and a corresponding end of file test, even though the OLD-MASTER file is read at the main sequence (see Figure 5.1).

Why must this read sequence be repeated at NO-UPDATE? _____ .

_____

_____

- - - - - - - - - - - - - - - - - - -

In the main sequence, after OLD-MASTER is read and an end of file test performed, the DETAIL file is then read. At NO-UPDATE we only wish to read OLD-MASTER and not DETAIL. Thus the READ OLD-MASTER sequence was repeated at NO-UPDATE.

32. Because of the relative inefficiency of input/output instructions, this duplication of the READ OLD-MASTER sequence is not considered good programming. Can you think of a method that could be used which would enable a branch to BEGIN at the NO-UPDATE sequence but which can avoid reading the DETAIL file? (Hint: this method was discussed in the last chapter and

is ideal for flip-flopping into and out of sequences.) _____

_____

- - - - - - - - - - - - - - - - - - -

If you said "by using switches," your perception is crystal clear!

33. By incorporating a SWITCH test between the OLD-MASTER and the DETAIL read sequences, we can control the main sequence. That is, at NO-UPDATE we can set SWITCH equal to 1. Then, at the SWITCH test between the two read sequences, we can branch to COMP-RTN if SWITCH is a 1 and, if not, we can proceed to the next sequential step. One major step must be added to this procedure. Can you determine what it is? _____

_____

- - - - - - - - - - - - - - - - - - -

SWITCH must be initialized at 0, at the beginning, and after every time it has been set to 1.

34. Redraw the flowchart in Figure 5.1 using this SWITCH concept.

- - - - - - - - - - - - - - - - - - -

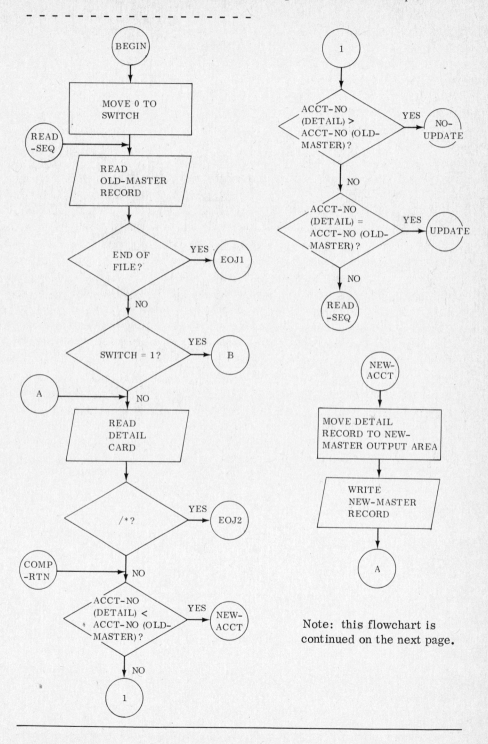

Note: this flowchart is continued on the next page.

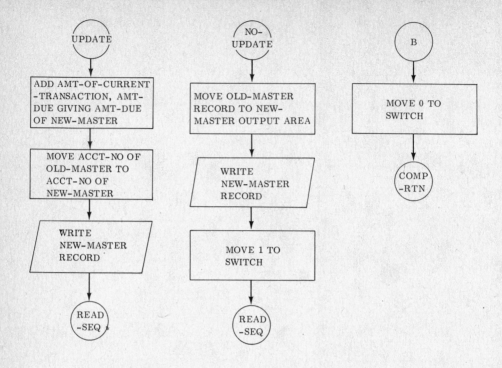

35. What is the purpose of using the SWITCH test in the preceding illustration? _____

_____

– – – – – – – – – – – – – – – – – – – –

The use of the SWITCH represents an efficient method of reducing the number of input instructions in the program.

36. The two end of job routines, called EOJ1 and EOJ2, of the update illustration also include additional READ commands. This, too, is somewhat inefficient. As a test of your understanding (and endurance), try to construct a flowchart of the above update procedure that eliminates these READ commands at EOJ1 and EOJ2. Use two switches—SWITCH1 and SWITCH2. (Hint: Let SWITCH1 = 1 when OLD-MASTER is at the end; let SWITCH2 = 1 when DE-TAIL is at the end. A branch to EOJ occurs only if both switches = 1. Do

not use a switch for eliminating a READ command at the NO-UPDATE sequence, since this might confuse the issue.) Now, try it.

-- -- -- -- -- -- -- -- -- -- -- -- -- -- --

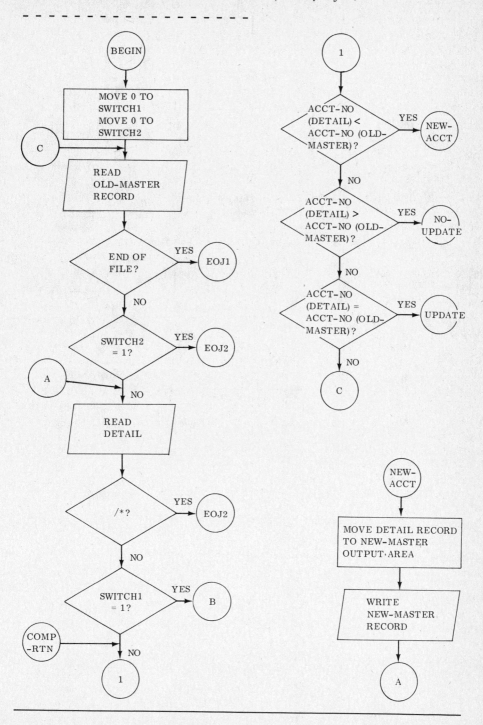

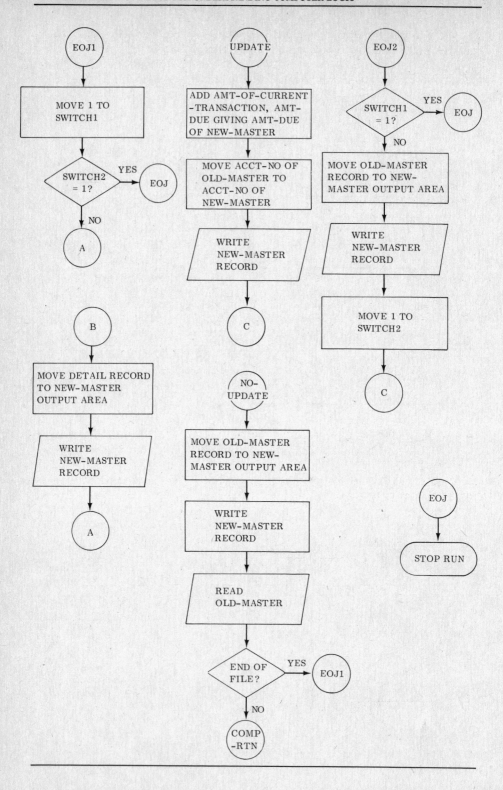

You might well call "foul" on that one! The intricacies of logic are enough to thwart even experienced programmers. Yet the application of switches to this sort of processing is not uncommon, so analyze this flowchart carefully. Be sure you understand it before you go on.

While your mind may be somewhat boggled by the use of switches, you can probably appreciate the flexibility which these one-position areas provide the programmer. That is, by using switches the programmer can branch into and out of routines with relative ease. From this point on, we will not dwell on switches since they may cloud the other elements of flowcharting and programming being emphasized. That is, our problems will not generally include switches, although many of them could indeed profit from the use of such switches.

One last point. Since the purpose of this section is to minimize input/output procedures, it should be mentioned that the above use of switches may be applied to the numerous WRITE instructions throughout the update procedure. Since the WRITE instructions are followed by different branch points, we cannot use a single procedure for writing records unless we incorporate switches to indicate branch points. If you're game for more practice, try rewriting the flowchart on your own, using switches with the WRITE instructions. (We haven't room to show the full flowchart here.)

The Merge Flowchart

37. A variation of the update flowchart is the merge flowchart. For this procedure, two files, each in the same specific sequence, are merged into a single sequential file.

Let us assume that the two input files are on two separate tapes and are called INPUT1 and INPUT2. They are each in ascending sequence by PART-NO, a field on both tapes. The PART-NO fields on both tapes will be unique. That is, if INPUT1 has a PART-NO of 187, then INPUT2 should not contain a record with the same PART-NO. Thus, if a record on INPUT1 has a PART-NO which matches a record on INPUT2, this will be considered an error condition and an error message should be printed. The purpose of the procedure is to merge two files containing distinct PART-NOs into a single sequential file.

Consider the following illustration which indicates the type of processing performed by a merge program. Do not proceed until you fully understand that records are written from both input tapes onto the output tape, which will also be in sequence by PART-NO.

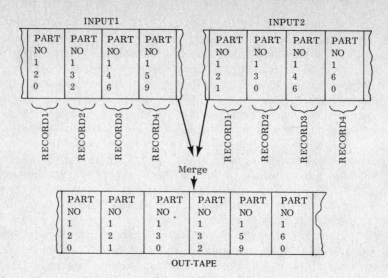

Note: The records with PART–NO 146
were not added to OUT–TAPE, since
they indicate an error.

First, we read a record from each input file. If PART–NO of INPUT1 is
less than PART–NO of INPUT2, the record from the _____ file is
written onto the new tape, called _____.

- - - - - - - - - - - - - - - - - - -

INPUT1; OUT–TAPE

38. After the INPUT1 record is processed, as above, we read another
_____ record.

- - - - - - - - - - - - - - - - - -

INPUT1 (The INPUT2 record has not been processed yet.)

39. Suppose the following illustration represents the first several steps of
the merge procedure.

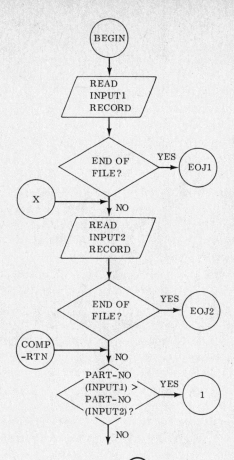

Draw the flowchart sequence required at (1)

- - - - - - - - - - - - - - - - - -

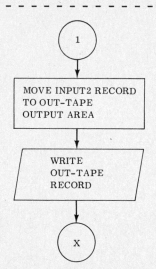

40. If PART-NO of INPUT1 is greater than (>) PART-NO of INPUT2, a record from _____ is written onto tape and another record is read from _____ .

- - - - - - - - - - - - - - - - - -

INPUT2; INPUT2

41. Assume that the following represents the next step of the routine labeled BEGIN in frame 39. Draw a flowchart segment for the processing required

at (2)

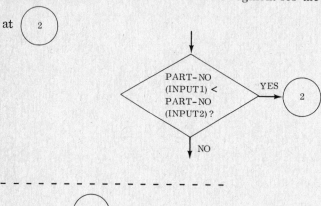

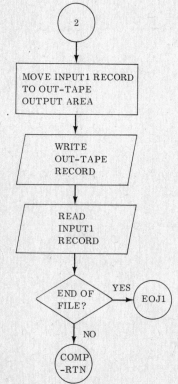

42. Rather than reading another INPUT1 record at the routine labeled 2, could we have branched to BEGIN, where an INPUT1 record is read? _____

- - - - - - - - - - - - - - - - - - -

No, because at BEGIN, an INPUT2 record is also read. In frame 41, we wish only to retrieve an INPUT1 record, since the previous INPUT2 record has not been processed as yet.

43. If a record from INPUT1 and a record from INPUT2 have the same PART-NO, what happens? _____

_____

- - - - - - - - - - - - - - - - - - -

An error message is written on the printer, and the records are not put on the tape; then both a new INPUT1 record and a new INPUT2 record are read.

44. Now, it's your turn to experiment. Draw the flowchart for the complete merging procedure, omitting for now the routines at EOJ1 and EOJ2.

- - - - - - - - - - - - - - - - - - -

See Figure 5.3. If you came close to the illustrated solution, smile—you're on your way! The logic inherent in these illustrations is not easy, and the concentration and perseverance necessary to achieve the proper results are traits which make a good programmer. If you had some difficulty, do not be discouraged; but do go back and review this section. Be sure you fully understand the merging flowchart before you go on.

45. Let us now consider the end of file routines. If a branch to EOJ1 occurs, there are no more records from the _____ file to process, but there may still be records from the _____ file to process. We need to process these latter records until what happens? _____

_____

- - - - - - - - - - - - - - - - - - -

INPUT1; INPUT2; until there are no more INPUT2 records, at which point we must terminate the run

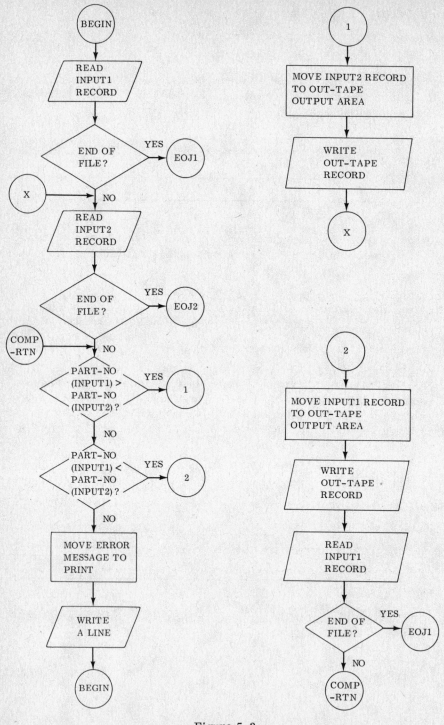

Figure 5.3

46. Draw the flowchart routine required at EOJ1.

- - - - - - - - - - - - - - - - - - -

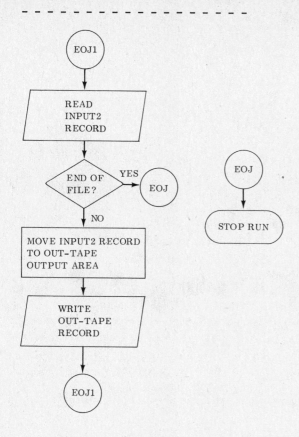

47. If a branch to EOJ2 occurs, there are no more records from the _____ file. But note that a record from INPUT1 has been read prior to the test for an end of file condition on INPUT2. This INPUT1 record must be processed. In addition, any other INPUT1 records must be read and processed until what

occurs? _____

_____

- - - - - - - - - - - - - - - - - - -

INPUT2; an end of file condition on INPUT1, at which point we must termin-
at the run

48. Draw the flowchart sequence required at EOJ2.

- - - - - - - - - - - - - - - - - - -

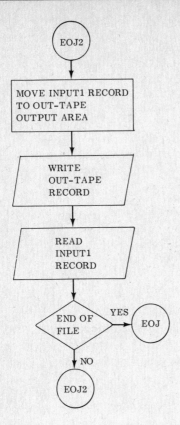

49. (True or False.) In any given run, it will be possible for the computer to branch to both EOJ1 and EOJ2. _____

- - - - - - - - - - - - - - - - - -

False. Only one of these two routines will be executed in a given run. Either we will run out of INPUT1 records first, at which point a branch to EOJ1 will occur, or we will run out of INPUT2 records first, at which point a branch to EOJ2 will occur.

50. Now it's time to try a flowchart of this magnitude on your own, without any assistance. If you're in doubt about the type of processing required, try some sample inputs and see if you can process them by hand. Try not to peek at previous flowcharts, unless it's absolutely necessary. Good luck, you're on your own. Draw an update flowchart using the following input files:

Detail card file		Master tape file	
1-20	Employee name	1-20	Employee name
21-25	Annual salary	21-25	Annual salary
26-80	Not used	26-50	Other data

Note: the tape file need not contain 80 character records.

Both files are in sequence by employee name. Use the field name EMP-NAME. Your flowchart should allow for the following.

      (1) The output file has the same format as the input master file.

      (2) For master tape records with no corresponding detail records (no match on employee name), create an output record from the input tape.

      (3) For detail records with no corresponding tape records, create an output record from the input card.

      (4) For master tape records with corresponding card records, take annual salary from card and all other data from tape.

- - - - - - - - - - - - - - - - - -

See Figure 5.4. Note that the input master record can be moved to output and then just a field from the detail record can be used to "replace" that input master field which is already in the output area.

51. Here's a tricky one. Two input files, called FILE1 and FILE2, are in sequence by DEPT-NO. They should each have one and only one record with the same DEPT-NO. That is, all records on FILE1 should have a corresponding record, with the same DEPT-NO, on FILE2. Where a match does not occur, print the erroneous record. No output files, except for a printed error report, are created. In a sense, then, this run is a validation to insure that the two files have matching DEPT-NOs.

    The hard part about this flowchart will be determining the sequence of READ commands, when an error occurs. A record from each file is read initially. If the DEPT-NO on each matches, we simply _____

_____

- - - - - - - - - - - - - - - - - -

read another FILE1 and FILE2 record

52. If the DEPT-NO does not match, we should print as an error the record with the lower DEPT-NO. Can you explain why? _____

_____

_____

- - - - - - - - - - - - - - - - - -

Because the record with the higher DEPT-NO may match the next record on the other file. For example, if FILE1 has a record with DEPT-NO 40 and the next record on FILE2 a DEPT-NO of 42, the record on FILE1 is considered the error, because the next record on FILE1 may have a DEPT-NO of 42.

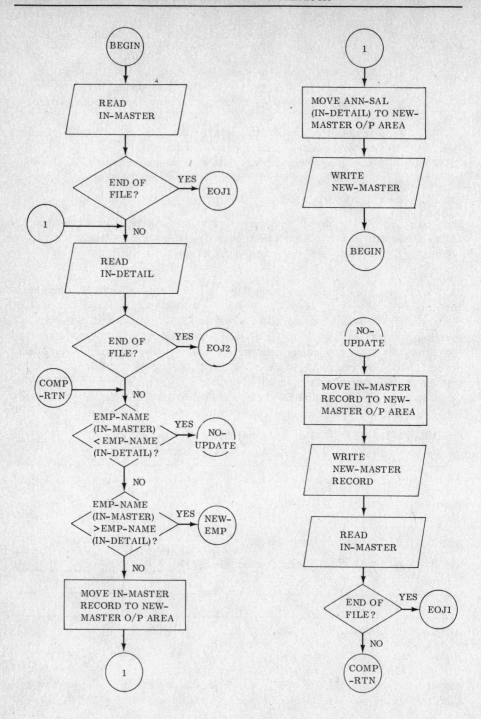

Flowchart is continued on the next page.

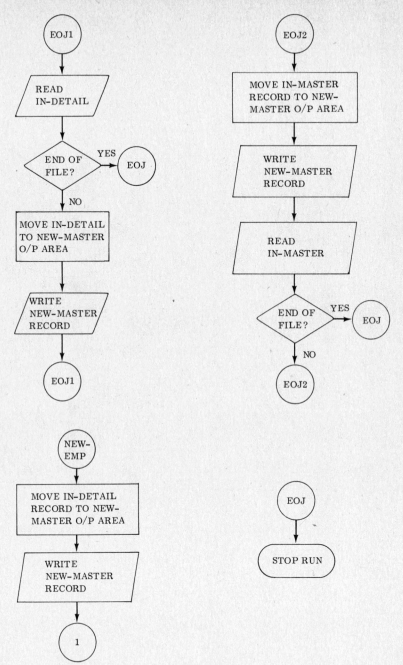

Figure 5.4

53. Once the record with the lower DEPT-NO is printed, which file is read?

_____

- - - - - - - - - - - - - - - - -

the file of the record just printed, here FILE1. That is, in the above example, a record from FILE1 only is read and a comparison is performed to determine if an end of file condition has been reached.

54. Okay, if you understand the concepts in the previous few frames, try to draw a flowchart of this matching operation.

- - - - - - - - - - - - - - - - -

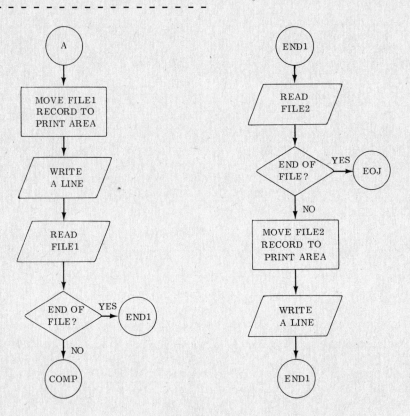

Figure 5.5

Note: Flowchart continued on next page.

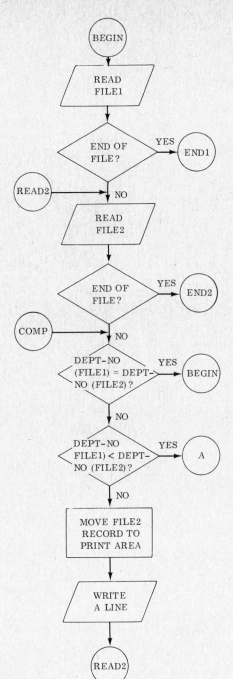

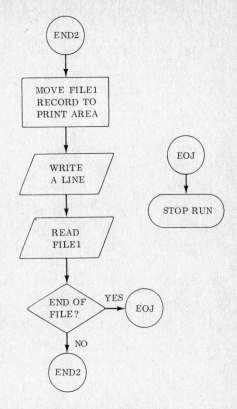

This completes our discussion of common programming techniques. If you understand the preceding routines, you are prepared to understand most of the applications you are likely to encounter in a business data processing environment. Learning the fundamental coding rules for any specific programming capability depends mainly on the ability to handle logic problems, and the material in this book can take you a long way in mastering the necessary logic.

If you're ready for a break, this is a good place to stop.

ILLUSTRATION OF AN INVENTORY PROGRAM

This and the following section, which illustrates a banking program, are designed to provide you with some insight into actual computer applications. Since the flowcharts are as "real-life" as you will find, they contain some "finishing touches" which we have not yet discussed.

55. We are to create an inventory program which uses inventory cards to produce a monthly reorder report. Each card that is read into the computer will have the following format.

ITEM NO	ITEM NAME	REORDER LEVEL	AMT IN STOCK	AMT ORDERED DURING THIS MO	COST OF ITEM	

The output will be a printed report with the following format.

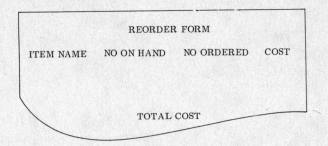

REORDER FORM

ITEM NAME   NO ON HAND   NO ORDERED   COST

TOTAL COST

The fields are calculated as follows.

    NO ON HAND = AMT IN STOCK + AMT ORDERED DURING THIS
            MONTH
    NO ORDERED = REORDER LEVEL - NO ON HAND (if reorder
            level is greater than number on hand)
          = 00 (if reorder level is less than or equal to number
            on hand)
    COST = COST OF ITEM x NO ORDERED
    TOTAL COST = SUM OF ALL COST FIELDS

The above definition of the problem was presented in much the same way as it might be in a data processing center. That is, from the above information, the programmer must construct a logical sequence of steps to produce the desired output. Our purpose here will be to construct a flowchart indicating that logical sequence of steps.

Before you draw the flowchart, you must understand the precise requirements of the program to be coded. To test your understanding, try to produce a sample of the output required, by hand, working with some input "test" data that you can construct yourself.

For example, let's consider the following to be the first inventory card that is to be read into the computer.

ITEM NO	ITEM NAME	REORDER LEVEL	AMT IN STOCK	AMT ORDERED DURING THIS MO	COST OF ITEM	
0026	WIDGET	500	450	000	100	

Note: COST OF ITEM is in dollars.

Using the above output format and the series of calculations required, try to construct, by hand, the first line of output, to see if you understand the operations required.

- - - - - - - - - - - - - - - - -

REORDER FORM

ITEM NAME	NO ON HAND	NO ORDERED	COST
WIDGET	450	50	$5,000

56. If you had some difficulty constructing the output, try one more. Suppose the following represents the second input data card.

ITEM NO	ITEM NAME	REORDER LEVEL	AMT IN STOCK	AMT ORDERED DURING THIS MO	COST OF ITEM	
0043	WIDGET	250	300	200	050	

Indicate what the second output line would look like.

- - - - - - - - - - - - - - - - -

ITEM NAME	NO ON HAND	NO ORDERED	COST
WIDGET	500	00	$ 0

57. The purpose of frames 55 and 56 is to help you understand the logic necessary to achieve the required output. The very first step in writing flowcharts is to understand this logic. Without a clear understanding of what you must accomplish, you may make serious mistakes. So you should always use this step-by-step method to test your understanding before you begin flowcharting.

Unlike previous chapters where we concentrated on compact, illustrative logic problems, the emphasis here will be on the whole program, and thus the whole flowchart as it would be drawn in a typical data processing environment.

Try your hand at the flowchart required for this inventory problem. Don't expect to get all the steps and don't be discouraged if you have some difficulty. This "real-life" business application requires integration of more steps than you are used to, and uses some seemingly new procedures. We'll examine these new procedures one by one later—but it will be most meaningful if you try drawing the flowchart yourself and then look at ours.

- - - - - - - - - - - - - - - - -

A suggested flowchart for this application appears in Figure 5.6. Study it carefully and compare it with yours. Then go on to the frames that follow.

58. How do you know which sequence in the flowchart represents the major sequence? _____

_____

- - - - - - - - - - - - - - - - -

The entry connector START or BEGIN usually identifies the main sequence.

59. What is the purpose of an instruction which moves zeros to TOTAL?

_____

- - - - - - - - - - - - - - - - -

to clear or initialize the field

60. Most computer systems do not automatically clear storage when a new program is read into the computer. This is because a computer may read and process several programs in storage at a given time. Thus, to automatically clear out storage each time a program is read might destroy the functioning of additional programs. So the programmer must clear out the storage areas for a particular program.

Because a common programming error is the omission of the instructions which initialize areas of storage, be sure to flowchart these initializing routines, as a reminder to prevent errors when the program is actually written.

Consider the flowchart which appears on page 255.

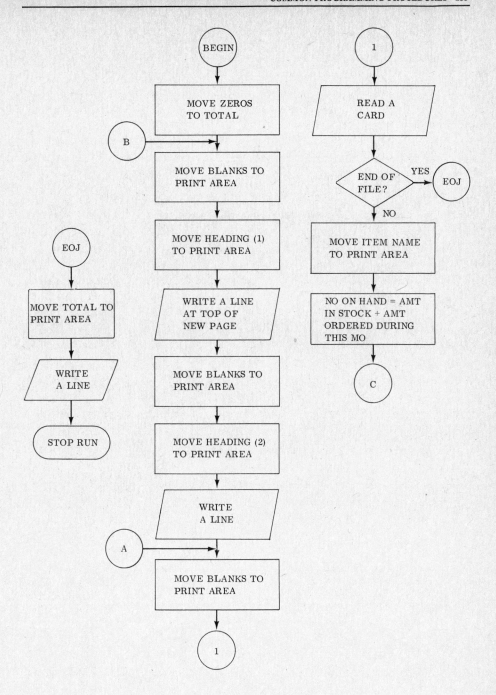

Note: Flowchart continues on next page.

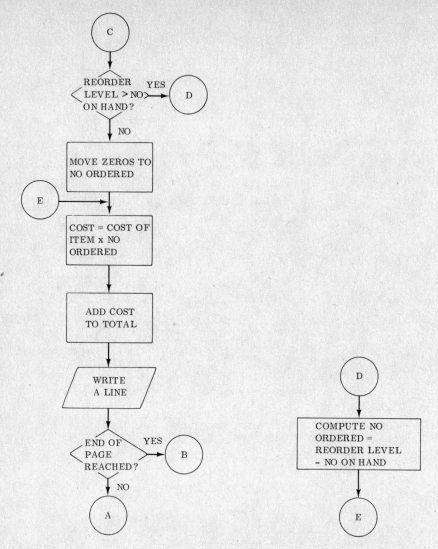

Figure 5.6

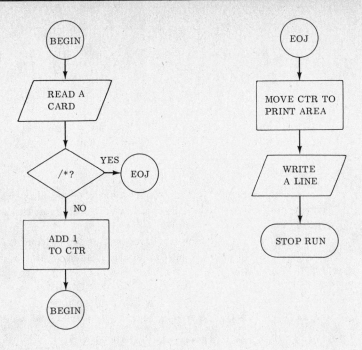

What will be the value of CTR at the end of the run? _____

- - - - - - - - - - - - - - - - - -

Undefined. The important point here is that the contents of CTR will depend
upon its initial value. If its initial value were zero, CTR would equal the
number of cards read. If it were not initialized at zero, the contents would
be unpredictable. If the program were coded precisely from the above flowchart, the failure to initialize CTR would result in erroneous processing.

61. Looking back at Figure 5.6, what is the purpose of the second instruction
in the main sequence? _____

_____

- - - - - - - - - - - - - - - - - -

Here, again, the print area is cleared or initialized by moving blanks or
spaces to it. Because most modern computers do not automatically clear
storage, the output area may also contain information from other programs.
Without a statement to clear the print area, the computer might produce
output with garbled information, instead of blanks, between the fields.

62. Here's a "think" question: Would the following be an appropriate alternative to the second instruction in the main sequence? _____

```
┌─────────────┐
│MOVE ZEROS TO│
│OUTPUT AREA  │
└─────────────┘
```

- - - - - - - - - - - - - - - - - -

No. Zeros are used to initialize arithmetic fields; blanks are used to initialize output areas. An output report looks better with blanks—not zeros—between fields.

63. The next two instructions in Figure 5.6 are part of a heading routine. All reports that are computer-produced should have headings at the top of each page to identify them.

Headings are generally of two types: (1) report headings and (2) field headings. All reports should have a report heading, such as REORDER FORM, MONTHLY SALES REPORT, or others. Most reports also identify the fields that are to print. ITEM NAME and NUMBER ON HAND are examples of field headings. In our flowchart, as well as in the program to be coded from it, such headings should be moved to the print area and written.

Every line that is to be printed corresponds to (how many?) _____ WRITE commands?

- - - - - - - - - - - - - - - - - -

one

64. On the next two pages, the flowchart in Figure 5.6 is again shown, this time in somewhat reduced form. Using a pencil, indicate by arrows the path to be taken by the flowchart if the following input card is read.

ITEM NO	ITEM NAME	REORDER LEVEL	AMT IN STOCK	AMT ORDERED DURING THIS MO	COST OF ITEM	
0036	WIDGET	600	250	200	200	

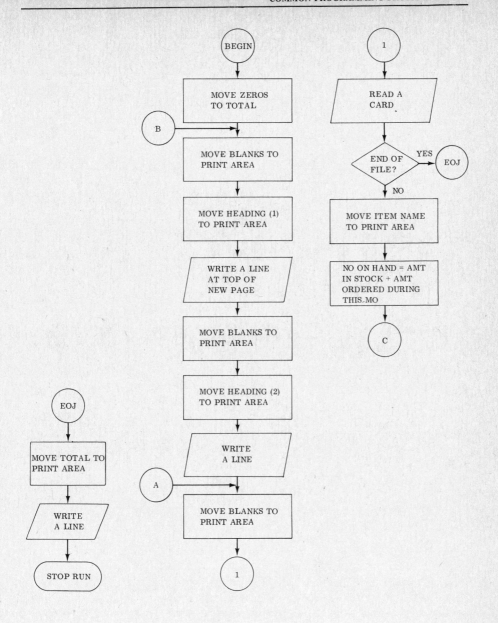

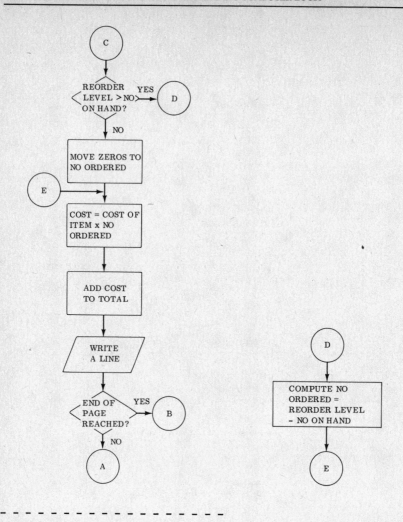

BEGIN→C→D→E→A

65. Computer-generated reports are printed on continuous forms. All such forms are connected but contain perforations which denote the end of each page. After all the pages are generated, these forms must be burst, or separated, into single sheets. (See Figure 5.7.)

Unless the computer is instructed to do otherwise, it will write each line and advance the paper, printing from one form to another, ignoring the fact that each is really an individual page. Although printing is physically performed from one continuous form to another, the computer must be instructed to observe page delineations. That is, each page should generally begin with a heading to identify the report. After the heading, or headings, data lines follow. The programmer generally instructs the computer to test for the end of a form after printing each data line. If this test is not performed, the computer will print each line of data on succeeding lines, ignoring actual page perforations and delineations. To avoid this, the programmer instructs the computer to test for an end of page marker and if it is reached, the computer is instructed to skip to a new page and write the heading again.

Using the flowchart in Figure 5.6, indicate the instruction that tests for an end of page, commonly called a page overflow test.

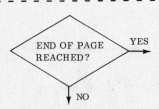

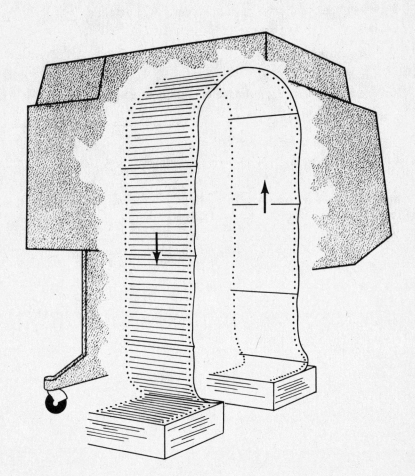

Figure 5.7.   Continuous forms.   Courtesy IBM.

66. What path is indicated if the end of page is reached? _____

_____

- - - - - - - - - - - - - - - - - -

The computer is instructed to proceed to that point in the program (here, in the flowchart) where a heading is to be printed on a new page.

67. What path is indicated if end of page is not reached? _____

_____

- - - - - - - - - - - - - - - - - -

The computer is instructed to proceed to that point in the program where another input card is read.

68. The first line of any report should generally contain a _____.

- - - - - - - - - - - - - - - - - -

heading, to identify the report

69. For report processing, to make certain that each page has a heading, what should we include in our program? _____

- - - - - - - - - - - - - - - - - -

a test for end of page (also called form overflow)

70. Now let's draw a flowchart for a slightly different inventory problem. The format for the input cards is as follows.

ITEM NO	ITEM NAME	AMT IN STOCK	REORDER LEVEL	COST OF ITEM	CODE

The output will be a printed report with the following format.

REORDER FORM

ITEM NAME   AMT TO BE REORDERED   COST

Your flowchart should allow for the following specifications.

_____

(1) If AMT IN STOCK is greater than or equal to REORDER LVL, nothing need be printed for that card.
(2) If AMT IN STOCK is less than REORDER LVL, calculate AMT TO BE REORDERED as (REORDER LVL – AMT IN STOCK) x (COST OF ITEM, where CODE = 1 (normal item).
(3) If AMT IN STOCK is less than REORDER LVL, calculate AMT TO BE REORDERED as 2(REORDER LVL – AMT IN STOCK) x COST OF ITEM, where CODE = 2 (frequently reordered item).
(4) Print a final TOTAL.

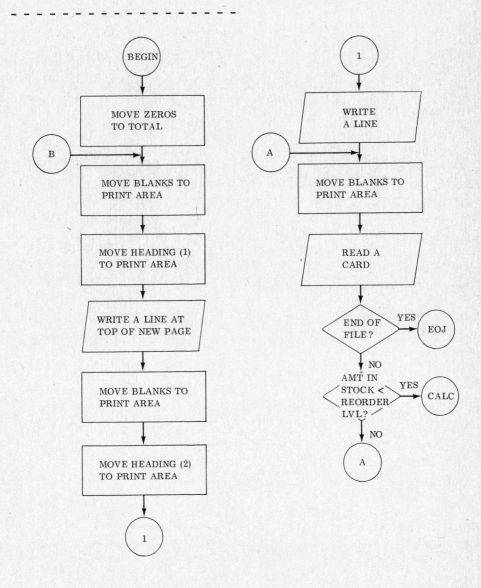

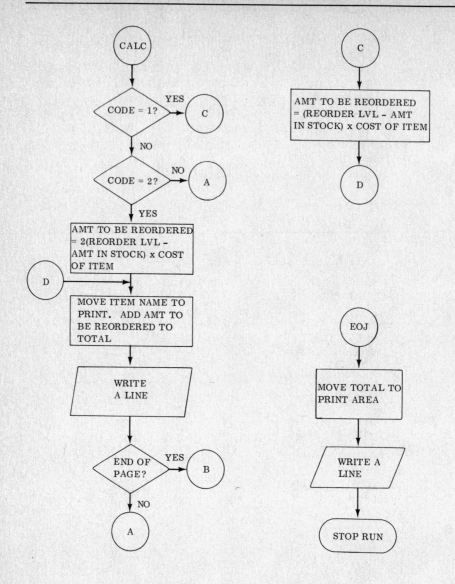

ILLUSTRATION OF A BANKING PROGRAM

71. A banking organization uses punched cards to store all transaction data for a given week. The card format is as follows.

CUSTOMER NAME	ACCOUNT NUMBER	CARD TYPE (B, W, D)	AMOUNT	

Cards will be in sequence by account number. Each customer will have one type B card, denoting his balance on hand at the beginning of the week. This will always be the <u>first</u> card with the given account number. In addition, there <u>may</u> be several D (deposit) cards and W (withdrawal) cards following a B card for a customer. The number and type of cards following a B card depend upon the number of transactions (if any) made during the week. Thus, all cards for a single account will appear together, with the B card being the first for the group.

Suppose that N. R. Brown, account number 0675, has $5,000 in his account at the beginning of the week. In the course of the week, he makes two separate deposits, one for $500 and one for $300. How many cards will be

entered into the system for this customer? _____ What card types would

they be? _____ Draw facsimiles of these cards.

- -

three; one type B card, two type D cards

CUSTOMER NAME N. R. BROWN	ACCOUNT NUMBER 0675	CARD TYPE D	AMOUNT 0300	

CUSTOMER NAME N. R. BROWN	ACCOUNT NUMBER 0675	CARD TYPE D	AMOUNT 0500	

CUSTOMER NAME N. R. BROWN	ACCOUNT NUMBER 0675	CARD TYPE B	AMOUNT 5000	

72. Suppose that J. C. Pennie, account number 6725, has made no deposits or withdrawals during the current week. Do you think there will be any cards

with his account number? _____ Explain your answer. _____

_____

_____

- - - - - - - - - - - - - - - - - - - -

Based on the information given, this is a hard question. If we are to assume that the card file contains <u>all</u> accounts, then there will be a B card for J. C. Pennie, which would contain his balance on hand. If, however, we are to assume that the card file represents only those accounts that had transactions during the current week, then there will be no cards with the given account number. When analyzing a problem, you should check details such as these, to be sure you are not including information you don't need—or leaving out information you should have.

73. Let us assume that the card file is a <u>master</u> file, containing all account numbers, even those that had no transactions during the current period.
    Suppose the following is the only card for R. H. Macie. Is it a valid input entry? _____

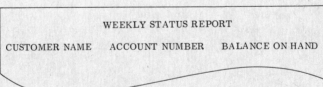

CUSTOMER NAME	ACCOUNT NUMBER	CARD TYPE	AMOUNT
R. H. MACIE	7332	W	4500

- - - - - - - - - - - - - - - - - - - -

No. W cards must follow B cards; if there is no B card for R. H. Macie, the entry is invalid.

74. The output of the program will be a printed report with the following format.

> WEEKLY STATUS REPORT
>
> CUSTOMER NAME   ACCOUNT NUMBER   BALANCE ON HAND

BALANCE ON HAND = BALANCE ON HAND (from B card) + DEPOSITS (from D cards) - WITHDRAWALS (from W cards)

Each line that prints corresponds to at least one input card, but sometimes will contain information from several cards. That is, although there may be a B card, two D cards, and three W cards for a particular account, only one output line will appear to indicate BALANCE ON HAND for that account.

Suppose the following is the first group of cards read into the computer. What will the first data print line look like?

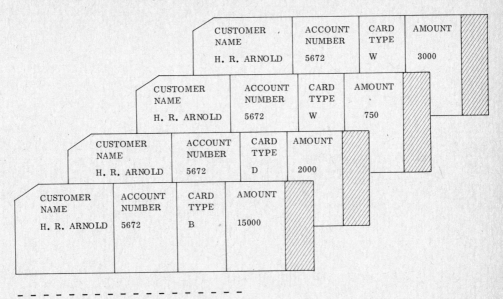

- - - - - - - - - - - - - - - - - -

H. R. ARNOLD   5672 $13250

75. The flowchart for this problem includes some new concepts you've not yet learned about. However, they will be most meaningful if you try to work out the logic yourself. So, first draw your own flowchart for this problem, and then compare it to Figure 5.8. Do not be discouraged if you have some difficulty. The new concepts will be clarified in the frames that follow.

- - - - - - - - - - - - - - - - - -

See Figure 5.8

75a In Figure 5.8, note that the headings are printed first, prior to any card processing. In your attempt, did you remember to include a heading routine?
    The major innovation in this flowchart is the use of a control break. That is, for a given account number, the number of input cards is unpredictable, depending upon the number of deposits and withdrawals made. Data cannot be printed until all the cards for a given account number have been read. To insure that all cards for a given account have been read and processed, a line is not printed until a B card with a new account number is read. That is, the new account B card creates a control break, which causes the previous account data to be written. Thus, except for the first card read, every B card that is read causes the printing of the previous account information. Exactly what happens to the very first B card that is read will be explained shortly.

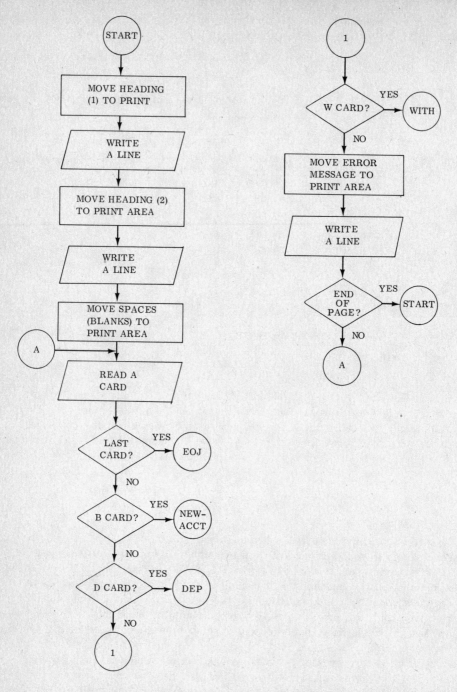

Note: Flowchart is continued on next page.

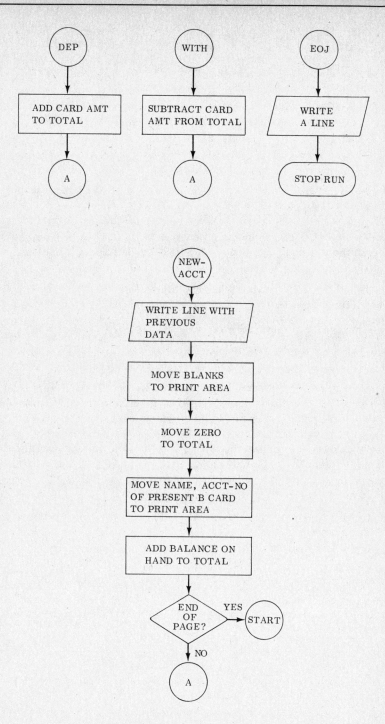

Figure 5. 8.   Program flowchart of a banking problem.

Consider the following input. (Note that the following is a shortcut method of indicating card data.)

CUSTOMER NAME	ACCOUNT NUMBER	CARD TYPE	AMOUNT
L. E. SMITH	11222	B	5000
L. E. SMITH	11222	W	300
L. E. SMITH	11222	D	200
L. F. SMITH	11456	B	1000
L. F. SMITH	11456	D	250

A line is printed after how many cards have been read? _____

- - - - - - - - - - - - - - - - - - - -

Four. The fourth card, which has a change in account number, causes the printing of the previous account number (11222) data.

76. The card in the input area when the first line is written (is, is not) _____ part of the first data line.

- - - - - - - - - - - - - - - - - - - -

is not

77. Thus, from the flowchart in Figure 5.8, we see that a B card causes a control break, denoted by a branch to NEW-ACCT. At NEW-ACCT, the previous account information is printed and the appropriate areas are re-initialized.

To be sure you understand how that works, follow some data through the process. Assume that the three fields are called NAME, ACCT-NO, and TOTAL. The B card that caused the control break to NEW-ACCT contains the following data.

NAME	ACCT-NO	TOTAL
L. P. RINQUIST	6758	$25000

The data in the three fields in the output area at the beginning of the NEW-ACCT routine is shown at (1) below. The numbers (1) through (6) correspond to the six instructions at NEW-ACCT. Indicate the changes to the three fields in the output area after each operation at NEW-ACCT is performed.

	NAME	ACCT-NO	TOTAL
(1)	R. Q. REYNOLDS	6754	$45000
(2)	_____	_____	_____
(3)	_____	_____	_____
(4)	_____	_____	_____
(5)	_____	_____	_____
(6)	_____	_____	_____

- - - - - - - - - - - - - - - - - - - -

(1)	R. Q. REYNOLDS	6754	$45000
(2)	(blank)	(blank)	(blank)
(3)	(blank)	(blank)	0000000
(4)	L. P. RINQUIST	6758	0000000
(5)	L. P. RINQUIST	6758	$25000
(6)	L. P. RINQUIST	6758	$25000

78. After a B card has been fully processed, a branch to A occurs unless what condition is reached? _____

- - - - - - - - - - - - - - - - - -

end of page or form overflow

79. An end of page condition will result in what type of operation? _____
_____

- - - - - - - - - - - - - - - - - -

printing of headings on a new page

80. If the B card is followed by a D card, what will happen? _____
_____

- - - - - - - - - - - - - - - - - -

Control will branch to DEP, where the CARD AMT will be added to TOTAL, and then branch back to A, where another card is read.

81. If a W card is read, what will happen? _____
_____

- - - - - - - - - - - - - - - - - -

Control will branch to WITH, where the CARD AMT will be subtracted from TOTAL, and then branch back to A, where another card is read.

82. According to the flowchart, if a card is neither a B, D, or W card, what will result? _____

- - - - - - - - - - - - - - - - - -

An error message will be printed.

83. Suppose that TOTAL were not re-initialized at zero at the NEW–ACCT routine. What would happen? _____

- - - - - - - - - - - - - - - - - -

_____

TOTAL would then contain a running total. That is, each time TOTAL would print, it would contain the total balance on hand for all previous accounts. At the end it would contain a final total. This is not what the program is required to produce!

84. Let us now return to the beginning of the run. We have said that except for the very first card, all B cards force a control break which causes previous data to print. Since there is no previous data when the first B card is read, we must ascertain what happens. Let's follow the flowchart through.

The first B card causes a branch to NEW-ACCT. At NEW-ACCT, a line is written, usually with previous account number data. In this case, what will

print? _____

- - - - - - - - - - - - - - - - - - - -

Blanks. Prior to the first read instruction, the print area was cleared; thus, the write instruction will result in the printing of a blank line.

85. After the first blank line is printed, the output area is initialized with the B card data, as it should be, and the program proceeds normally. Thus, in this case we do not need to insert a special first card routine, because the normal flow adjusts very nicely to the first card requirements.

There is a very important lesson inherent in this flowchart. For programs that require control breaks, you should draw the flowchart considering the normal flow of logic. Most often, the first card routine can be made to fit the normal flow pattern, as in the above, where the only variation was that a blank line printed.

Consider the following input cards and output format.

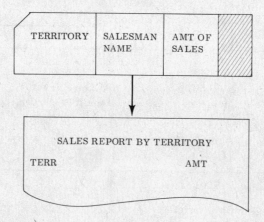

The purpose of the program is to print a sales report with total amount of sales for each territory.

Consider the following input cards.

TERRITORY	SALESMAN NAME	AMT OF SALES
11	S. NEWMAN	12000

TERRITORY	SALESMAN NAME	AMT OF SALES
11	Q. VINCENT	34000

TERRITORY	SALESMAN NAME	AMT OF SALES
03	S. ANDREWS	12350

TERRITORY	SALESMAN NAME	AMT OF SALES
03	T. SMITH	6000

TERRITORY	SALESMAN NAME	AMT OF SALES
03	J. BROWN	43250

How many output lines will be printed? _____

- - - - - - - - - - - - - - - - - -

two, one for territory 03 and one for territory 11

86. Construct the first two lines of data.

- - - - - - - - - - - - - - - - - -

SALES REPORT BY TERRITORY

TERR	AMT
03	61600
11	46000

87. Each time a territory changes, what should happen? _____

_____

- - - - - - - - - - - - - - - - - -

a control break, where previous data must be printed

88. Now, first review the flowchart in Figure 5.8 to make certain that you understand a control break routine. Then, as best you can, try to construct a flowchart for this problem.

- - - - - - - - - - - - - - - - - -

See Figure 5.9 for a suggested solution

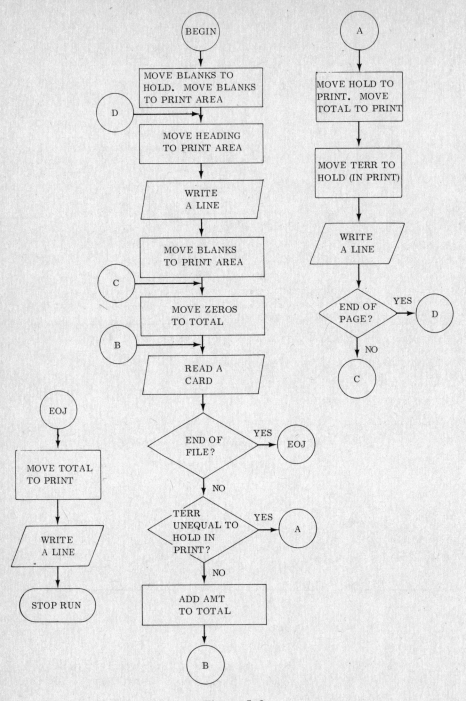

Figure 5.9.

89. Using Figure 5.9, what would the first data line look like? _____

_____

_____

- - - - - - - - - - - - - - - - - - - -

It would contain all blanks except for the TOTAL field which would contain
zeros. Thus the first line might appear as:

0000

SELF-TEST

1. Draw a flowchart for the following simplified accounts receivable billing
program. This program will utilize, as input, a master file with information
on all charge accounts for a particular department store. The input is on tape,
as shown below.

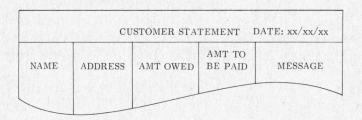

NAME	ADDRESS	ACCT NO	TYPE OF ACCT	AMT OWED	NO OF MOS IN ARREARS

The output is a monthly statement or bill submitted to the customer.

CUSTOMER STATEMENT DATE: xx/xx/xx				
NAME	ADDRESS	AMT OWED	AMT TO BE PAID	MESSAGE

The operations to be performed are as follows.

(1) <u>Compilation of billing data</u>. If TYPE OF ACCT contains a 1 (regular
charge), the entire bill is to be paid each month. In this case, AMT OWED
is transmitted to the output field, AMT TO BE PAID, with no interest computed.
    If TYPE OF ACCT is a 2 (budget charge) then 1/12 of AMT OWED plus
INTEREST CHARGE (1% of entire AMT OWED) is recorded on the bill as AMT
TO BE PAID.
    In each case, NAME, ADDRESS, and AMT OWED are placed directly on
the customer statement from the master tape. DATE is obtained from a control card, which is the only card read. The information from this control card
is placed in the computer in a field called DATE-IN. Thus DATE-IN is used
to transmit the month and year to the Customer Statement.

(2) Determination of charge status. The field called NO OF MOS IN ARREARS
denotes the number of months since a payment has been made to an account

that has a balance. If two months have elapsed (a 2 is in the field), a message REMINDER—YOUR ACCOUNT IS IN ARREARS is to print on the statement. If three months have elapsed (a 3 is in the field), a message WARNING—YOUR CHARGE PRIVILEGES HAVE BEEN SUSPENDED is to print. A separate monthly run provides a listing of all customers that have not made payments in three months. This list is then distributed to sales personnel who are told not to honor the customers' charge cards.

2. Consider the following card input.

STATE CODE	CITY CODE	DISTRICT CODE	AMT OF SALES	

The output is to be a printed report that lists the total amount of all sales figures for each city and the total amount of all sales figures for each state. At the end of the report a final total is to print. Draw a flowchart to accomplish these tasks. Assume that the cards are in sequence by city codes within state codes. That is, for STATE-CODE 01, there may be ten CITY-CODEs (e.g., 01-10). The cards will be in sequence such that all 01 city codes for state code 01 will be first, then 02 city codes for state code 01 will follow. (Hint: branch with NO decisions, if you find that technique easier.)

3. The following represents two tape files to be used as input.

FILE1

PART NO	INVOICE NO	UNIT COST	QTY ON HAND	

FILE2

PART NO	INVOICE NO	UNIT COST	QTY ON HAND	

Draw a flowchart that prints only those records from either file that are not matching records. Assume that each file is in sequence by PART-NO.

4. The following represents two tape files to be used as input.

DEBIT FILE

TRANS NO	CUST NAME	AMT OF TRANS	DEPT NO	ITEM NO	

CREDIT FILE

TRANS NO	CUST NAME	AMT OF CREDIT	DEPT NO	ITEM NO	

Assume that both files are in sequence by TRANS-NO. Draw a flowchart that will result in the merging of the two files into a single output file. If the files contain a matching record, consider this an error; print both records and do not put them on the output tape.

5. Draw a flowchart of an update procedure which reads in the following master and detail files.

MASTER	STUDENT NO	STUDENT NAME	STATUS	DATE OF BIRTH	ADDRESS	NO OF CREDITS	AMT IN ARREARS

DETAIL	STUDENT NO	STUDENT NAME	STATUS	NO OF CREDITS	AMT IN ARREARS	

Assume that all detail records have corresponding master records. If this is not the case, print the error. An output master tape is to be created which contains the same record formats as the input master but which also incorporates detail records. That is, change the master record using data from the detail record. Draw a flowchart of the required operations.

Answers to Self-Test

1.

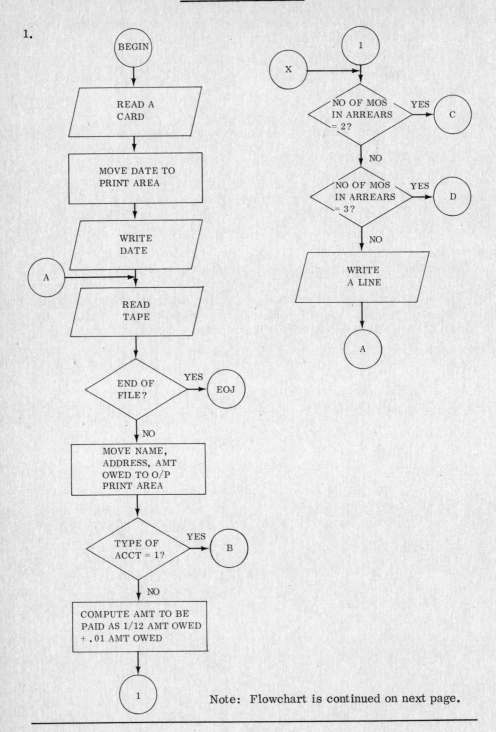

Note: Flowchart is continued on next page.

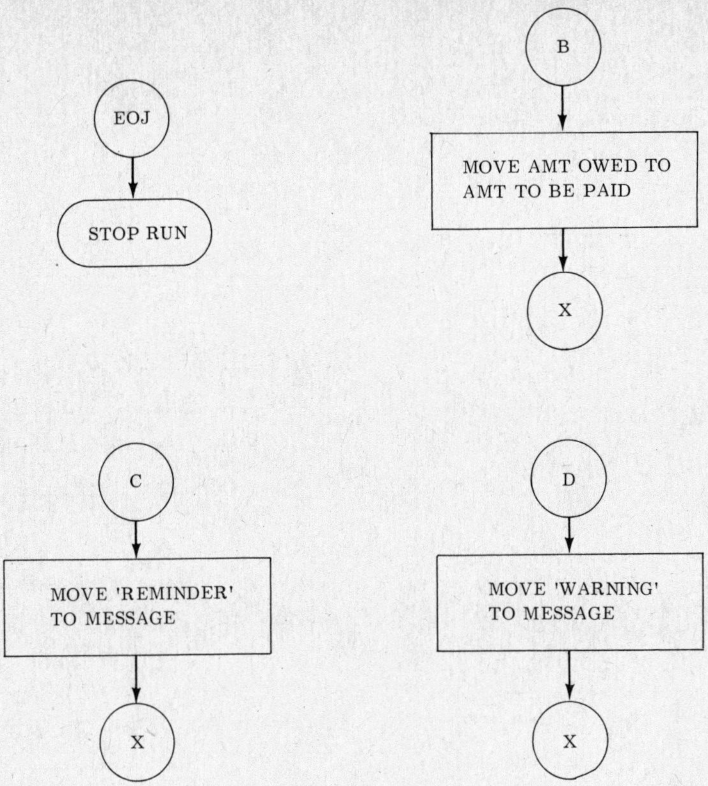

EOJ

↓

STOP RUN

B

↓

MOVE AMT OWED TO
AMT TO BE PAID

↓

X

C

↓

MOVE 'REMINDER'
TO MESSAGE

↓

X

D

↓

MOVE 'WARNING'
TO MESSAGE

↓

X

(frames 55–70)

2.

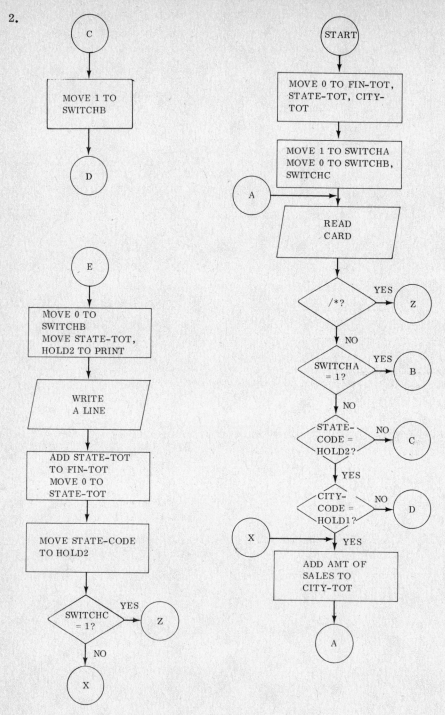

Note: Flowchart is continued on next page.

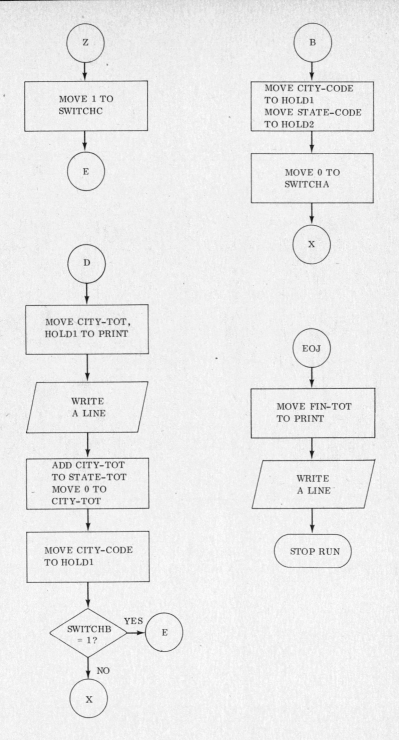

(frames 71–89)

3.

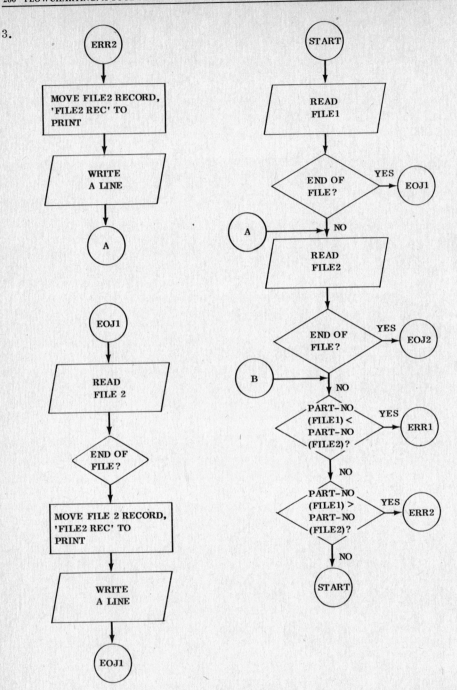

Note: Flowchart is continued on next page.

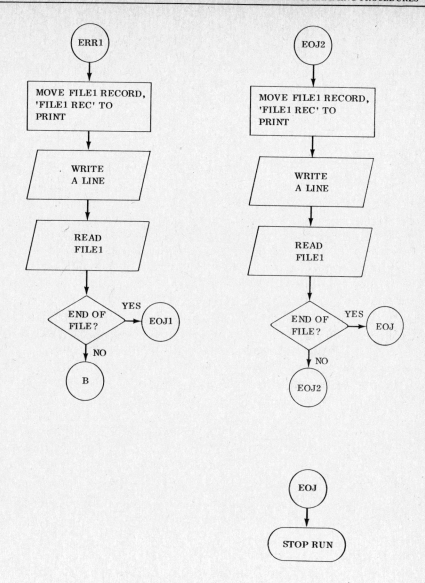

4.

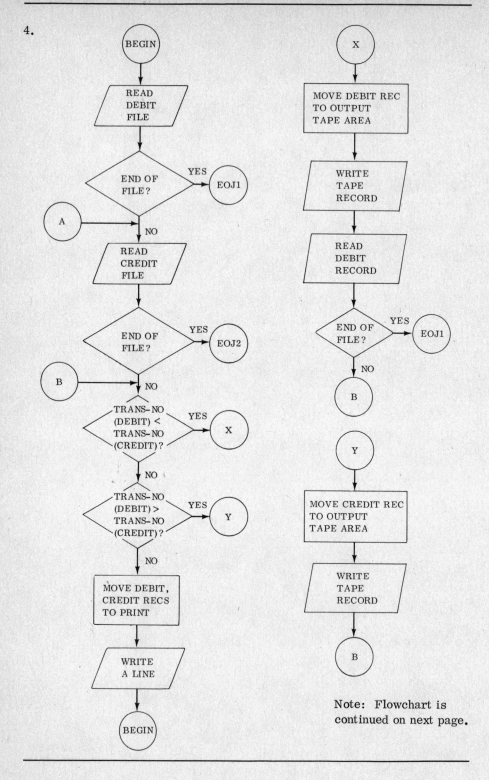

Note: Flowchart is
continued on next page.

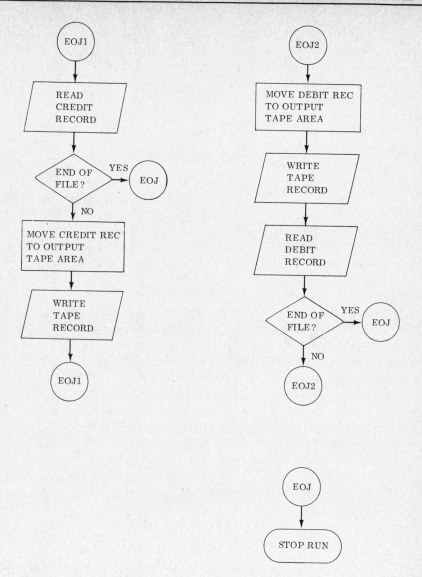

5.

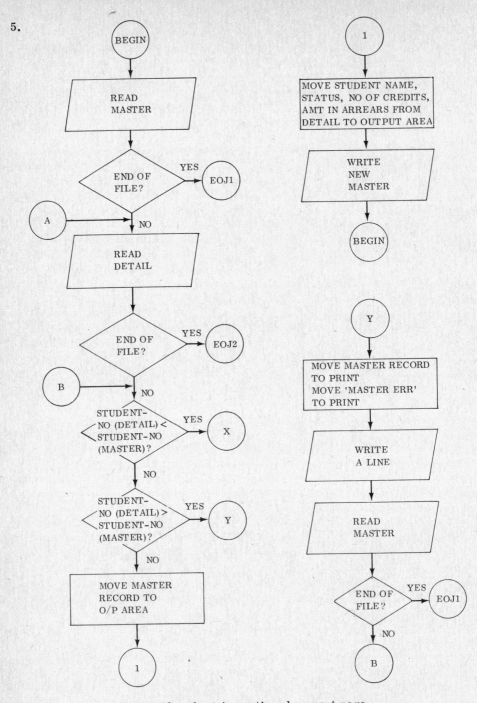

Note: Flowchart is continued on next page.

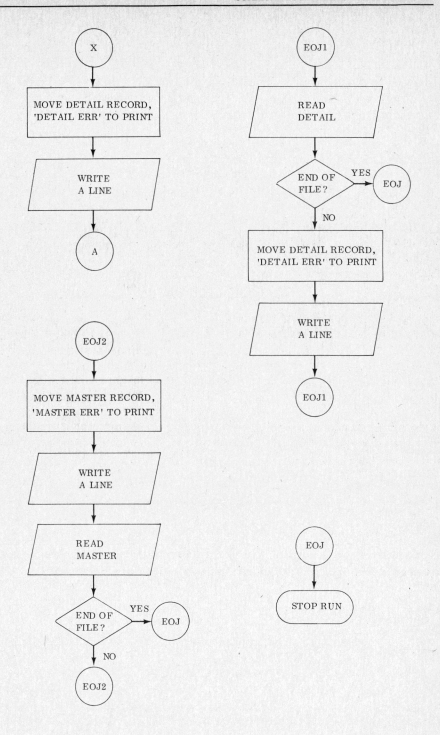

(frames 1–54)

CHAPTER SIX
Tables and Table Look-ups

Most intermediate and high-level computer processing requires, at some point, the use of tables. Table handling is a common feature of every major computer language.

Tables are required to provide for the repeated occurrence of items in storage. Suppose, for example, that a program is to create bills to be sent to a company's customers throughout the country. The program might require, as input, a listing of sales tax figures for all counties and states. This listing will need to be stored in the computer. The listing or table could then be accessed for each customer record. According to the customer's address, the corresponding sales tax figure could be extracted from the table in storage. That is, a table look-up could be performed to determine a sales tax figure, usually a percentage, which is a function of the customer's address.

Such tables, or arrays as they are also called, are required in more complex scientific problems as well. The topic is akin to matrix algebra, a subject familiar to mathematicians.

As you will see, tables or arrays provide enormous flexibility in computer processing. In this chapter, you will learn how to:

- store, access, and interpret tables or arrays;
- flowchart applications using tables or arrays.

1. A table or array is a series of entries used to store information of a repetitive nature. Before considering the mechanics of table handling by computers, let us begin with a discussion of table handling by people. Suppose that the following is a table of federal income tax deduction percentages.

SALARY LEVEL	TAX DED.
1	15%
2	18%
3	20%
4	22%
5	25%
6	27%
7	30%

The table is used to indicate the percentage of an employee's gross pay that is to be deducted for federal income tax. The tax percentage used depends upon the employee's salary level. For salary level 4, for example, 22% of gross pay is withheld for federal income tax.

How much is withheld if an employee's salary level is 2? _____ If it is 6? _____

- - - - - - - - - - - - - - - - - - - -

18%; 27%

2.   Using computer terminology, the procedure that is used to access such a table, once it is in storage, and to withhold the appropriate amount, is called a table look-up. Suppose we store the preceding table in the computer as seven independent tax deduction entries, each two positions long (plus decimal point). In storage, the above table might appear schematically as:

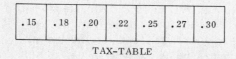

TAX-TABLE

Note that 15% = .15; 18% = .18, and so on. Each entry in the table, from left to right, corresponds to a salary level.

If an employee's salary level is 4, which entry would we access in the table to determine the federal income tax to be withheld? _____

- - - - - - - - - - - - - - - - - - -

the fourth entry, .22

3.   The sixth entry in the table corresponds to a salary level of _____.

- - - - - - - - - - - - - - - - - -

6

4.   Let us assume that the table or array is called TAX-TABLE. Suppose that an employee who earns $15,000 a year has a salary level of 3. To obtain the federal income tax to be withheld for the given salary, the following operation is required.

```
MULTIPLY 15000 BY
TAX-TABLE (3)
GIVING FED-TAX
```

That is, the third element of TAX-TABLE, called TAX-TABLE (3) contains the appropriate percentage, in decimal form. The tax entry multiplied by $15,000, which is the employee's gross pay, will yield the required federal tax.

In most computer languages, the qualification of (3) applied to TAX-TABLE is called a <u>subscript</u>. It denotes the specific element of TAX-TABLE which we wish to access. (More about subscripts later.)

Suppose that an employee at a salary level of 2 earns $12,500 a year. Draw a flowchart symbol with the operation required to obtain the federal tax to be withheld for the given salary.

- - - - - - - - - - - - - - - - - -

```
MULTIPLY 12500 BY
TAX-TABLE (2)
GIVING FED-TAX
```

5. Many intermediate and high-level computer programs require areas established in storage which are to be used for the repeated occurrence of established items, as in the preceding illustrations. That is, suppose we wish to read into storage 50 population figures, one for each state, and each ten positions long. Rather than defining 50 separate storage areas, each ten positions long, we can instruct the computer to establish a 500-position <u>table</u> or <u>array</u>, arbitrarily called ISTATE, to be segmented into 50 parts. The area in storage would appear schematically as below.

ISTATE (1)	ISTATE (2)	. . . . . .	ISTATE (50)

To establish such an area in the COBOL language, for example, we could say:

ISTATE OCCURS 50 TIMES

In the FORTRAN language, the required statement might appear as:

DIMENSION ISTATE (50)

In PL/I, it is written

DECLARE ISTATE (50)

The programming entries show that little effort is required to establish such an array or table of fields in most programming languages. The effort required to use these fields, however, is a bit more complicated, and we will devote the rest of this section to it.

To access any one of the 50 table entries in storage, we must use identifying numbers called <u>subscripts</u>. Write an operation to move the third state population figure from ISTATE to a field called HOLD.

- - - - - - - - - - - - - - - - -

```
MOVE ISTATE (3)
TO HOLD
```

6. We can use, in this case, integers from 1 to 50 as subscripts, since the table has 50 entries. To say, for example, MOVE ISTATE (0) TO HOLD or MOVE ISTATE (51) TO HOLD would result in an error.

It is also possible to use field names as subscripts, providing that those field names have integer values. Thus, the following is valid and will result in the same processing as MOVE ISTATE (3) TO HOLD.

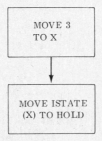

The appropriate element from ISTATE would be moved to HOLD, as long as X has an integer value ranging from _____ to _____. ISTATE is called a _____.

- - - - - - - - - - - - - - - - - - -

1; 50; table or array (The importance of using variables or field names as subscripts will become clear in a little while.)

7. Let us return for a moment to our TAX-TABLE.

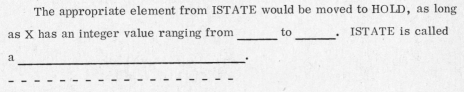

TAX-TABLE

Suppose that input cards are to be read in with the following format.

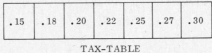

Remember that a field name can be used as a subscript. Now, here's a "think" questions. For each card read into the computer, what element in TAX-TABLE is to be accessed? _____

- - - - - - - - - - - - - - - - - -

TAX-TABLE (SALARY-LEVEL). If you answered this question correctly, congratulations! If you did not, here's a brief explanation: Suppose that the first card read had a 1 in the field called SALARY-LEVEL. We would then multiply the card's salary figure by TAX-TABLE (1) to obtain a federal tax. If the next card had a 2 in SALARY-LEVEL, the card's salary figure would be multiplied by TAX-TABLE (2) to obtain a federal tax. In effect, the subscript used with TAX-TABLE will be the same as the contents of the field called SALARY-LEVEL. Since we can use field names as subscripts, TAX-TABLE (SALARY-LEVEL) would provide the required entry.

8.   Now let's return to our 50 state population figures contained within the table or array called ISTATE. Suppose we wish to determine a total U.S.A. population. That is, we must sum all 50 ISTATE figures in a field called TOTAL. The common procedure for performing the addition of these 50 figures is a loop. You will recall that a loop performs a series of instructions repeatedly until a certain condition is satisfied. We will establish a subscript called CTR (an abbreviation for counter). CTR will be initialized at 1; the first state population figure will be added to a total; then the CTR will be incremented by 1. This series of instructions will be repeated until what condition occurs? _____

- - - - - - - - - - - - - - - - - -

until CTR exceeds 50, at which point all ISTATE figures have been added

9.   CTR is a variable subscript that varies from _____ to _____. You should initialize TOTAL at what value? _____

- - - - - - - - - - - - - - - - - -

1; 50; 0 (Remember, the storage area of most computers is not automatically cleared when a program is read in; thus, each program must clear out all arithmetic fields prior to processing.)

10. With frames 8 and 9 to guide you, draw a flowchart of the required routine, branching to a sequence called WRITE-RTN when all the additions have been completed.

- - - - - - - - - - - - - - - - - -

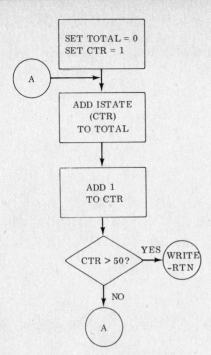

11. Let's try a variation of the above flowchart, in case you are still a little shaky. Suppose we wish to accumulate the first 25 ISTATE figures in an area called ACCUM. Draw the required flowchart.

- - - - - - - - - - - - - - - - - -

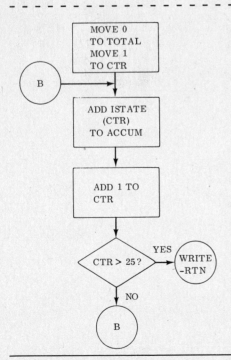

12. All high-level programming languages, such as COBOL, FORTRAN, and PL/I, have "shortcut" methods for performing the loops described in frame 11. COBOL, for example, uses PERFORM operations; PL/I and FORTRAN use DO loops. Hence, you may come across flowcharts describing these shortcuts that differ substantially from the flowcharts illustrated here. Fear not—if you can master the techniques described in this guide, you will understand the shortcut methods of any language and its flowcharting variation, in a very short time. The routines described here can be performed in any programming language; but note that most of these languages also have additional methods of handling arrays.

Thus far, we have assumed that the arrays or tables are already stored in the computer. Each program must, however, provide for reading this information into storage. Suppose we wish to read the 50 elements of ISTATE into storage, where each punched card contains a single 10-position population figure. How many cards must be read to fill the table? _____

- - - - - - - - - - - - - - - - - -

50—each card contains one population figure

13. A routine is necessary, which will repeat a procedure 50 times. What is the procedure required? _____

- - - - - - - - - - - - - - - - - -

to read a population card and store the figure in ISTATE

14. Suppose that the first card's population figure is to be stored in ISTATE (1), the second card's population figure is to be stored in ISTATE (2), and so on. Suppose we initialize CTR at 1, and each time we read a card we increment CTR by 1. When CTR is 5, the _____th card figure must be moved to ISTATE (no.) _____.

- - - - - - - - - - - - - - - - - -

fifth; (5)

15. Using a loop and a field called CTR as a subscript, draw a flowchart of the required operations to read the 50 elements of ISTATE into storage. When all the table cards have been read, branch to a routine called DATA.

- - - - - - - - - - - - - - - - - -

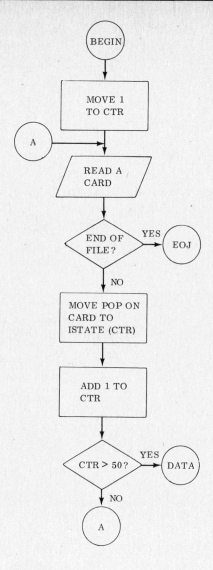

16. You might assume that the end of file condition would not be reached since 50 cards are required to fill up the table. As a protective measure, however, an EOF (end of file) test should be included with every READ statement. If, accidentally, only 48 cards were included in the deck and no EOF test were indicated, the computer would "hang up" on its 49th attempt to read a card.

Some flowcharts incorporate an operation that establishes the table, such as the following.

This operation is often included because of the fact that the actual programs must contain instructions that set up the table. These are sometimes referred to as DECLARE or DIMENSION statements or OCCURS clauses, depending upon the programming language. For purposes of this guide, however, we will only incorporate the executable statements, not the statements that establish tables.

Now that we know how to accumulate data in an array, let's draw some flowcharts using arrays. Suppose that the population figures are entered into the array ISTATE in alphabetic order; this is, ISTATE (1), the first entry in the table, refers to the population of Alabama, ISTATE (2) corresponds to the population of Alaska, . . . ISTATE (50) corresponds to Wyoming's population.

California is the fifth state, in alphabetic order. Draw a flowchart step to move California's population to an output area called POP1.

- - - - - - - - - - - - - - - - - - - -

```
MOVE ISTATE
    (5)
  TO POP1
```

17. Now let's get a bit more sophisticated. In the next frame, we will try to draw a flowchart routine to find the largest state population figure. Place this figure in an area called HOLD, and, at the end, branch to WRITE-RTN. First, some hints. You will need to establish a variable subscript which tests each entry in the table to determine which is the largest. HOLD should be in-itialized at zero. Then each succeeding figure should be compared to HOLD.

(a) If the figure is greater than the one at HOLD, what should be done?

(b) If the figure is not greater than the one at HOLD, what should be done?

(c) How many such comparisons are necessary? _____

- - - - - - - - - - - - - - - - - - -

(a) It should be moved to HOLD, because it now represents the largest.
(b) The subscript should be incremented and the next figure tested.
(c) 50—one for each state figure.

18. Now try to draw the required flowchart.

- - - - - - - - - - - - - - - - - - -

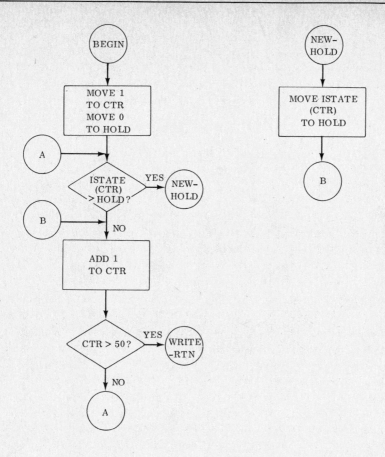

19. Draw a flowchart that will print the number of states that have population figures in excess of 1 million. Place this number in a field called TOTAL, and then print it.

– – – – – – – – – – – – – – – – – – – –

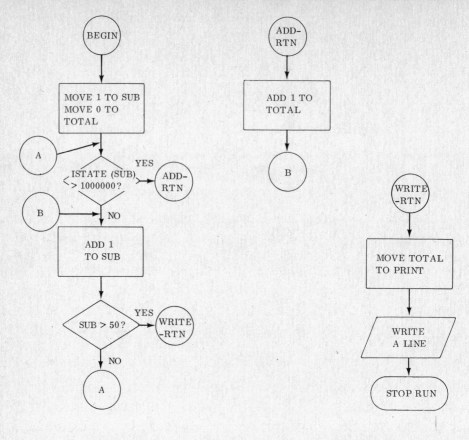

20. Let us now leave population tables and go on to a benefits table. Suppose that we wish to accumulate in storage a table corresponding to the following:

BENEFITS TABLE

NO OF YRS EMPLOYED	NO OF EMPLOYEES	WEEKS VACATION	EXCUSED DAYS
1	XXXX	XX	XXX
2	XXXX	XX	XXX
.			
.			
.			
40	XXXX	XX	XXX

NO OF YRS EMPLOYED will not be an entry in the table. Instead, NO OF YRS EMPLOYED will correspond to the subscript. The fifth grouping in the table, for example, will refer to five years of employment. The table in storage will look something like:

| NO OF EMPLOYEES (1) | WEEKS VACATION (1) | EXCUSED DAYS (1) | NO OF EMPLOYEES (2) | WEEKS VACATION (2) | EXCUSED DAYS (2) | . . . . |

	NO OF EMPLOYEES (40)	WEEKS VACATION (40)	EXCUSED DAYS (40)
. . . .			

The X's indicated in the table denote the number of positions in each field. WEEKS VACATION, for example, is a two-position field.

How many storage positions will be required for the entire table? _____

- - - - - - - - - - - - - - - - -

360 positions (For each NO OF YRS EMPLOYED, nine storage positions will be required (4 + 2 + 3). Remember that the actual NO OF YRS EMPLOYED is not an entry. Since there are 40 such years indicated, 40 x 9 or 360 positions are required.)

21. Let us assume that data for the table will be read in on cards with the following format.

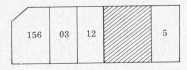

Each card corresponds to a particular NO OF YRS EMPLOYED. That is, the first card (the card with CARD NO 1) will have figures on NO OF EMPLOY-EES, WEEKS VACATION, and EXCUSED DAYS corresponding to one year of employment. The second card will have figures for two years of employment, and so on through forty cards.

Suppose the following card is read into the computer.

| 156 | 03 | 12 | | 5 |

This card has appropriate figures for how many years of employment? _____

- - - - - - - - - - - - - - - - -

five (it is card number 5)

22. An employee employed by the company for five years is entitled to how many weeks vacation? _____ How many excused days? _____ How many employees have worked for the company for five years? _____

- - - - - - - - - - - - - - - - -

03; 12; 156

23. Draw a flowchart of the routine required to read forty cards and to accumulate the data in the benefits table in storage. At the end, branch to
NEXT-STEP.

- - - - - - - - - - - - - - - - - - - -

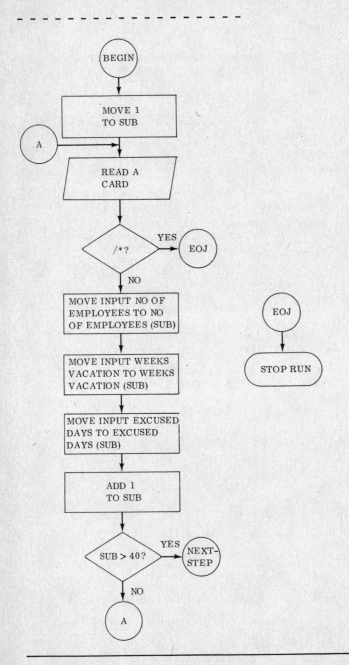

You may have come up with a more efficient solution. If so, good for you!
Read on.

24. Can you think of a way to make the flowchart more efficient? (Hint: We
really don't need a field called SUB for a subscript.) _____

_____

_____

_____

- - - - - - - - - - - - - - - - - -

Since CARD NO on each input card corresponds to the number of years of
employment, it can be used as a subscript: MOVE INPUT NO OF EMPLOY-
EES TO NO OF EMPLOYEES (CARD NO). In a way, this is a more reliable
method, because the cards need not be in sequence. For example, suppose
the first card has CARD NO 4 and the second card has CARD NO 6. Using the
old method (illustrated in frame 23), the first card's data would be entered
into the first storage area and the second card into the second storage area.
But using the CARD NO as a subscript, each card would be placed in its appropriate place in storage.

25. Now that we have read the table into storage, we can access it for processing. Draw a flowchart sequence which prints the number of weeks vacation to which an employee with nine years of service is entitled. Label this
routine NEXT-STEP. At the end, branch to RTN2.

- - - - - - - - - - - - - - - - - -

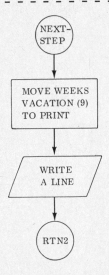

Because the ninth entry of WEEKS VACATION in the table corresponds to nine
years of service, the MOVE operation above will produce the desired results.

26. Draw a flowchart sequence (RTN2) that will find the total number of employees. Place the result in a field called TOTAL and print. Then branch to RTN3.

- - - - - - - - - - - - - - - - - - -

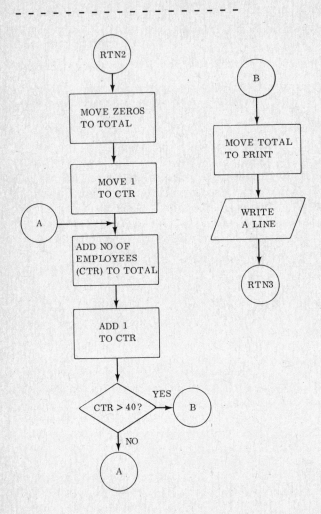

27. Is the following a correct alternative to the routine in frame 26? _____

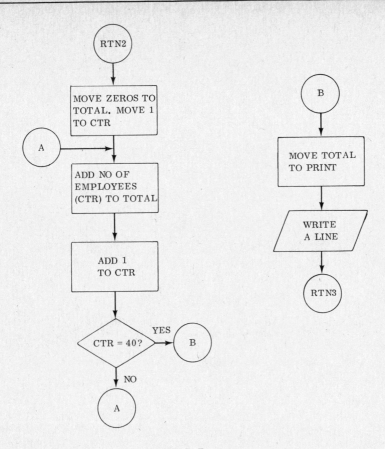

- - - - - - - - - - - - - - - -

No. Only 39 additions, instead of 40, will be performed. The routine using CTR = 40 would be okay if the addition of 1 to CTR were performed <u>after</u> the instruction which tests CTR for 40.

28. Is the following a correct alternative to the routine in frame 27? _____

- - - - - - - - - - - - - - - - - -

Yes, it's fine. Follow the logic flow through to insure that you understand the mechanism of the loop. You can now see that there are numerous ways of flowcharting this sort of illustration.

29. The following flowchart has an error in it. When programmed and test-ed, the output will be incorrect. The error is characteristic of the type of errors made by programmers. See how good a sleuth you are by trying to "debug" the flowchart.

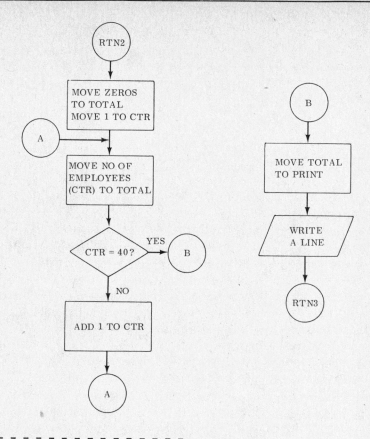

- - - - - - - - - - - - - - - - - - -

Bet you were looking for a looping error, in which case you ignored the obvious. That would be the natural inclination of many programmers. The error, however, lies in the fact that the NO OF EMPLOYEES (CTR) is <u>moved</u> to TOTAL, when it should be <u>added</u> to TOTAL. If you found the error for yourself, you're a good troubleshooter. If not, let this be a lesson—the obvious is often overlooked!

30. Here's a flowchart problem that's a bit more difficult. Find the number of years an employee must be employed to accumulate more than 100 excused days. (The exact number of excused days to which an employee is entitled is given in the table—find the excused days entry which is greater than 100.) Place the result in a field called WORK and then print. Assume that the excused days entries increment with each year of employment. That is, an employee with x yrs of service is entitled to fewer excused days than an employee with x+1 number of years of service. When finished, have the computer branch to RTN4.

- - - - - - - - - - - - - - - - - -

Here is a simple flowchart to do the job. (If you added an error routine to yours, good for you!)

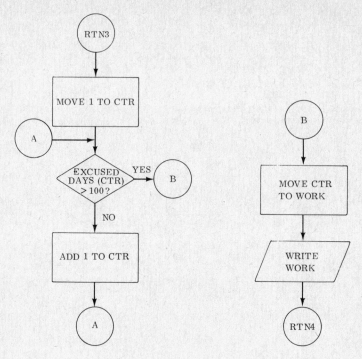

In this flowchart every EXCUSED DAYS field in the table will be compared to 100 until one exceeds it. If the fifth entry exceeds 100, then 5 is printed, because 5 represents the total number of years which the employee must be employed in order to accrue more than 100 excused days. The trick here is that CTR contains the number of years of service and is the field which must be printed.

31. There is, however, a potential hazard with the above flowchart. Try to guess what it is. _____

_____

— — — — — — — — — — — — — — — — — — —

Suppose no EXCUSED DAYS entry on the table has a numeric value in excess of 100. In such a case, the computer will test all 40 fields and keep incrementing CTR attempting to test a 41st field, a 42nd field, and so on. You see, the computer will not automatically stop at 40 entries unless it is told to. It will continue to seek out EXCUSED DAYS (41), EXCUSED DAYS (42), and so on, when CTR contains these values. Eventually it will "hang up."

32. Redo the flowchart in frame 30 to eliminate the possibility of this potential hazard. If the table has no excused days entry over 100, branch to ERR-RTN and print the message NO ENTRY ON TABLE FITS DESCRIPTION.

- - - - - - - - - - - - - - - - - - - -

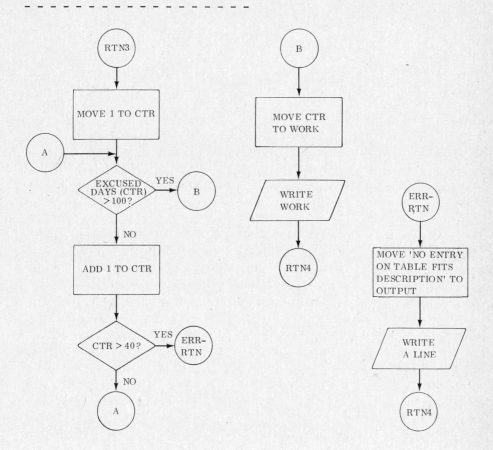

33. We are now ready to draw a flowchart for a full-fledged table look-up procedure. Such a procedure requires the reading in of table data and the processing of data according to a specific pattern. Once the table data is read in, we then read in ordinary input data. Entries on the input must be compared to the table entries until a match is found. In general, input data is compared against table entries in a table look-up procedure.

Consider the following table.

TAX TABLE

LOW SALARY LIMIT	HIGH SALARY LIMIT	STATE TAX RATE	FED. TAX RATE
00000	01200	0%	2%
01201	02200	2%	5%
02201	03000	3%	6%
03001	05000	10%	12%
.	.	.	
.	.	.	
.	.	.	
.	.		
99000	99999	30%	50%

Our first task will be to read such a table into storage. After that, we will read salary cards and determine an employee's tax rate by performing a table look-up.

Suppose an employee earns $1,250. According to the above table, what would be his state tax rate? _____

- - - - - - - - - - - - - - - - -

2%—his salary falls within the limits of 01201 and 02200

34. Suppose an employee earns $3,222. According to the above table, what would be his state tax rate? _____

- - - - - - - - - - - - - - - - -

10%

35. The computer is instructed to compare the salary on the input with each high salary in sequence, beginning with the first entry. If the input salary compares less, the corresponding tax rate can be extracted from the table. Suppose INPUT SALARY < HIGH SALARY (CTR) yields a YES. Which TAX

RATE figure do we tell the computer to access? _____

- - - - - - - - - - - - - - - - -

TAX RATE (CTR). The point here is that CTR will provide the corresponding TAX RATE.

36. Following is a full job description as might be provided at a computer center. Pretend that you are the programmer and draw the flowchart to insure your understanding of the logical integration of elements. Good luck!

<u>Job description</u>: Monthly take-home pay is to be computed for each employee of Company ABC.

A tax table must be read from 20 input cards, with the following format.

1-5	Low limit salary
6-10	High limit salary
11-13	State tax percentage (.xxx—three positions to right of decimal point)
14-16	Federal tax percentage (.xxx—three positions to right of decimal point)
17-80	Not used

Example:

Low limit	High limit	State tax	Federal tax
06700	09800	020	100

These figures denote that state tax is 2% and federal tax is 10% for the salary range $6,700-$9,800.

Following the tax cards are detail employee cards containing the following information.

1-20	Employee name
21-25	Annual salary
26	Number of dependents
27-80	Not used

Annual take-home pay is computed as follows.

(1) Standard deduction = 10% of annual salary up to $10,000.
(2) Dependent deduction = 750 x number of dependents.
(3) FICA (social security tax) = 5.85% of salary up to $13,200.
(4) Net salary = Annual salary - standard deduction - dependent deduction - FICA.
(5) Find tax of net salary in tax table.
(6) Annual take-home pay = net - (state tax% x Net salary) - (federal tax% x Net salary)
(7) Monthly take-home pay = Annual take-home pay/12

Print employee name and monthly take-home pay (all fields are dollars and cents figures).

Note: For ease of annotating flowcharts, call table figures STATE TAX and FED TAX, to be subscripted by a value, and call the computed tax figures S-TAX and F-TAX.

- - - - - - - - - - - - - - - - - - -

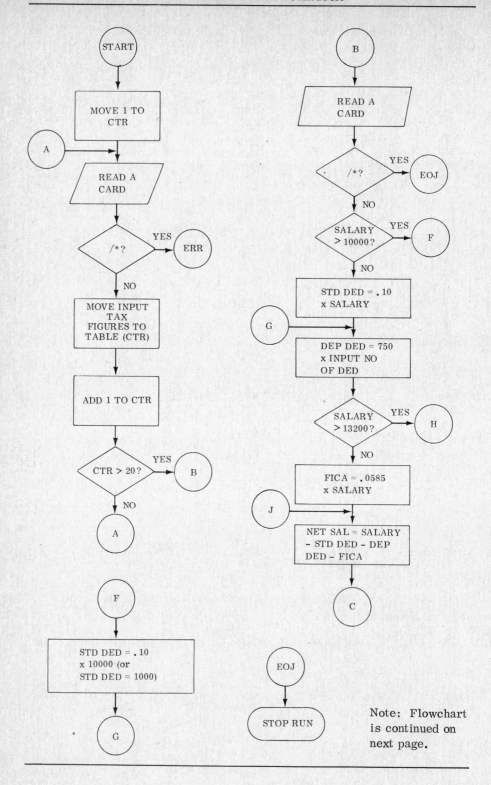

Note: Flowchart is continued on next page.

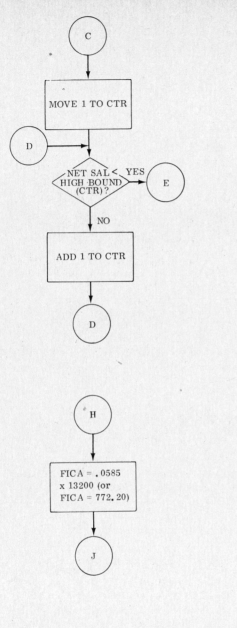

(C)

MOVE 1 TO CTR

(D)

NET SAL <
HIGH BOUND
(CTR) ? → YES → (E)

NO

ADD 1 TO CTR

(D)

(H)

FICA = .0585
x 13200 (or
FICA = 772.20)

(J)

(E)

MULTIPLY STATE TAX
(CTR) BY NET SAL
GIVING S-TAX
MULTIPLY FED TAX
(CTR) BY NET SAL
GIVING F-TAX

ANNUAL TAKE-HOME =
NET SAL - S-TAX - F-TAX
DIVIDE ANNUAL TAKE-
HOME BY 12 GIVING ITEM

MOVE NAME, ITEM
TO PRINT

WRITE
A LINE

(B)

(ERR)

MOVE ERROR
MESSAGE 'TOO
FEW TABLE
CARDS' TO PRINT

WRITE
A LINE

STOP RUN

SELF-TEST

1. A program is to read ten cards with the following format into a table.

    1-5   Salary
    6-8   Tax
    9-80   Not used

The table will appear in storage as:

TABLE-1

SAL (1)	TAX (1)	SAL (2)	TAX (2)	. . . . . .	SAL (10)	TAX (10)

(a) Is the following a correct solution for the preceding?   Explain your answer.

_____

_____

_____

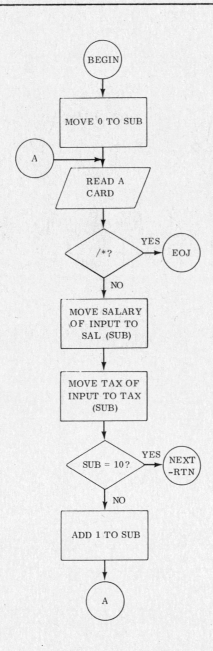

(b) Is the following a correct solution? Explain your answer.

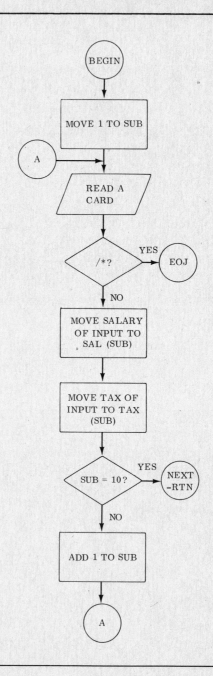

(c) Is the following a correct solution? Explain your answer.

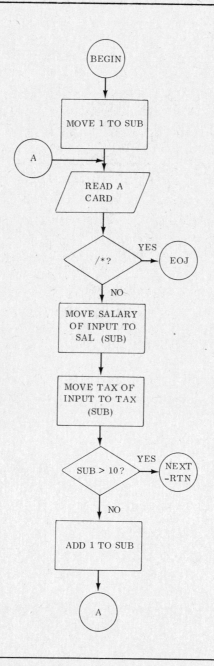

(d) Is the following a correct solution? Explain your answer.

_____

_____

_____

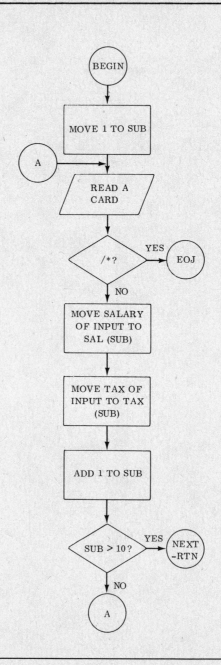

2.   Draw a flowchart to print twelve transaction amounts, one for each month of the year and, in addition, a grand total for the year. The input is as follows.

        1-5   Transaction amount
        6-30   Not used
        31-32   Month number (1-12)
        33-80   Not used

Note: An undetermined number of cards will serve as input, but only 12 totals are to be printed. The input cards are not in sequence.

3.   Each input card for a program which creates tape records of sales will have the following format.

        1-5   Amount of sales—day x
        6-10   Amount of sales—day x + 1
        11-80   Not used

Twenty cards will serve as input, representing 40 daily figures. The first card will have sales amount for day 1 in card columns 1 through 5, the sales amount for day 2 in card columns 6 through 10. The second card will contain amount of sales for day 3 in card columns 1 through 5 and the amount of sales for day 4 in card columns 6 through 10, and so on.

   Draw a flowchart to create 40 tape records, each five positions long. The first tape record should contain sales amount for day 40, the second record should contain sales amount for day 39, and so on.

Answers to Self-Test

1.   (a) It is incorrect. SUB is initialized at 0; after the first card is read, SALARY of input is moved to SAL (0), an invalid move.
    (b) Okay
    (c) It is incorrect. The decision symbol which compares SUB to 10 and branches on a "greater than" permits 11 entries to be moved to the table.
    (d) Okay. This solution corrects the above by relocating the step that increments SUB by 1.
(frames 20-36)

2. See flowchart on following two pages.

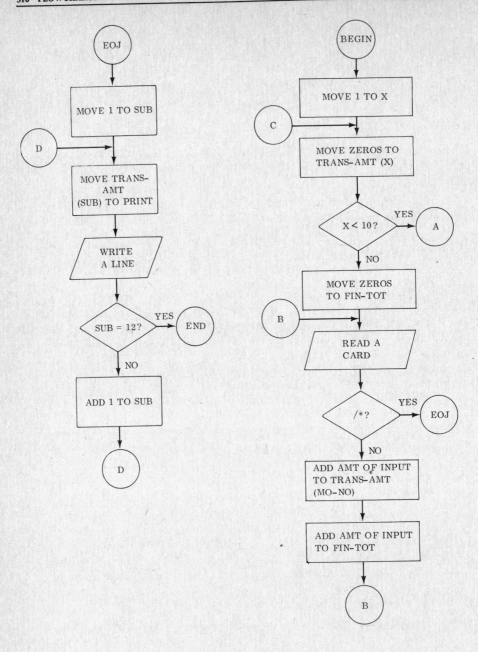

Note that we used MO–NO as an input field. You may have
done something different, but this is the most efficient.

Flowchart is continued on next page.

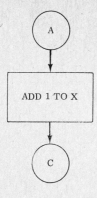

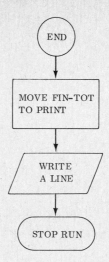

(frames 1–19)

3.

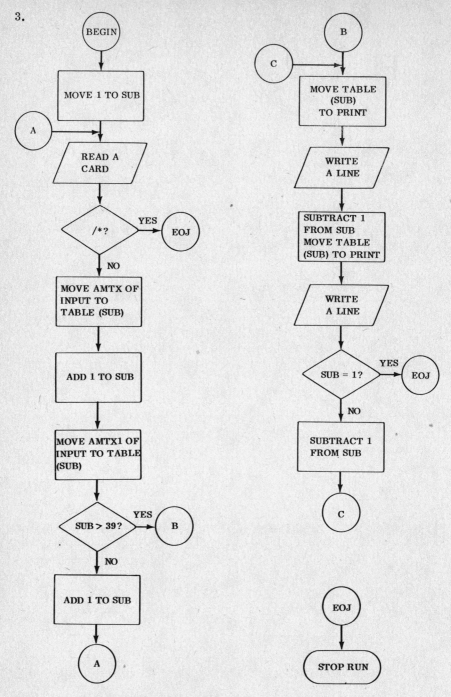

Note: When a branch to B has occurred, SUB contains 40 and is, then, ready to be used to print the entries in reverse order.

(frames 20–36)

CHAPTER SEVEN
Flowcharting and Other Programming Tasks

Now that you have flowcharted complex problems and interpreted typical business applications, you will be able to program in any computer language, once you have learned the basic rules of that language. This chapter will show how flowcharting relates to programming and to the overall job flow. It will use the COBOL language to illustrate specifically how a flowchart can be used to create a computer program. When you complete this chapter, you will be able to:

- identify how flowcharting and programming relate to the flow of data;

- identify the types of languages and translations used in data processing;

- explain the tasks of compiling, executing, and debugging a program.

FLOWCHARTING THE PROBLEM—REVIEW

1. You will recall that a programmer draws a flowchart <u>before</u> constructing a program. Often the steps involved in achieving a job's requirements are intricate and detailed. Before writing the set of instructions (the program), the programmer must outline the logic required. In this way, the programmer will avoid omitting necessary instructions or including illogical functions.
   A standardized method for outlining the logic to be used in a program is

a pictorial representation called a _____ . In your own

words, what does this pictorial representation illustrate? _____

_____

_____

- - - - - - - - - - - - - - - - - - - -

a program flowchart (I hope you answered this question correctly!); indicates the program elements and how they will logically integrate

_____

CODING THE PROGRAM

2.   Once the programmer has outlined the steps of a program in a flowchart and is satisfied that they logically integrate, he or she can begin to write the set of instructions. That is, the programmer can begin to code the program. Programs are coded on sheets of paper called coding or program sheets. See Figure 7.1 for an illustration of a sample coding sheet.

When the coding has been completed, the program must be converted to a form that is readable by the computer. Typically, this is done through key-punching of cards, though the instructions may also be put onto magnetic tape or magnetic disk.   Each line of a coding sheet generally corresponds to a single flowcharted operation and is punched into a single punched card. The entire deck of program cards, called a source program, is then read by a card reader of a computer system. (You may remember that, although there are machines that could read data printed on coding sheets, they are very costly and are not often used in computer centers.)

A deck of cards is keypunched from _____. In your

own words, explain the process of keypunching.   _____

_____

_____

- - - - - - - - - - - - - - - - - - - -

coding sheets
Keypunching is the process of converting instructions from coding sheets (or other source documents) to a machine-readable form, in this case punched cards.

Translating the Program

3.   It may seem to you that once the deck of program cards has been key-punched, we're ready to run the program. Unfortunately, it's not that simple. Computers can operate on, or execute, programs only if they are coded in actual or absolute machine language. Each computer has its own actual ma-chine language. Machine language is complex and the average programmer is rarely familiar with it. Absolute machine languages require:

(1) Complex operation codes. An ADD instruction, for example, may be a "58" code in absolute machine language; a MULTIPLY instruction might be a "4J." If the programmer were to code his or her program in actual machine language, he or she would have to remember such complex codes.

(2) Actual machine addresses. For example, an ADD instruction which adds two input fields must place the result or sum in a third field. In absolute machine language, this third field, as well as the first two fields, is an actual machine location. So to program in this language, the programmer must keep track of actual machine locations, a cumbersome and difficult task.

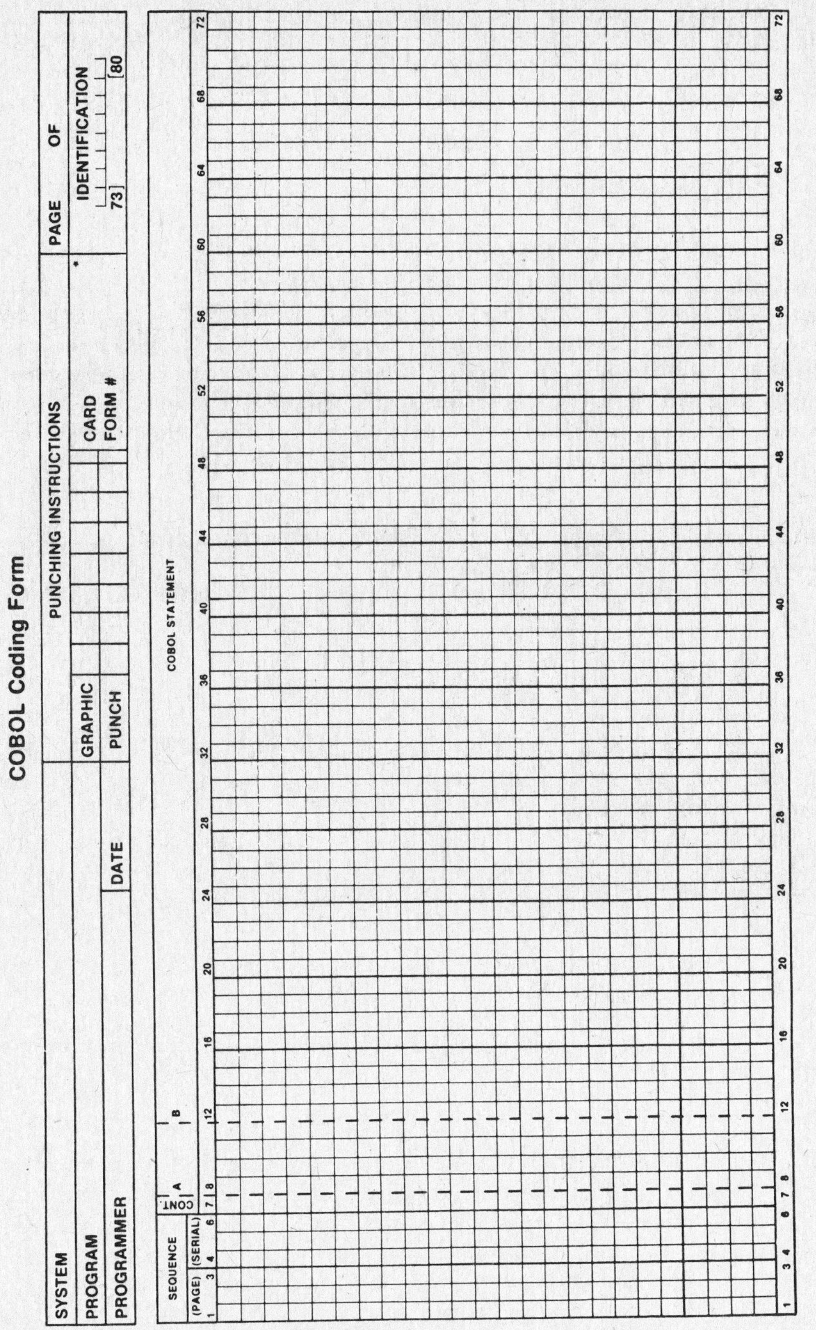

Figure 7.1. Sample coding sheet.

Why is programming in an actual machine language complex and cumber-some? _____

_____

- - - - - - - - - - - - - - - - - - - -

because the programmer must remember complex operation codes and keep track of actual machine locations

4. Few programmers code in the machine's own language. The alternative is <u>symbolic programming language coding</u>.

A programmer can code far more easily in a symbolic programming language. It uses symbolic operation codes such as ADD or +, in place of actual machine operation codes. Similarly, in place of actual machine addresses, symbolic programming languages permit the use of symbolic locations such as HOLD, RESULT, and SUM—the types of symbolic locations that we have been using in our flowcharts. Thus, we can code ADD TAX TO TOTAL rather than something like 2R 40683220. The overwhelming majority of programs

are coded in a symbolic programming language rather than in an _____

_____.

- - - - - - - - - - - - - - - - - - - -

actual or absolute machine language

5. Note that a symbolic program, although easier for a programmer to code, cannot be run or executed by the computer as is. It must first be converted to absolute machine language.

Programs can be executed by the computer only if they are written in what type of language? _____

- - - - - - - - - - - - - - - - - - - -

absolute machine

6. What must be done to programs written in a symbolic programming language before they can be executed? _____

_____ What does the phrase "execute a program" mean? _____

- - - - - - - - - - - - - - - - - - - -

they must be converted into absolute machine language; run the program—that is, take input data, process it, and convert it to output data

_____

7.   Thus, a program written in a symbolic programming language requires
two phases.

> (1) Translation phase. The program must be translated into actual
> or absolute machine language.
> (2) Execution phase. Once translated, the program is run or
> executed.

As indicated, most programs are coded in a _____

language. This program, written on coding sheets, must be converted to a

form that can be accepted by the computer, such as _____.

- - - - - - - - - - - - - - - - - -

symbolic programming; cards or tape

8.   The program written in symbolic programming language is called a source
program. A source program keypunched into cards is called a source deck.

Are source programs executable? Explain. _____

_____

- - - - - - - - - - - - - - - - -

No. They must be translated into machine language before they can be run.

Types of Translations

9.   All symbolic programming languages must be translated into machine
language before they can be run or executed. The computer itself performs
this translation. That is, the computer reads the source program as input
and translates it, producing the absolute machine language program as output.
   High-level symbolic programming languages are relatively simple to code
but require rather complex computer translations. Low-level symbolic programming languages are harder to code but require a simpler translation process.
   With high-level languages, such as COBOL, FORTRAN, PL/I and BASIC,
this translation process is called a compilation. The computer manufacturer
supplies a special program, called the compiler. The compiler reads the
source program written in a symbolic programming language, and produces
as output a machine language equivalent, called the object program.
   Thus, the compiler is a program that reads, as input, the _____

_____ and

translates it to output, which is the _____ program.

- - - - - - - - - - - - - - - - - -

_____

source program deck—that is, the symbolic language program; object program (absolute machine language program)

10. A process which translates a source deck into an object program is called compilation. The program which performs this translation is called the

_____.

- - - - - - - - - - - - - - - - -

compiler

11. In your own words, explain how a source program is related to its equivalent object program. _____

_____

_____

- - - - - - - - - - - - - - - - -

The source program written in symbolic programming language goes through a translation process called compilation, which produces the equivalent object program written in actual machine language.

12. FORTRAN, COBOL, and other high-level programming languages require unique compilations. That is, a FORTRAN compiler must be used to translate FORTRAN programs, a COBOL compiler must be used to translate COBOL programs, and so on. Each computer requires a compiler program that can read the specific symbolic program and convert it to its own machine language. Since individual computers each have their own unique machine language, the compiler for each machine will be different.

Can the compiler used to translate a COBOL program be used to translate a FORTRAN program? _____

- - - - - - - - - - - - - - - - -

no, each computer language has its own compiler

13. Can the compiler used to translate a COBOL program on a Honeywell computer be used to translate the same COBOL program on an IBM computer?

_____

- - - - - - - - - - - - - - - - -

no—since each computer has its own machine language, the compiler program must be geared to each individual computer

14. Low-level programming languages, called assembler languages, are similar to machine language. Because assembler languages are so similar to

machine language, they require only a simple translation called an <u>assembly</u>. An assembly is not as complex as a high-level compilation.

In the assembly process, a special program called an <u>assembler</u> translates an assembler language program into _____

_____.

- - - - - - - - - - - - - - - - -

an object program in machine language (All translation programs convert programs into machine language object programs.)

15. While an assembler language requires the simplest translation process, it requires the <u>most</u> programming effort. High-level languages require less programming effort, but the conversion process is more complex.

Which is easier for the programmer to code: machine language, high-level language, or low-level language? _____

- - - - - - - - - - - - - - - - -

high-level language

16. Which is easier for the computer to translate: high-level language or low-level language? _____

- - - - - - - - - - - - - - - - -

low-level language

17. The translator—assembler or compiler—is a program that is usually on a magnetic tape or magnetic disk file of programs, ready to be accessed by the computer. The control system of the computer calls for these translator programs as needed. When a translator is read into storage, it then calls for the source program as input and begins the translation.

What is the difference between a compilation and an assembly? _____

_____

_____

- - - - - - - - - - - - - - - - -

A compilation is a relatively complex translation process required for translations of high-level languages. An assembly is a simple translation process, required for translations of low-level languages which are more like machine language.

Debugging

18. As we have seen, the technique of flowcharting, before coding programs, minimizes the number of logic errors. Unfortunately, however, logic errors can, and usually do, occur even in programs written by top-notch programmers who draw meticulous flowcharts. Programming is a detailed and rigorous job, and very susceptible to errors or "bugs."

To insure that mistakes are detected before the program is actually used by the data processing center, it must be <u>tested</u> for logic errors.

(True or False.) Programs that are written after the corresponding flowcharts have been drawn need not be tested. _____

- - - - - - - - - - - - - - - - - - -

false—all programs should be tested

19. What type of error is detected by testing a program? _____

- - - - - - - - - - - - - - - - - -

logic errors

20. Another term for a program error is _____.

- - - - - - - - - - - - - - - - - -

bug

21. What do we mean by "testing a program"? The programmer creates artificial or "test" input data, designed to include all possible conditions that can occur in normal input data. The program is then given the test data as input in a trial run. In this way, the computer detects logic errors and the programmer can correct them. This process of detecting and correcting logic errors in a program is called <u>debugging</u>.

After a program has been fully debugged—and this could take several trial runs—it may be turned over to the data processing staff to be run on a regularly scheduled basis. That is, the programmer gives the program to the computer personnel, along with necessary explanations of its requirements (called documentation). At this point, the programmer can take a well-earned coffee break before beginning the next assignment!

Assume that a program has been turned over to the data processing center by the programmer. After running several times on a regular basis, it suddenly aborts or "bombs out." What explanation would you give? Assume that the computer has been checked and the input has been checked, and both are okay.

are okay. _____

_____

- - - - - - - - - - - - - - - - -

_____

If both the input and the computer are okay, then chances are the error is in the program. Very likely, the programmer did not fully test his program. That is, test data was probably not inclusive enough to provide for all contingencies. This sort of occurrence sometimes necessitates waking the programmer in the middle of the night! (Many regularly scheduled jobs are run during the night shift.)

22. What does the term "debugging" mean? _____

_____

- - - - - - - - - - - - - - - - - - -

The process of detecting and correcting logic errors in a program is called debugging.

23. (True or False.) Good programmers require very little time to debug programs. _____

- - - - - - - - - - - - - - - - - - -

False. Depending upon the magnitude and complexity of the job, even the best programmers often require a good deal of time to debug a program.

24. What is the purpose of testing a program? _____

- - - - - - - - - - - - - - - - - - -

to eliminate all of the logic errors

25. What should be considered when creating input "test" data? _____

_____

- - - - - - - - - - - - - - - - - - -

All possible conditions for which the program tests must be included to insure that the program, in its entirety, functions properly

INTRODUCTION TO COBOL PROGRAMMING

26. To illustrate the relationship between flowcharting and programming, we will use a program that has been coded from a flowchart. For this purpose, we will use a program written in the COBOL language, because it is widely used and because its Englishlike nature makes it very easy for non-programmers to understand the logic.

Definition of the problem.

 A computer center of a company is assigned the task of calculating weekly wages for all nonsalaried personnel. The following represents the card input.

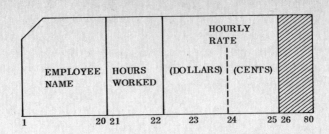

WEEKLY-WAGES is computed as HOURS-WORKED times HOURLY RATE. The output will be a magnetic tape with the following format.

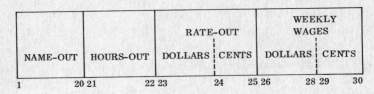

The input to the system will be called EMPLOYEE CARDS. The computer will

calculate WEEKLY-WAGES from the two input fields _____

and _____ .

- - - - - - - - - - - - - - - - -

HOURS-WORKED; HOURLY-RATE

27. The input data along with the computed figure will be used to create the output tape file called PAYROLL-FILE. In COBOL, the names of the files are important.

Figure 7.2 represents a flowchart of the operations required. The problem and flowchart have been kept relatively simple, to facilitate your understanding of the COBOL program.

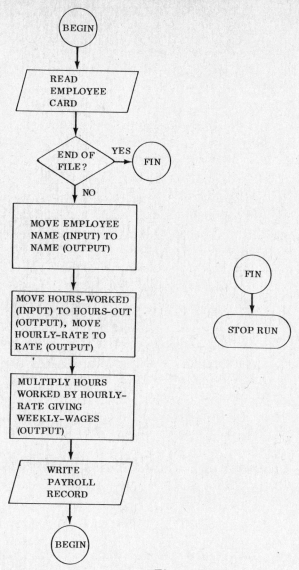

Figure 7.2

Once the input and output record formats have been clearly and precisely defined, the program may be written. You will recall that a program is a set of instructions and specifications that operate on input to produce output. Figure 7.3 is a simplified COBOL program which will operate on employee cards to create a payroll tape file with the computed wages.

Note that the program is divided into four major divisions. The first major division is IDENTIFICATION DIVISION, coded on line 01. What are the other three divisions? _____

- - - - - - - - - - - - - - - - - - - -

IBM

COBOL PROGRAM SHEET

System	SAMPLE
Program	SAMPLE
Programmer	N. STERN

Form No. 220-1664-1 U/R 050
Printed in U.S.A.

Punching Instructions | Graphic | | Punch | | Card Form # | |

Sheet ___ of ___

Identification
SAMPLE01
73 · · · 80

```
SEQUENCE
(PAGE)(SERIAL)  A  B
 3  4  6  7  8  12
01  IDENTIFICATION DIVISION.
02  PROGRAM-ID. 'SAMPLE'.
03  ENVIRONMENT DIVISION.
04  FILE-CONTROL.  SELECT EMPLOYEE-CARDS ASSIGN TO READER.
05                 SELECT PAYROLL-FILE ASSIGN TO TAPE 11.
06  DATA DIVISION.
07  FD  EMPLOYEE-CARDS
08  01  EMPLOYEE-RECORD
09      02  EMPLOYEE-NAME        PICTURE A(20).
10      02  HOURS-WORKED         PICTURE 9(2).
11      02  HOURLY-RATE          PICTURE 9V99.
12  FD  PAYROLL-FILE
13  01  PAYROLL-RECORD
14      02  NAME-OUT             PICTURE A (20).
15      02  HOURS-OUT            PICTURE 9(2).
16      02  RATE-OUT             PICTURE 9V99.
17      02  WEEKLY-WAGES         PICTURE 999V99.
18  PROCEDURE DIVISION.
19  BEGIN.  READ EMPLOYEE-CARDS AT END GO TO FINISH.
20          MOVE EMPLOYEE-NAME TO NAME-OUT. MOVE HOURS-WORKED TO
21          HOURS-OUT. MOVE HOURLY-RATE TO RATE-OUT.
22          MULTIPLY HOURS-WORKED BY HOURLY-RATE GIVING WEEKLY-WAGES.
23          WRITE PAYROLL-RECORD.
24          GO TO BEGIN.
25  FIN.    STOP RUN.
```

* A standard card form, IBM electro C61897, is available for punching source statements from this form.

Figure 7.3

ENVIRONMENT DIVISION, DATA DIVISION, and PROCEDURE DIVISION, coded on lines 03, 06, and 18 respectively

28. Every COBOL program <u>must</u> contain these four divisions in the aforementioned order. The IDENTIFICATION DIVISION here has only one entry, the PROGRAM-ID. That is, the IDENTIFICATION DIVISION of this program merely serves to identify the program.

The ENVIRONMENT DIVISION assigns the input and output files to specific devices. EMPLOYEE-CARDS, the name assigned to the input file, will be processed by a card reader. Similarly, PAYROLL-FILE is the output file assigned to a specific tape drive.

The DATA DIVISION describes, in detail, the field designations of the two files. The input and output areas in storage are fully described in the DATA DIVISION. The File Description, or FD, for EMPLOYEE-CARDS defines the <u>record</u> format called EMPLOYEE-RECORD. EMPLOYEE-RECORD has three

input fields. What are they? _____

- - - - - - - - - - - - - - - - - - -

EMPLOYEE-NAME, HOURS-WORKED, and HOURLY-RATE (coded on lines 09, 10, and 11 respectively)

29. Each field has a corresponding PICTURE clause denoting the size and type of data which will appear in the field. The EMPLOYEE-NAME field is an alphabetic data field containing 20 characters. PICTURE A(20) indicates the <u>type</u> of data (A denoting alphabetic information) and the <u>size</u> of the field (20 characters). Similarly, HOURS-WORKED is a two-position numeric field. PICTURE 9(2) indicates the type of data, 9 denoting numeric information and (2) denoting a two-position area. HOURLY RATE is a three-position numeric field with an <u>implied</u> decimal point. PICTURE 9V99 describes a three-position numeric field (indicated by the three 9's) with an implied or assumed decimal point (indicated by the V) after the first position. Thus 125 in this field will be interpreted by the computer as 1.25. The decimal point does <u>not</u> appear on the input document but is nonetheless implied.

Similarly, the output file called PAYROLL-FILE has a record format called PAYROLL-RECORD, which is subdivided into four fields, each with an appropriate PICTURE clause. What four fields are contained in PAYROLL-

RECORD? _____

- - - - - - - - - - - - - - - - - - -

NAME-OUT, HOURS-OUT, RATE-OUT, and WEEKLY-WAGES (coded on lines 14-17)

30. If any constants or work areas were required in the program, they, too, would be described in the DATA DIVISION. Notice that the first three fields in PAYROLL-RECORD will be taken directly from each input record. The last field, WEEKLY-WAGES, must be computed. Look at the PICTURE

clause for WEEKLY-WAGES. Can you tell the size of the field and the type of data? _____

_____

- - - - - - - - - - - - - - - - - - -

It is a five-position field (indicated by the five 9's) with an implied decimal point after the third position (indicated by the V), and it contains numeric data (a 9 indicates numeric data).

31. The PROCEDURE DIVISION contains the set of instructions or operations to be performed by the computer. Each instruction is executed in the order in which it appears unless a GO TO statement, or a <u>branch</u>, alters the sequence. Note that the PROCEDURE DIVISION in the program is divided into two paragraphs, BEGIN and FIN.

Now compare the flowchart (Figure 7. 2) and the COBOL program (Figure 7. 3). The flowchart corresponds to what DIVISION of the COBOL program?

_____

- - - - - - - - - - - - - - - - - -

PROCEDURE DIVISION

32. From examining the COBOL program, you should be able to see how programs need rigorous detail and planning <u>in addition to</u> a logically integrated flowchart. That is, the flowchart should make the coding of the actual instructions much easier, but there are still other parts of the program which must be carefully constructed.

The COBOL instruction READ EMPLOYEE CARDS AT END GO TO FIN corresponds to <u>two</u> flowchart operations. Can you determine which ones?

- - - - - - - - - - - - - - - - - - -

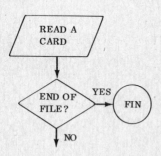

The actual correspondence between flowcharts and programs depends on the nature of each specific language. The use of the COBOL language in the preceding frames was designed to give you a basic familiarity with the interrelationship between flowcharts and programs.

THE SYSTEMS FLOWCHART

33. The programmer's tasks, which we have been describing, represent only one facet of a data processing procedure. Usually, programmers are given individual assignments which are part of an integrated procedure, or sys- tem. A system, in a business sense, is an organized method for accom- plishing a business function. A payroll system, for example, may require several programs, such as an edit, a weekly update, a monthly update, and a sort, which combine to make the system function effectively and efficiently.

A system generally requires a series of programs which, when integrat- ed, combine to make the entire process function properly. Can you define,

in your own words, what an accounts receivable system is? _____

_____

- - - - - - - - - - - - - - - - - -

An accounts receivable system is an organized method of processing accounts receivable information.

34. Do you think that an accounts receivable system would consist of one pro- gram or more than one? _____

- - - - - - - - - - - - - - - - - -

probably many more than one

35. The systems analyst is the person who analyzes the elements of a system, assesses the requirements of the system, and determines if these require- ments are properly met in the existing system. If not, he or she must deter- mine whether a revised, usually computerized, set of procedures would meet those requirements and would be justifiable in cost. If computerized opera- tions can ultimately save the company money, the company may ask the sys- tems analyst to design a more efficient and effective system.

Can you determine, then, the two major facets of the systems analyst's

job? _____

- - - - - - - - - - - - - - - - - -

analysis and design (The analyst first analyzes present operations and then designs more efficient, usually computerized, systems.)

36. If a new design is required, the analyst must assign specific aspects of the system to people who are responsible for coding solutions to specific prob-

lems. These people are called _____.

- - - - - - - - - - - - - - - - - -

programmers

37. A common tool used by the systems analyst for communicating ideas on a new design and its processing requirements is called a systems flowchart. The systems flowchart, like its more detailed counterpart, the program flowchart, depicts the relationship between inputs, processing, and outputs within the whole system. It is a general representation of the information flow within the total system.

A systems flowchart depicts the logical integration of elements within a system, while a program flowchart depicts the logic in a program. How does a program relate to a system? _____

- - - - - - - - - - - - - - - - - - -

Usually, several programs are integrated into a whole system.

38. Programs are written to facilitate the processing of data within a total business installation. The systems analyst is responsible for analyzing and redesigning systems, where applicable. Figure 7.4 shows a sample systems flowchart for an updating procedure of an accounts receivable system in a department store.

Which is more detailed: a systems flowchart or a program flowchart?

_____

- - - - - - - - - - - - - - - - - - -

The program flowchart is far more detailed.

39. Systems flowcharts are drawn by _____ while program flowcharts are drawn by _____.

- - - - - - - - - - - - - - - - - -

systems analysts; programmers

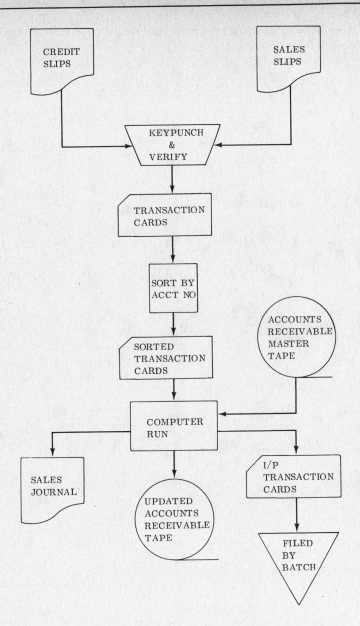

Figure 7.4. Updating procedure of an accounts
receivable system in a department store.

40. Are the symbols used in a systems flowchart the same as those used in a

program flowchart? _____

- - - - - - - - - - - - - - - - - -

no, most are different, as you may have already noticed

41. As a final question, let's pull together all parts of the data processing procedure. Below are various steps in the total procedure. Write the steps in proper sequence.

> translate program
> assign specific problem to programmer
> debug program
> flowchart information flow in system
> code program
> execute program
> convert instructions to source program
> flowchart logic of problem
> obtain object program

- - - - - - - - - - - - - - - - - -

(1) flowchart information flow in system
(2) assign specific problem to programmer
(3) flowchart logic of problem
(4) code program
(5) convert instructions source program
(6) translate program
(7) obtain object program
(8) debug program
(9) execute program

SELF-TEST

1. Which of the following three sequences of operations is correct? _____

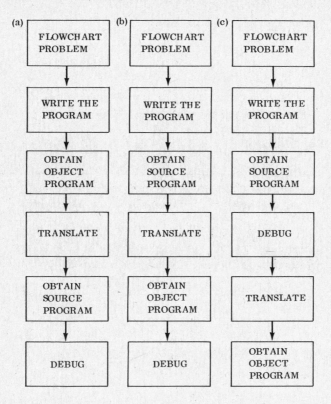

(a)
FLOWCHART PROBLEM
↓
WRITE THE PROGRAM
↓
OBTAIN OBJECT PROGRAM
↓
TRANSLATE
↓
OBTAIN SOURCE PROGRAM
↓
DEBUG

(b)
FLOWCHART PROBLEM
↓
WRITE THE PROGRAM
↓
OBTAIN SOURCE PROGRAM
↓
TRANSLATE
↓
OBTAIN OBJECT PROGRAM
↓
DEBUG

(c)
FLOWCHART PROBLEM
↓
WRITE THE PROGRAM
↓
OBTAIN SOURCE PROGRAM
↓
DEBUG
↓
TRANSLATE
↓
OBTAIN OBJECT PROGRAM

2. Programmers usually write programs in what type of language? _____
_____ Why? _____

_____

3. In order to be executed, a program must be in what language? _____

_____

4. What is the relationship between a source program and an object program?

_____

_____

_____

_____

5. What is the difference between a high-level and a low-level programming language? _____

_____

_____

6. Name and describe two types of program translators discussed in this chapter. _____

_____

7. What does it mean to "debug" a program? _____

_____

8. (True or False.) The systems analyst provides the programmer with job requirements from which the programmer must create a program. _____

9. What should the programmer consider when creating input "test" data?

_____

_____

Answers to Self-Test

1. (b) is correct (frames 1–7, 18–25)

2. symbolic programming language; because the programmer can code more easily with symbolic language than with machine language, which requires learning complex operation codes and remembering exact storage locations. (frames 2–7)

3. actual or absolute machine language (frames 2–7)

4. A source program is written in symbolic programming language; it must be translated into machine language, producing the corresponding object program. (frames 2–8)

5. A high-level programming language is easier for the programmer to code but requires a more sophisticated translation process; a low-level programming language is more complex for the programmer to code but easier for the computer to translate. (frames 9–16)

6. compiler—a translator used to translate a high-level program; assembler—a translator used to translate a low-level program (frames 9–17)

_____

7. Debugging is the process of detecting and correcting logic errors during a trial run.   (frames 18–25)

8. true   (frames 33–40)

9. The input test data should include all possible conditions for which the program tests.   (frames 18–25)

Index